MR. AND
MRS. PRINCE

☞ Several likely Negro Men, Women, Boys and Girls, some of which Arrived about a Week ago to Sold by Hugh Hall.

MR. AND MRS. PRINCE

How an Extraordinary Eighteenth-Century Family Moved Out of Slavery and into Legend

GRETCHEN HOLBROOK GERZINA

RESEARCHED WITH ANTHONY GERZINA

Amistad

An Imprint of HarperCollins Publishers

HarperCollins books may be purchased for educational, business, or sales
promotional use. For information please write: Special Markets Department,
HarperCollins Publishers, 10 East 53rd Street, New York, NY 10022.

FIRST EDITION

Designed by DEBORAH KERNER

Library of Congress Cataloging-in-Publication Data has been applied for.

ISBN 978-0-06-051073-2

08 09 10 11 12 ID/RRD 10 9 8 7 6 5 4 3 2 1

FOR ANTHONY

· ·

Our book—our adventure

Know all men by these Presents that I Aaron [...]
the County of Hampshire and Province of the Ma[ssachusetts]
England Yeoman for sundry good Considerations [...]
have Manumitted Released and forever Disch[arged ...]
servant or Slave named Abijah alias Prin[ce ...]
services or servitudes of any kind or nature [...]
Heirs or assigns or to any Person or Persons cl[aiming ...]
vice by any Power or Authority Derived from [...]
and I do hereby Renounce all my Right Title [...]
now have or heretofore had unto the said [...]
forever by these Presents. In Witness where[of ...]
my hand and Seal the Ninth Day of May [...]
Year of his Majesties Reign annoque Domin[i ...]
=dred and fifty one _____

Signed Sealed & Delivered In Presence of }
Eben.r Barnard Ashel Sexton
Rec.d August 27 — 1751 and Recorded [...]
                                     p.r Edwar[d ...]

l off Northfield in

husetts Bay in new

hereunto moving

my Negroman

rom any further

troever to me or any

ng Right to his Ser-

ny Heirs or Assigns

Interest which I

h alias Prince

Gave hereunto Set

the Twenty fourth

thousand Seven Hun-

Burt & Seal

the Original

chon Reg'r

In the checkered lives of Abijah Prince and Lucy Terry is found a realistic romance going beyond the wildest flights of fiction.

—GEORGE SHELDON, 1896

CONTENTS

LIST OF ILLUSTRATIONS

The Prince

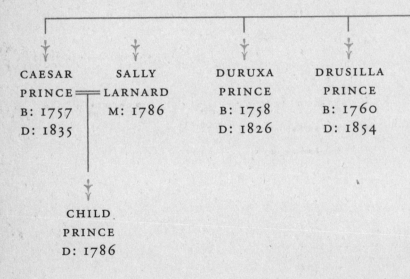

ABIJAH PRINCE
B: 1705–1706
D: 1794

CAESAR PRINCE ══ **SALLY LARNARD**
B: 1757 M: 1786
D: 1835

DURUXA PRINCE
B: 1758
D: 1826

DRUSILLA PRINCE
B: 1760
D: 1854

CHILD PRINCE
D: 1786

Note: Festus Prince and Lucy Holman had three children. One of them was named Festus, after his father, but we can't be sure which of the sons had this name. We assume the elder. The final Festus Prince could therefore be the son of either of these two. In the absence of concrete evidence, it is not certain that he belongs to the family, but all circumstantial evidence points to it.

Family Genealogy

LUCY TERRY
M: 1756
B: 1724–1726
D: 1821

FESTUS PRINCE	LUCY HOLMAN	TATNAI PRINCE	ABIJAH PRINCE	ANNA HARRIS
B: 1763	M: 1805	B: 1765	B: 1769	M: 1789
D: 1820		D: 1820	D: 1793	

DAUGHTER PRINCE	FESTUS (?) PRINCE	SON PRINCE	CHILD PRINCE
B: 1806– 1810	B: 1807– 1812	B: 1810– 1820	B: 1790 D: 1790

FESTUS PRINCE
B: 1847
D: 1920

MAP OF THE PARTS OF NEW ENGLAND WHERE THE PRINCES' STORY
TAKES PLACE. *Courtesy of Simon Gerzina and Carrie McBride*

A QUEST

When I stood on my front porch in Guilford, Vermont, and looked across the big meadow lying beneath Owl's Head and Pulpit Mountains, I could just make out the property bordering Packer Corners. On the other side of these mountains, more than two hundred years ago, this was the home of two former slaves, Abijah Prince and Lucy Terry, and their six children.

What used to be their farm is now eerie in its deserted quietness. Long and utterly uninhabited, the land is crisscrossed with crumbling stonewalls covered with ancient moss. Trees have fallen and others have grown, and yet it seems that at any moment Abijah himself will step out from behind a tree and wipe his brow, for it was he who cleared the property and built a home there. Abijah Prince and Lucy Terry were true New England settlers: hardworking and cash-poor but, like all the other self-made people in this formidable place, eager to acquire land as soon as it became available and to provide for their family. One important thing set them apart from the others: Bijah, as he would be known—it rhymes with Elijah—and Lucy were black.

In western New England in the 1700s, their romance and marriage blossomed and endured, taking Abijah Prince and Lucy Terry out of slavery and into legend. At a time when the burgeoning American slave trade was dominated by Rhode Island, when blacks outnumbered whites in the South, when southern slaves were denied the right to marry or to read or to keep their children, these two not only married, acquired property, and raised a family, but gained a lasting reputation for Bijah's tenacity and Lucy's gift for words. Today Lucy Terry is known as the nation's first documented African American poet.

"In the checkered lives of Abijah Prince and Lucy Terry," George Sheldon wrote more than one hundred years ago in his history of Deerfield, Massachusetts, "is found a realistic romance going beyond the wildest flights of fiction." He wasn't the first to write about Bijah and Lucy, but thanks to him, their story came to public attention, spawning a century of efforts by amateur historians to find the rest of the story, most of which they got wrong, and which this book definitively corrects. It's easy to see how this happened, with people so hungry for stories about our hidden, undocumented past and forgotten ancestry. Like all good fiction, this begins with a love story and the triumph of good over evil. It is Romeo and Juliet, David and Goliath, Moses and Pharoah, all rolled together, but taking place in colonial and revolutionary America, with black people as the heroes.

I fell in love with Lucy and Bijah from the moment I first heard of them. How could I not love a woman who arrived in New England from Africa as a small enslaved child in the early 1700s and reputedly went on to argue successfully cases before the Vermont and U.S. Supreme Courts? How could I not love the man who, as a grizzled veteran of the French and Indian Wars, extricated himself from lonely slavery in a tiny Massachusetts town and then helped the much younger Lucy to her own freedom? She was said to be smart and magnetic, to have a way with words, a poet; he was determined and entrepreneurial enough to become a landowner. Together they raised a family of proud and patriotic children, along the way showing everyone just how hard they would fight to keep what was theirs, whenever and wherever that right was challenged.

Here is the story as I first read it, before I knew how much of it was wrong. This is still more or less the way it appears in most accounts people read. In 1730 a five- or six-year-old African girl named Lucy Terry arrived in Deerfield, in what was then part of the New England frontier, among a few largely unprotected settlements in the far west of the Massachusetts Bay Colony. Lucy arrived as the property of Ebenezer and Abigail Wells, a childless couple who had the little girl baptized. She was very popular, known for her gift for words and storytelling. Deerfield had suffered several disastrous attacks before Lucy arrived, but in 1746, after more than two decades of relative peace, another Indian attack on a group of Deerfield farmers and their children brought death and terror to the village. In its aftermath, Lucy composed her only surviving poem, a singsongy ballad commemorating this "Bars Fight." The poem wouldn't be published for another hundred years but was passed down through repetition and memory.

In 1756 Lucy married Abijah Prince, the former slave of the Rev. Benjamin Doolittle of Northfield, who freed Bijah and arranged for him to acquire land in that town. Several years later, another Deerfield resident, David Field, was said to have fulfilled his father's promise by giving Bijah one hundred acres in Guilford, Vermont, where the Princes eventually moved and established a farm. As Bijah grew old, their unscrupulous neighbors set fire to their hayrick and drove animals onto their property in an attempt to ruin their crops and run them off their land. Lucy fought back with her finest weapon—her tongue—fending off repeated attacks and legal challenges with an awe-inspiring articulateness, taking their case all the way to the Vermont Supreme

Court and arguing it herself—and she won. At the founding of Williams College, trying to gain a place for one of her sons—two of whom had served in the Revolutionary War—she argued in front of the trustees for three hours, quoting biblical chapter and verse. Unmoved, at the end of her oration they still refused to admit a black student.

After Bijah's death in 1794, the legend continues, Lucy moved with her grown children to another large property that Bijah had acquired across the state in Sunderland, eighteen miles from Bennington, close to the New York border. Once again a neighbor tried to evict them from their land, and once again Lucy fought back. Everything I read said that she took a case all the way to the U.S. Supreme Court, again arguing it herself, and again winning.

The story I first heard a dozen years ago, passed on like a game of telephone with facts altered and misunderstood as they went from person to person, always ended with the moving account of how, until her death in 1821, the nearly blind Lucy made an annual pilgrimage across Vermont to visit Bijah's grave to continue the long conversation with the man she loved. The story had everything to fascinate—not only a heroic and forgotten couple but a rewriting of the history of slavery in America. Two hundred years before I was born, they had lived near where I had grown up in western Massachusetts, in towns where even today few black families live. Then they had moved to the very town I moved to before I knew of them. How could I *not* go looking for them?

On a second look, Bijah and Lucy's story seemed entirely one of gaps, a fool's mission made up of the thinnest net of provable truths. Many have hunted for more information on the Princes in the more than one hundred years that have passed since Sheldon wrote his book, but no one has been able to verify more than a handful of facts; the rest have been either missing or contradicted. I held little hope of discovering anything more. Biographers of the long-dead rely upon the written word, spending years poring over letters, journals, and published works. But what if those things do not exist? What if no one was even sure that your subjects were literate? As Hermione Lee writes, "Biographies are full of verifiable facts, but they are also full of things that aren't there: absences, gaps, missing evidence, knowledge or information that has been passed from person to person, losing credibility or shifting shape on the way." She wonders what to do "with the facts that can't be fixed, the things that go missing, the body parts that have been turned into legends and myths?" Even the Princes' bodies have gone missing, Bijah's plowed under by a Vermont farmer a century after his burial, and Lucy's grave never located. But as the recent discoveries of African burial grounds in Manhattan and Portsmouth, New Hampshire, prove, the African American presence is long and deep, with miraculous things still waiting to be discovered. If a net is a series of holes held together by string, as it's been defined, I was determined to look for the strings.

After two years of researching their story on my own, my husband, Anthony, joined me in the hunt for the details of their lives, and the simple story turned into a life-changing experience for both of us. A former marketing manager for an international corporation, he had been downsized a few years earlier. We gave up our other home and moved into the one we'd had built in Guilford, and Anthony threw himself into the rural life. Though he has an MBA, he was no researcher or academic; he is a white guy with only an average knowledge of African American history. He looked bewildered when we first walked into the library at Historic Deerfield and I put an account book in front of him. Within weeks our roles were reversed. Soon it was he who walked me through the archival materials, who read them in a fresh way that only someone who was seeing something new could have done. He made important deductions and connections, and between us the true story of Bijah and Lucy and their children opened up.

Yet at the same time, the more we learned about the Princes, the more complicated the story of how race and slavery operated in eighteenth-century rural America became. So much has been written, filmed, and discussed about southern slavery in the nineteenth century that we have all but erased many of those slaves' forebears, those who helped to make America before it was even a country. More than two hundred years after Bijah's death and nearly as many since Lucy's, the Princes and their children are at the heart of what it means to be American. There is a growing body of literature around slavery in New England, and we have to read their story against the entire body of colonial and revolutionary history. If the details tell of particular lives, they also can be seen as the bolder strokes of a new nation coming into being, shaped and altered by a new terrain and new human encounters. From the early French and Indian battles in which Bijah fought and which Lucy memorialized in poetry, through the Revolutionary War in which two of their sons fought, up to nearly the Civil War and emancipation, their story goes against much of what we think we know about African Americans in early America—and indeed about America itself.

Their world was geographically small; once Lucy arrived as a child from Africa, it was encompassed by western Massachusetts and southern Vermont. There is no evidence that either of them knew the nearest major cities of Boston, New York, or Philadelphia, let alone the South. Bijah's birth around 1706 predates the United States itself by seventy years. Yet their lives and the remarkable way in which they chose to live them are part of a history few have imagined ever existed or could be found. By detailing the history of a family that was able to accomplish much of what most settlers of that area strived for and the lives of African Americans who in many ways were as Puritan in their values as the next family, and who were even arguably an accepted part of the community yet were nonetheless nearly ruined by the effects of slavery, this book shows how morally complex New England slavery was long before the Civil War.

Our search for Bijah and Lucy lasted for more than seven years and took us all over several states. This book records a pilgrimage, a quest to honor them by piecing together their story from the long-hidden facts tucked away in old account books, town meeting minutes, court dockets, and other records in New England, New York, and Washington, D.C., almost everything written in quill pen and fading eighteenth-century script. Over time we touched papers the Princes had touched, stood on their land, discovered their community, deciphered their illnesses, discovered what became of their children, and pieced together a story that had lain dormant for centuries.

We had no idea, at least at first, that we were probably compiling the most complete story ever known about an eighteenth-century African American family. It isn't always a happy story, but it is a remarkable one that changes perceptions of early American history. It also changed my life in a way that I never anticipated, for it revealed my own family history and the completely unexpected connection between my story and theirs.

PART ONE

Bijah

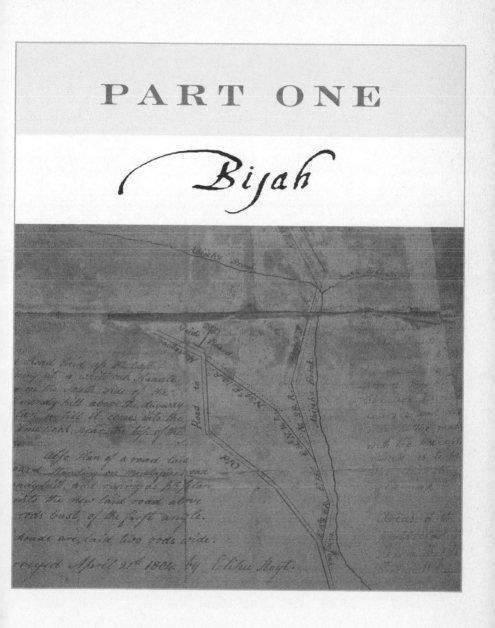

CHAPTER ONE

THE ATTACK

On Tuesday, October 4, 1785, half a dozen men, later described by the courts as a "mob," armed themselves with clubs and crashed through a farm gate and into the Guilford, Vermont, house of Abijah and Lucy Prince. Several of the attackers had wrangled with the Princes in court on and off over small debts and trumped up transgressions. For months, financed and encouraged by the Princes' nearest neighbor, they hounded the former slaves, but the elderly Bijah and Lucy not only refused to be intimidated but responded to every assault with defiance. Only five months before, Lucy had left behind her eighty-year-old husband to guard the house while she traveled north to take their complaints to the highest governing body of the independent republic of Vermont, and she powerfully impressed the Governor and Council with the first speech they had ever heard by an African American. She returned with an order of protection, but it had no effect against the thugs who were now breaking down her door.

They made their way inside, brutally beating the Princes' hired man, a mulatto. Bijah and Lucy escaped harm, but the attackers set fire to their hayrick as they raced off. No hay could mean no food throughout the coming winter for the livestock, and therefore no food for themselves, or transportation, or way to make a living. It was likely to mean poverty, starvation, and failure. Others might have given up, but Bijah and Lucy had not faced a lifetime of warfare and the struggle for their own freedom in order to be run off their hundred acres. Instead, they went straight to the authorities and lodged complaints. Within days, arrest warrants were issued for all six attackers. One absconded, but the others were locked up, and all eventually ended up before the law, with three of the Princes and a large number of others subpoenaed to testify against them.

The Princes, as we shall see, were no strangers to the courts. Had they lived in the South, they would not have been allowed to testify against whites, let alone file charges. So much of how they became who they were depended upon the fact that they lived in New England, a place of contradictions. Slavery was firmly ingrained in the economy and social network of many of the states, but the principle of legal fair play also prevailed, sometimes awkwardly, alongside enslavement in a complicated world inhabited by Africans, Indians, and Europeans. In the stories about the Princes, Lucy always appears as the one who repeatedly acted as a lawyer, but it would turn out that it was Bijah who taught her to pursue her rights through the courts. How did he learn this? To understand that we begin where his life began, nearly eighty years before the attack, and long before the state of Vermont was even imagined.

It was Bijah's luck, or perhaps his misfortune, to enter life in this complex, violent, and troubled part of New England, far from the cities of Boston and Philadelphia, and farther still from the yet-to-be-developed southern plantations. In an interesting historical coincidence, he was born about three hundred years ago, in 1706, the same year as Benjamin Franklin, another self-made man who left his home to begin a new life. Their life spans were almost exactly parallel—Franklin died just four years before Prince at the end of the century—but aside from Franklin's eventual opposition to slavery and the fact that they both came of age in Massachusetts, they occupied different universes. Franklin was completely urban: when he left the family home in Boston, he set out for the city of Philadelphia, and he later spent years in Paris serving the American cause. He abandoned his wife for years and was a largely absent father. Bijah lived in the country and in small towns, clearing land and building a house with his own hands, fighting in an earlier war, and devoted to his family. Black and white, rural and urban, their paths never crossed, but they both lived out important versions of a new country.

Tradition says that Bijah began his journey in Wallingford, Connecticut, near New Haven, just after the time when the Congregationalist descendants of the Puritan settlers had bought out, killed, or decimated by illness the native population with whom they came to trade. Yet how can one be sure? Although the early New Englanders were meticulous record keepers, if you were black, your name—such as it was—was put on paper only if you had dealings with a court, if you were bought or sold or inherited, or if you were baptized. If you ran away, newspaper advertisements might describe your height, coloring, distinguishing features, the clothes you ran off in, and your facility with the English language, since English might be your second or even third language. If you did none of these things, you probably faded into obscurity as another "John Negro" or "Coffee" or "Mary" whose origins or fate seemed negligible, your tastes and your life unremarked. In New England you were likely to be given a first name that was English or biblical, just as were the whites, but rarely a last name, unless occasionally that of an owner. Abijah Prince's first name comes, like most Puritan names, from the Old

Testament and was prescient: one of the biblical Abijahs was appointed by his father to become a judge. Many male slaves were named Prince, but very few from three hundred years ago had both a first and last name; Bijah wore his name proudly, insisting in later years on signing his full name rather than an X on legal documents.

He may have gotten his last name from a slave owner, or his father may have been named Prince. Two entrepreneurial ship captains near New Haven, Samuel Prince and Josiah Prince of Milford, Connecticut, made many runs up and down to the Caribbean on their "coasters." The owners of this sort of trading sloop often dealt in slaves on a small scale, for themselves or for friends. They carried supplies grown on several Connecticut slave plantations to feed slaves on West Indian plantations, returning with rum, molasses and sugar, and other products.

Armed with nothing but conjecture, a couple of dates, and an eventual master's name of Doolittle, I began, far too confidently, to try to track down Bijah's origins in Connecticut and headed for the state library. The Connecticut State Library is a haven for researchers on family history, with some of the most knowledgeable librarians in the field. It occupies the bottom floors of a courthouse in Hartford, protected by stern armed guards and metal detectors. Having written several histories, I was at home in libraries all over America and England; I had researched biographies and thought I knew my way around archives. Yet now, a neophyte among a crowd of family researchers, I found that I knew nothing about the vital records, church records, manuscripts, computer terminals, microfilms, and secondary materials that form the backbone of genealogical research. I had never heard of the Barber or Corbin compilations. Accustomed to the hush of university libraries and the help of reference librarians,

I was at sea among the seasoned amateur searchers of their families' pasts who chatted so loudly and familiarly about their discoveries at the large tables. On a good day, the state librarians try to make up for this array of materials with enthusiasm and knowledge. On a bad day, with genealogists occupying most of the seats and microfilm readers, you're on your own. Somehow believing that no one else had thought to look for Bijah in Connecticut, I sat down to plow through the records. Hours later I was humbled.

There was a black Abijah Prince in the Connecticut census, but he was there in 1790, by which time my elderly Bijah had been living in Vermont for years. There were many black people listed under the heading of "Negro," with no last name, but the dates and names were similarly wrong. Among the many mentions of other early black inhabitants were the happy but uncommon records of black marriages and the impossibly sad records of slaves being sold or put in their owner's will as property, their lives signed away in the formal and chilly legal language of the 1600s and 1700s. It was a relief not to find Bijah's name there.

Knowing from the legend that Bijah was taken to Northfield, Massachusetts, by a young Wallingford minister named Benjamin Doolittle, I turned to this family, which began in America with a patriarch appropriately named Abraham, the first of his American tribe. Thirty years after the Pequot Wars, in which Connecticut and Massachusetts colonists and soldiers massacred much of that Indian nation and sold the survivors into slavery on Barbados, Abraham Doolittle—or Dowlittel, as he spelled it— founded Wallingford, surveying and laying out the new settlement. He occupied a world that remained dangerous, but into which the English never hesitated to expand, and he became its earliest and most important citizen. I was certain that such a prominent early family had left papers behind and that perhaps the sale of a slave boy might be mentioned in them. A few weeks after my fruitless visit to the Connecticut State Library, I drove to the Connecticut Historical Society in suburban West Hartford. There I made a mistake that I soon learned not to repeat: I told the librarian that I was researching a black man's history.

A strange thing happens when you tell some librarians and archivists that you are looking for an African American. They hear that phrase and cannot go past it, separating out black and white American histories as though they were not interconnected. "We have so little on African American history," she said sadly. "I wish we had more. Have you looked at our website?" She checked her computer, only to report that there was nothing in the Doolittle files about black history. With coaxing, she finally produced the Doolittle file, a surprisingly slim folder containing nothing of interest except a highly romanticized history of Abraham, "the ancestor of all the Doolittles in America," written by one of his proud Victorian descendants. I made a copy to read at home.

I learned that Abraham Doolittle was a Puritan who arrived in Boston in about 1640 with his brother, John, just twenty years after the *Mayflower* landed in America. Men of good sense, courage, and faith, the Doolittle brothers were in their early twenties when they left England, and over the next decades they would be called to public work. John repeatedly held the positions of constable, tithing man, and surveyor in eastern Massachusetts, while Abraham and his wife, Joan, left almost immediately for New Haven, where he was among the first proprietors, allotted an acre and a half in the new village and more acreage outside of it.

Within two years of his arrival in New Haven, Abraham Doolittle became sheriff, and from that followed a series of public offices. When plans were laid to found the new colony of Wallingford a dozen miles away on a hill overlooking the Quinnipiac River, Abraham was the man chosen to head the inspection party into a land that was still wooded and full of wolves, moose, and deer— and native people. It was not a bucolic place, yet in his vision it was already transformed into orderly squares and rectangles, with a main street running through the middle and a church. As far as the new village and surrounding fields might spread, he knew that the new settlers would always push up against dangers that they did not control. His was a world of masters and servants, of oppositions between civilized people and savages, between original sin and a striving toward redemption.

As time went on, he held nearly every important job in the new community of Wallingford: treasurer, explorer of the surrounding area, surveyor of highways, cofounder of the first church, and selectman. Along the way he was given more and more land and the rank of sergeant. In 1675, during King Philip's War, he had his house fortified in the usual way—with a wall of sixteen-foot-tall logs, sharpened to points, to keep out Indian attackers. He died in 1690 at the age of seventy, fifteen years before Bijah was born: a man of substance, honored by those in New Haven and in the now-prospering town and revered by his descendants, including the man whose account I was reading. Ten of Abraham's children survived into adulthood. Some of his grandchildren suffered from great "weakness and infirmity," but his son John married three times in an era when men frequently outlived their exhausted wives.

One of John's sons, Benjamin, is at the heart of Bijah's story. Born in 1695 to John's second wife, Mary Peck, Benjamin was a mentally quick and physically able young man educated at Yale.

Like the more established Harvard, Yale still had relatively few students, all men, many of them descended from the first settlers, and nearly all of them Congregationalists, and they were taught by tutors scarcely older than their students. The college was in flux, so seniors in his class were allowed to go where they preferred to finish their degrees, and Benjamin chose Wethersfield. Like many of his fellow students, he studied religious doctrine and medicine, for it was common for young graduates to minister to both the souls and the bodies of their congregations.

Positions for these young graduates were plentiful, since one of the first desires of those establishing new settlements in western Massachusetts and what is now known as the Pioneer Valley, which snakes up the Connecticut River into nearby present-day Vermont and New Hampshire, was to convince a clergyman to settle among them. When Benjamin graduated from Yale in 1716, he was asked to try life in a largely unprotected establishment lying north of the older towns of Springfield and Northampton, Massachusetts. A month before he left the calm and relatively cultured safety of Wallingford for the decidedly riskier life of a minister in an area under repeated attack by the French, who disputed ownership of much of the territory, and their Indian allies, Benjamin married. It would take a strong and adventurous woman to embark upon such a precarious life, and he had found just such a one in Lydia Todd, a twenty-year-old schoolteacher from a prominent North Haven family. Her parents, Samuel Todd and Susanna Tuttle, were able to provide Lydia with a handsome dowry of £165, an enormous amount in a time when ready money was rare and banks nonexistent. Lydia would prove to be every bit as hardy and self-reliant as Benjamin hoped. They married in October 1717 and headed to Northfield shortly afterward, taking with them Bijah, a twelve-year-old slave boy, a common gift for a newly ordained minister.

As I put down the Doolittle family history, I was speechless. I had just understood an astonishing and wholly unexpected fact: when Lydia Todd married Benjamin Doolittle, a member of my ancestral family became the owner of Abijah Prince.

CHAPTER TWO

BIJAH'S LIFE
WITH THE DOOLITTLES

When I looked over the Doolittle records, I noticed again that Lydia Doolittle's maiden name was Todd and that her mother had been a Tuttle. I am descended from Connecticut Tuttles on my mother's side and hadn't thought much about it before then. Tuttles in New England are like rocks in Vermont: so ubiquitous that they seem to grow from the soil. In Lydia's day, families commonly had up to a dozen children, and each child went on to have another dozen. It was this rapid population growth that fueled the desperate acquisition for land, often farther and farther away from the original colonial settlements.

Somehow these Tuttles caught my attention, however, and their names seemed familiar. I turned to my mother for her genealogical expertise. For decades my sister and I had mocked her obsession with genealogy, a passion she caught long before the family genealogy craze came into full swing. At times her bed was so covered with forms and papers and binders that our father fitted himself onto a narrow strip of mattress to sleep while she worked. Even today, at over eighty, she goes off for weeks at a time by bus to do her research in distant states and volunteers at the local history room of her library. Her Connecticut, Michigan, and Ohio ancestors proved a source of endless discovery, and she had traced their roots back to Britain and Germany. She tried for years to find as much as she could about my father's African American family, getting as far back as the early nineteenth century. This time, however, it was her family, my white ancestors, whom I needed to understand. I got into the car and drove down to the house where I grew up in Springfield, Massachusetts, where she still lives.

"Don't get your hopes up," she warned as she pulled out her volumes of notebooks and binders with their meticulously researched and recorded family lines, each full of hard-earned and verifiable facts. She sniffs at lazy genealogists who search only on the Internet and put down conjectures and assumptions without the documents and cross-checks that prove them correct or not.

Line by line, we traced back our lineage. Lydia's grandfather was my many-times-great-grandfather. Incredibly, there on the chart were Lydia Doolittle, her parents, and their parents and siblings. "I'll be darned," said my mother. Lydia's uncle—her mother's brother—was our direct ancestor. Our direct ancestors no doubt saw Bijah during family visits in Wallingford and Northfield when he moved there with Lydia and Benjamin; they stood in the same room; they gave him orders; they saw him grow from a boy into a man, living in that isolated and often dangerous place.

In 1718, one year before Daniel Defoe published his novel *Robinson Crusoe* in England, young Bijah must have felt as though he were stranded on a desert island when he arrived in Northfield, Massachusetts. Despite cajoling, bribes, and threats, only a dozen families had moved to the settlement, and the empty lots around the village square were held by absentee landowners and speculators who declined to settle into what they described as a "Puritan outpost." It was only in the previous year that a gristmill, sawmill, and dam had been built; before that, ox teams hauled grain and boards all the way from Hadley. Twelve-year-old Bijah moved onto a nearly empty street, into a nearly empty town; the nearest black person, a slave named Caesar, lived on a farm miles away on the outskirts of the town.

As the townspeople gathered to welcome their new minister and his bride, they could not help glancing skeptically at Bijah and wondering how long the worldly newcomers would last in this rugged fledgling village. In many New England towns, owning a slave would have signaled his entry into professional life. But that was not Northfield's way.

Benjamin Doolittle's predecessor, twenty-one-year-old James Whitmore, had remained just six months, perhaps because his only compensation had been an annual salary of £25, room and board for him and his horse, and the opportunity to preach outdoors, since there was no meetinghouse. To attract someone like Doolittle, they offered to build a house of sixteen feet by twelve feet, hardly an attractive inducement for a young man accustomed to life in prosperous Wallingford and about to start a family. Luckily for him, but unfortunately for another family, just before Doolittle's arrival another house became available when its owner drowned in the Connecticut River. The town offered to build a meetinghouse and added substantial land and money to the original proposition: another seventy acres of land, a sum of £100 to be paid out over three years, an annual salary of £55 for six years, firewood for six years, and after that, "as much wood as each man might cart on sled in one day of each year." The Doolittles and their servant—for those living in this part of the world eschewed the unpleasant word "slave"—moved into the house almost directly opposite Cap. Benjamin Wright, an old Indian fighter who had led scalping expeditions and ordered the murders of native babies to prevent them from developing into full-grown enemies and who was now Northfield's leading citizen. It was a good deal on both sides. Doolittle had negotiated a good contract, and the town gained a young man committed to the fledgling community and to their religious doctrine. The twenty-eight-year-old minister opened the first town meeting, held in the new meetinghouse, with a prayer.

Over the years the Doolittles put together a handsome household, containing no fewer than ten beds, several of them with mattresses and bolsters and fine sheets. They put pictures on the walls, cloths on the tables, and curtains on the windows. Benjamin and Lydia eventually accumulated fourteen parcels of land, ranging from five to four hundred acres each, and sold off lots from time to time at a profit. Over the years the house became more crowded as Lydia gave birth to eleven children and soldiers boarded with them. It is unlikely that Bijah got to sleep in any of the ten beds, although he probably had a place by the cooking fire, in the attic, or with the male children. He came to adulthood in a household thick with people and possessions, both practical and fine, as an insider who was also an outsider, at the beck and call of more than a dozen people.

Was it my distant relative Lydia, the former schoolteacher, who taught Bijah to read? Somehow he learned to do so, and to write a bit too, in an unpracticed hand. Doolittle bought a primer when his first child, Oliver, was five, and perhaps Bijah sat with them in the evenings while Lydia taught the letters to her growing family. At first Lydia taught her children at home, but as time went on and the town grew, a small school opened for six months each year. As a slave, Bijah could never have attended school; he was more valuable as a laborer in the fields and woods, and he learned every aspect of rural and community life. He raised flax, hoed corn, harvested grain, and tended horses, oxen, cows, and pigs. He learned to fish, hunt, and handle a scow and a canoe. He knew how to ride a horse and handle a gun. He trained himself to watch for chances to learn new skills, easy enough when one was the only servant to a family with large landholdings. All of these skills were crucial when he eventually struck out on his own.

Except for a twenty-year period ending in 1746, Northfield and the neighboring towns faced frightening attacks and threats as the French and Indians sought to drive the western New England settlers off the land. Based in Quebec, raiders traveled down the St. Lawrence River, into Lake Champlain, overland to the Connecticut River, and on into territory that France wanted to claim for itself. Just as upsetting to the Protestant settlers of New England was that the French and their Algonquin nation allies were all practicing Catholics. During war years no one was safe, and any sound or shape was taken for an enemy. Ebenezer Field, a blacksmith who had arrived from Deerfield only three years earlier, was mistaken in the twilight for a native and shot by his Northfield neighbors. They rushed him to Deerfield, but he died in the town he had so recently left. Indians stabbed a portly old white woman in the back as she walked home in the twilight. During these times families went to their fields with armed lookouts, and men attended the long Sunday meetinghouse services wearing pistols. It may have been the practice on southern plantations, where blacks far outnumbered whites, to deny slaves the use of firearms, but on the Massachusetts frontier all men needed to know how to shoot and to protect the colony. Bijah would spend much of his life in places defined by strife.

The governor of the Massachusetts Bay Colony, recognizing Northfield's unfortified vulnerability during these first years of

Doolittle's ministry, approved the building of a garrison to be permanently staffed by ten soldiers who had to board with town residents. Doolittle was allowed a private guard of two soldiers, who lived in his house. On October 9, 1723, when a group of twenty Indians attacked the lower fort at Northfield and seventy more attacked a group of men going from one fort to another, the governor ordered fifty men out to the area. Another forty men were ordered out to protect Northfield, Deerfield, and Brookfield in response to an "evil [that] grows worse daily."

A year later a major conference among the English and Indians took place in Deerfield, signaling a peace that would last for twenty years, until 1744. Lydia gave birth to her fourth child, a daughter they named Eunice, only a few weeks after the tracks of thirty native people were found near the town. But for the most part peace prevailed, and a generation grew up knowing no fear of raids. During these years Doolittle spent more and more time away from home at Fort Dummer in both his capacities as parson and physician, for which he was paid a salary on top of what his congregation paid him. Bijah undoubtedly accompanied him on some of these errands.

As time passed and the fear of raids faded away, Doolittle faced growing antagonism from his congregation, and some of the hostility concerned Bijah. Though over the years he successfully argued for salary increases, which he received, Doolittle's long absences, growing wealth, and increasing absences rankled those who paid his salary. Twice they tried to suspend his free deliveries of firewood, and twice he got the deliveries reinstated. No one denied that a good doctor was necessary to tend to the soldiers who were so essential to the town's defenses, but they knew that he was well paid for his services elsewhere, while neglecting the needs of his flock. By 1739 to 1741, when he had been living in Northfield for more than twenty years, he was traveling regularly between there and Fort Dummer, making more than £50 a year for this military work in addition to his £75 annual salary as minister.

Some of the fruits of this income were visible; he may have been a hardy frontiersman used to roughing it in freezing forts and on his own land, but he and his family also loved nice clothes, good food, and material possessions. On Doolittle's shopping excursions, he and his daughters brought home fine fabrics, ribbons, and linen handkerchiefs. Bijah, too, became known in the shops, occasionally making his own extremely modest purchases, and he must have relished the trips to Deerfield, which, although small, had a substantial slave population. Kept regularly away from others of his own race except when he made such excursions to other towns, Bijah found himself further isolated by belonging to a highly prominent yet increasingly unpopular man.

Northfield's opposition to its busy minister grew, and by 1739 he was formally accused of religious heterodoxy. The townspeople had many accusations in their arsenal: his two professions, prolonged absences, and religious doctrine were all targeted. To drive him out they threw at him whatever might stick. Among these was a serious charge that concerned Bijah: after twenty years in Northfield, Doolittle's slave-owning status still rankled with them. With one or two exceptions, no other residents, even those with a reasonable income, owned slaves, and Doolittle's practice of renting out Bijah's labor to others and thereby profiting from the unpaid labor of another seemed yet another example of his greed. The case went before magistrates, who urged the town to work out its difficulties, but the discontent did not fade. Ultimately, no less a luminary than the famous Northampton minister Jonathan Edwards, himself a slave owner who brought many black people into his own church through conversion and baptism, finally came to Doolittle's defense, arguing that those who complained the loudest about Negro slavery also directly benefited from slavery whenever they hired Bijah from Doolittle. Their objections had less to do with sincere antislavery sentiments than with their personal objections to their pastor, Edwards declared. The controversy died down, but ironically it was Edwards who was eventually forced out of his Northampton ministry; he moved to Stockbridge later becoming president of the College of New Jersey, now known as Princeton University, taking his slaves with him. The people of Northampton, however, had no uncertainties concerning their feelings toward slavery, and the black population continued to grow. Eventually Bijah and his children would come to find real community there, but as a slave in Northfield he lived a life of labor and racial solitude.

The last ten years of Benjamin Doolittle's life were ones of strife and loss in which he grieved over the consecutive losses of four of his nine children and the return of war. The cruelest death was that of his firstborn son, who, unlike the others, had survived the dangers of childhood diseases only to be killed at the battle of Louisburg on Cape Breton when the English wrested the fort away from the French. Doolittle's poem "On the Death of My Children" showed him resigned to God's will, but at the same time he railed in his war journal against the failure of the colony to properly supply and protect people and forts closer to home. When King George's War broke out in 1744, he was so alarmed that he had his house bulletproofed, lining it with oak planks three inches thick. As Doolittle became more and more preoccupied with his personal and professional griefs, Bijah, now a man approaching middle age, began fending more and more for himself, taking odd jobs here and there, including hanging out the town flag. Then, at the beginning of January 1749, while repairing fence posts, Doolittle had a heart attack and died.

After the minister's death, Col. Timothy Dwight, up until the previous year judge of the probate court and now judge of Hampshire County Court, made up the probate list. With Lydia as his administrator, Dwight settled Doolittle's accounts and debts. It was an extensive and exhaustive list, but Bijah's name did not appear on it, suggesting that Doolittle had freed the slave who had grown to middle age in his service. But he had not.

Instead, Bijah seems to have been left nearly forgotten by his master, too great an embarrassment to ignore during Doolittle's troubles, and yet too valuable to be let go. Why was Bijah left in a limbo that allowed him movement but not freedom? We can only assume that a slave was too valuable an asset, even to a relatively wealthy widow like Lydia and her well-off children, to be simply freed.

After spending two years trying to piece together the Princes' lives, I had read all the histories of the various towns I knew they had lived in: Wallingford, Connecticut; Deerfield, Massachusetts; and in Vermont, Guilford and Sunderland. I had been to historical societies and spoken to librarians and local historians. I had tracked down the elderly descendants of Benjamin Doolittle, still living in Northfield hundreds of years later. They knew the story well but had little to add, hoping instead that I might unearth something new. Before closing the file on Bijah's early life, I looked once more at Lydia's family history, just to make sure that Bijah had not been given to her in a will or as a marriage gift. Though that search came up empty as well, I found myself interested in this young woman who gave up safety, society, and comfort to move to the Massachusetts frontier with her new husband. It was in a letter written by one of her grandchildren that I learned about her later life and discovered that she was, even then, the devoted and feisty woman she promised to be at her marriage. I never knew what she thought about slavery, but she never owned another slave in her long life.

I did learn that after Benjamin's death Lydia outlived two more husbands. Her third wedding, to the widower Japhet Chapin of Chicopee, took place when he was eighty-two and she was eighty. They were so vigorous that they rode on horseback from Chicopee to Northfield in one day, a total of forty miles, without tiring. She wore a beautiful sky blue riding hood made especially for the wedding. When Chapin later fell ill and became delirious, he thought she was his first wife and kept asking for the widow Doolittle to call on him. Without turning a hair, she left the room and changed her clothes and returned as Lydia Doolittle instead of Lydia Chapin. The pleasant visit over, she left the room and changed back to her original clothes, and he told her all about the visit Mrs. Doolittle had paid him. He died seven years after their marriage. Both mentally and physically strong, she impressed everyone with her morality and intelligence, and it seemed that she could go on forever. She did not die of old age. Instead, she slipped and fell while lifting one of her great-grandchildren off a table and injured her lungs. She was ninety-two.

In December 1719, a year or so after Lydia, Benjamin, and Bijah left Wallingford for Northfield, the night sky put on a display all over New England, causing great alarm. Undulating stripes of white light lit up the heavens from east to west across the horizon. Behind a veil of white, the mountains and stars were still visible.

Thinking that it looked like the light that a burning house throws off, those watching believed that the sky itself was on fire. The spectacle lasted for an hour, subsided, but then returned at eleven o'clock, this time with a blood-red color pulsing through the streaks. People stood outside, their mouths open in dread, until the clouds finally obscured the fiery sky. The lights reappeared just before dawn, and "those who saw it say it was then most terrible." The northern lights are a common sight in the Northeast and Canada, but this is the first recorded instance of them in America, and those who now saw them for the first time were filled with foreboding and wondered whether the heavens were lighting up with an indecipherable message.

This is what I felt myself as I discovered my family's part in Bijah's story. It was as though I had gone to a family dinner and discovered that I was in the wrong house. I felt shocked and ashamed, and with that shame came a deep desire for atonement and an even more urgent desire to recover their story—not for myself but for the Princes, who, I was certain, had been nudging me along their path. I had to keep going, and now I knew that I needed help: the academic year was about to resume, and with it came the end of a generous grant that had given me a year to research them. I turned not to a research assistant but to my husband, Anthony, who by now had been drawn into the story and also longed to see where it led. No amount of searching produced any more mentions of Bijah in connection with the Doolittle family, but we were convinced that they had not freed him. We began to piece together his next years, a period of time that up to now had remained a blank in the legend that surrounded him.

What he did—two years before Doolittle's death—was to take his life into his own hands. At over forty years of age, Bijah left Northfield and carefully forged a series of alliances with influential whites known as the "river gods" of western Massachusetts and with a parallel community of free and determined black people that we came privately to call the "Negro network." He initiated this sea change by doing what any unhappy man who needed to leave a small town would do: on March 1, 1747, Abijah Prince joined the army.

He traveled for four years and by the end of that time was a changed man with an unanticipated new life.

CHAPTER THREE

BIJAH GOES TO WAR

It is hard to imagine two men who differed more than Abijah Prince and Elijah Williams. In 1747, when he left Benjamin Doolittle's house, Bijah was a forty-one-year-old slave, although he had a certain limited freedom of movement. He was a black man with neither property nor family. We don't know what he looked like, but men of the laboring class dressed simply in breeches and stockings, topped by long shirts and wide-brimmed hats. He smoked a clay pipe and could read; he could write some too—they were taught as separate skills in those days. He longed not for the fripperies of upper-class fashion but for the same basic things that all men wanted: property, family, independence. All these he would get over the next two decades, one way or another, through Elijah Williams, a clergyman's son, shopkeeper, and businessman who knew Doolittle, Bijah, and Lucy. Doolittle sometimes shopped at his store, and as prominent men from neighboring towns, they and their slaves often encountered each other on the streets and in the shops. Northfield was a rustic place, and some who needed supplies liked to make the twenty-mile trip to the more convivial town of Deerfield.

We don't know what Elijah looked like at thirty-five, but if his half-brother Stephen's portrait shows a family resemblance, he was a full-faced, self-satisfied man with small features and a healthy appetite. He was a merchant who wrote in an elegant hand, wore

good wigs and had them refurbished regularly, built a fine house and filled it with select furnishings from Boston, Europe, and Asia, dressed himself and his family in the latest London fashions, and felt keenly the need to serve politically and militarily—with an eye to turning a buck on the side if possible.

Part of an enormously influential Massachusetts Tory family, Elijah Williams was Harvard-educated and had completed most of the work for a master's degree. His father was the Rev. John Williams, the most famous redeemed captive from the 1704 French and Indian raid on Deerfield, in which more than one hundred residents were killed or marched to Canada for ransom; Elijah was one of the children of John's second marriage. One of his cousins left money to found the school that became Williams

College. Several members of the family were high-ranking military officers, several were prominent ministers, and another was a judge. The Williamses, along with several other families, made up a group known as the "river gods" because they prospered in commerce, based at that time on the Connecticut River. Elijah wasn't one of the most prominent members of his clan, but he lived in a big house on the Deerfield common, next to the meetinghouse and across the road from the Wellses, the family who had come to own Lucy Terry. Williams's family and his family's slaves saw Lucy every day in their comings and goings. Living in such a small place, Elijah undoubtedly encountered Bijah too over the years, particularly when Benjamin Doolittle and Bijah traveled to Deerfield to conduct Benjamin's business.

Just before King George's War of 1744–48, Elijah worked as a surveyor, raised cattle, and kept a successful shop in an old cider mill with a sign reading TO ALBANY on its outside corner next to the street, much in the way modern highway signs remind us of the last gas station in the state. There he sold everything from essentials like flax, tobacco, rum, and rye to little luxuries like chocolate, snuff boxes, and lace. One of his big sellers was his father's memoir of the 1704 raid, *The Redeemed Captive.* On his substantial acreage he grew hay and grain and raised livestock, which he not only sold locally but sent to markets in Connecticut by river and east to Salem and Boston. He was also an ambitious entrepreneur who dipped his fingers into many pots, a business practice that eventually led to his financial downfall. He was to find the war years particularly profitable, for he not only served as captain of a group of "snowshoe men" but supplied the goods for several units. Though something of an operator, Elijah Williams was also a fair man, and respectful of others. All of this was to Bijah's good, but it took countless hours of research before I realized just how much the two men benefited each other.

As time passed, my stack of photocopies grew, but no new material surfaced. I visited libraries and historical societies from Guilford to Hartford. I made dozens of phone calls, some to people who were reputed to be experts on the Princes but who had little or no information on them other than what had been published by others. Then I made my first visit to the Pocumtuck Valley Memorial Association, or PVMA, the Deerfield library and museum that George Sheldon had founded with his archival hoardings. The library, now directed by David Bosse, is on a quiet, tree-shaded street only a block or so from the Wells house. It is a peaceful place to work, with three librarians, but because the library's website showed only two or three items with Bijah's name on them in a few account books, I expected to spend only a couple of days with its collection. I stayed three years.

On my first visit, I was greeted by Martha Noblick, a thin woman with a long braid and glasses, who quickly expressed some frustration with my vagueness. I had become secretive about "my" Bijah and Lucy, defensive about looking for slaves when other librarians had been dismissive about finding anything, and worried about encountering other seekers on the same trail. "If you would just say something about what your project is, what you're looking for," she finally said, "I might be able to help you better." As soon as I told her, she clapped her hands together in delight. "Oh, that's wonderful!" Soon carts of account books came down from the stacks, and others on microfilm, and I learned to read the browning eighteenth-century script. The library director showed me how to decipher the old accounting style and the different currencies.

In those days, away from real cities, little hard money exchanged hands; like all colonial villages, Deerfield was cash-poor. You might buy rye at one of the shops and then have a farmer pay the shopkeeper for you after you worked two days for the farmer. If you helped butcher a pig—a job assigned a monetary value—you went home with meat that also had a price, but no coins changed hands. All the shops, businesses, and even households kept meticulous accounts with prices, debits, and credits faithfully entered. And miraculously, in Deerfield many of those account books still survive, thanks in large part to George Sheldon's Victorian foraging. On that first day at the PVMA I sat down at a microfilm reader and found, within an hour, Bijah's account at a store.

I spent much of that summer reading the ledgers of Elijah Williams and others in the community. The account books and daybooks told the story of daily life in Deerfield: when someone was building a house or an addition, it showed in the hiring of someone to help make mortar. The books showed who was harvesting flax and having it "hetcheled," or drawn through a board of nails to make it into smooth fibers for spinning and weaving. They showed who carried loads of firewood, who made trips to the mill, who stopped at the tavern for a drink, and who bought needles and thread, as well as who married, who had babies and had them baptized, and who died. More importantly, they offered glimpses into slave life, particularly the lives of those whose labor was hired out regularly. Titus and Cato, slaves of the stern Deerfield minister Jonathan Ashley, seemed always to be working for someone else, though they were never compensated for their work; Ashley was paid for their time. Yet they too had accounts at the shops and the taverns, bringing in furs they'd trapped and getting a fair price, occasionally buying rum, hunting equipment, including bullet-making supplies, and small indulgences like shoe buckles. Compensation for the work of slaves, free blacks, and whites was the same, regardless of their status: two shillings a day for ordinary labor. Bijah appeared with some pleasing frequency throughout these years, and Lucy only occasionally.

These accounts called into question nearly everything I thought I knew about American slavery. We tend to associate slavery with the South, and we envision sprawling plantations under an unrelenting sun, with pillared big houses and compounds of slave cabins, guarded by overseers with whips and guns. Here was something so different that at times I had to remind myself that, though less violent, it was slavery just the same. In both the North and South, children and parents were sold away from each other, and freedom came only when a white person granted it. In the North, slaves shared living quarters with their masters and mistresses, often sleeping with the children. They ran away in large numbers, just like their southern counterparts, and they worked in the fields and houses of their owners and were hired out without receiving pay. Unlike southern slaves, however, they traveled between towns and villages easily, could marry, learned to read, and had to attend church. In eighteenth-century rural New England, slaves themselves carried arms for hunting, military service, and protection against enemy attacks. Still, the level of their despair became clear as I read also of slave suicides in these isolated villages, so silent and lonely as they lay shrouded in deep winter snow. The cabins of the South at least offered companionship, something that Bijah, the determined survivor, lacked for the first half of his life.

On March 1, 1747, Abijah Prince was one of nine men who enlisted in Capt. Elijah Williams's company in Deerfield. The hierarchy of command reflected the pervasive power of the Williams family throughout Massachusetts Bay Colony: Capt. Elijah Williams reported to Maj. Ephraim Williams, who reported to Lieut. Col. William Williams, known among his not always satisfied men as "Colonel Bill." This was now the third year of King George's War, one of a series of European wars of succession that had begun in the previous century and spilled over to America when a king or pontiff died. When the English took the French privateers' haven of Louisburg in the Maritimes in 1745—the same battle in which Benjamin Doolittle's eldest son was killed—enlistees like those in Elijah's company assembled in Deerfield, expecting to be sent to Canada. Adventure-seeking recruits, they looked forward to it, and indeed the possibility of another Canadian excursion encouraged many men to enlist.

Bijah followed the wave of enthusiastic 1746 recruits, and he may have enlisted for an even earlier stint. (Men generally signed up for several months, not years, at a time, but could continue to reenlist.) At the beginning of April 1747, a month after Bijah joined up, Elijah shut down his store on the street, using it only as a commissary, while his company waited a month in town for the expected deployment north. The month in Deerfield gave Bijah plenty of time to get better acquainted with Lucy, now a woman of twenty-two or twenty-three.

When they got their deployment, the soldiers were disappointed to learn that instead of heading north to Canada, they were being posted farther west into the frontier, only about twenty-five miles away. That winter the legislature had ordered one hundred men to Fort Massachusetts and another hundred to Fort Number 4 when reports came in that the French were outfitting their men for winter travel with "Mittons," "Slays," and "Snow Shoes." Elijah's "snowshoe men"—they did their winter scouting on snowshoes—probably made short day trips all winter to the line of small forts dotting the frontier's rim from today's southern Vermont and western New Hampshire and into western Massachusetts. Now, in late May, Bijah and twenty-four others were ordered to make up a company and march to the "blockhouses west of the Connecticut River." Earlier attacks and fire had left it in great need of rebuilding, and the men were needed to guard supplies as they came in from Albany and Fort Hoosuck. Hardly on a Canadian adventure, the men were again disappointed.

It was just as well that Bijah didn't go to Canada. If they had lost, or if he had been taken in battle, he might well have been another unredeemed captive. White captives found themselves lingering for years in prisons in Quebec and in England. Black soldiers fared worse and were sometimes sold into slavery.

Not marching north didn't mean that Bijah saw no action, however. There are varying accounts of a skirmish his company engaged in on May 19. In one, a convoy of 102 men from the crew rebuilding Fort Massachusetts was sent to Albany to retrieve supplies and deliver them to the fort. Elijah's men were part of a guard sent to meet them after another guard helped them safely across the Hoosuck River. Several squadrons went out to make sure that the coast was clear and the wagons would be able to pass safely. Ordered to make their way back to the fort in a tight unit prepared for action, they instead relaxed and took their time, walking out of formation and "stringing along." They had been warned against such lax behavior, but they must have figured that since the fort was burned and the killings and captivities already over, they were in little danger.

They were wrong. Scouts had seen the convoy days earlier and knew their movements. Suddenly Bijah and the others found themselves ambushed and in a furious battle. They managed to push the enemy back into a swamp. Meanwhile, someone had alerted the fort, and soldiers there fired a cannon, dispersing the natives and French, who left all their supplies—blankets, clothing, weapons, even a mirror—behind in the retreat. The toll: three Massachusetts men wounded and a Deerfield man captured, ten Indians killed, and one "Indian's scalp, about as big as three fingers," taken. There were two battles of ten or fifteen minutes until reinforcements came from the garrison.

In another version, the fight took place at the fort while the men were at work, Colonel Bill among them, when "an army of the enemy came upon them, with a design to beat them off, and frustrate their purpose," and they were saved by the timely arrival of the supply convoy.

In either scenario, after this skirmish Bijah and the others weren't kept as busy as they should have been, and in June several of the enlisted men wrote to Deerfield to complain. They had readily enlisted when the Canadian expedition was proposed, they said. Instead, they were at Fort Massachusetts, then sent to Number 4, "where we were 6 or 7 weeks and underwent the hardships of Seige by the Enemy." From there they went back to Fort Massachusetts to rebuild it and found themselves underutilized; they were wearing out their clothes, however, in scouting rounds of twenty to forty miles a day and were unable to afford to replace them. Furthermore, they hadn't been paid, and their families were suffering; some even had had to hire men to carry on their civilian work at home at a higher rate than the king was paying for their military service.

By October, Bijah's hitch was up. Williams sat down to reckon accounts at the end of the month, and Bijah was paid an enormous amount of money: just under £160, nearly the amount of Lydia Doolittle's marriage portion, a vast sum for a slave—which at this time he still was. But even here the accounts contain

LIEUT. COL. JOSEPH DWIGHT, COMMANDING OFFICER AT
FORT MASSACHUSETTS IN 1747. *Courtesy of Berkshire Museum, Pittsfield, Massachusetts.*

mysteries—did he actually receive his pay, and how was he supplied? Bijah is listed right along with the other enlisted men, his salary falling in the normal range for such service. Unlike the other soldiers, however, he had no store debts—sums charged against soldiers' salaries for supplies and personal purchases. The only other person who is similarly listed separately, and with no debts, is another slave, Caleb Sharp (sometimes known as Sharp Caleb), a mixed-race black and native man with a Deerfield master. Perhaps Elijah, knowing that Bijah was a slave, held the money back to give to Doolittle. What is clear is that Elijah and Bijah had formed some sort of alliance. One can't call it real friendship, since their social situations were so vastly different. Patronage, based on mutual respect earned during military service and on long acquaintance, seems more likely.

With the signing of a treaty between England and France in 1748, Elijah finally made good on a long-held desire to leave Deerfield and move to Enfield, situated halfway between the larger cities of Springfield, Massachusetts, and Hartford, Connecticut, and therefore a suburb of two cities in two different colonies. It was at that time part of Massachusetts but would soon defect to Connecticut. The end of the war had provided a good excuse to leave Deerfield, but he now had an even more compelling reason to leave: his wife (also named Lydia), unable to recover from a long disease, had found an Enfield doctor whom she trusted. He visited his half-brother, Rev. Stephen Williams, in Longmeadow several times that spring to check the place over, and he finally settled the whole family in Enfield in early May 1748. With nothing to keep him in Deerfield, he shut down his big house and moved his family and his store, taking Bijah with him.

Over the next three years, both men took on new lives. Elijah quickly rose to prominence, serving as town clerk from 1749 to 1751 and as a selectman for the same years. When Enfield decided to secede from Massachusetts and join Connecticut in 1749, he was instrumental in that upheaval, becoming a member of the Connecticut General Assembly. Indeed, he was continually elected and they were glad to have him. The store did well in the new location, and some of his most regular customers were members of the Terry family.

Bijah functioned as a general helper. He ran errands and was greatly trusted by everyone. Sometimes he was asked to carry cash to Enfield from customers in other towns. He delivered goods to Deerfield, probably on horseback or by cart. He repaired fences. He bought supplies and delivered them to the store. He may well have worked behind the counter when Elijah was on one of his many trips to Boston or Hartford. Nor was Bijah alone, for Elijah had at least two other employees, both of them white: Pedajah Field, son of a Northfield horse doctor, and a young Enfield man named Asahel Sexton. Bijah had daily companionship, a great deal of freedom of movement, and perhaps a nest egg from his military earnings. His pay may have been the simple and common arrangement of food, clothing, and shelter in exchange for labor, for he had no account at the store, and Elijah paid for expenses such as having Bijah's shoes mended.

Elijah's happiness at starting life anew was short-lived, for Lydia's health was not improving. She was "near her end" at the beginning of January 1749, and her death a few weeks later threw Elijah into deep despondency. He remained inconsolable for a time. Lydia was, like Elijah, only thirty-six years old. Their ten-year-old daughter Eunice had also been sick for some time, and Elijah paid someone to nurse her for over a year, until the month after Lydia's death. Perhaps in an attempt to offer his brother something other than spiritual comfort, Stephen in March gave Elijah his Deerfield lands, his share of their patrimony. Like so many widowers with young children, Elijah remarried only a year after Lydia's death. He gave life in Enfield another year, then gave up the experiment. In May 1751 he moved back to Deerfield and reopened a store and tavern there, taking Bijah, Pedajah, and Asahel with him. On May 9, 1751, shortly after they returned to Deerfield, a significant gathering occurred, probably at Elijah's tavern.

For all his travels, Bijah at this time was still a slave. Doolittle had not freed him. Elijah was not Bijah's master, but like so many others of his time and class, he expressed no general opposition to slavery. Neither did his brother Stephen, a kind as well as pious man whose diaries are full of concern for his own slaves. When Stephen's slave Stanford, who suffered from pleurisy, fell deathly ill in January 1752, his limbs swollen, Stephen and his wife prayed constantly for him and sat by his bed while he was sweated for his fever. As in other western Massachusetts families, his wife kept a medical chest and carefully nursed everyone in the household. Nothing worked this time, however, and Stanford died on a sorrow-filled evening at the end of the month. They prayed to have their "affections weaned," yet his burial the next morning found them despondent as "Stanford [was] laid in dark Silent Grave ye place where ye Servant is free a^c his master." The minister's Harvard biographer recalls him as being "thoughtful of the needs and comforts of his black people."

On the other hand, another of his other slaves, Cato, had a tendency to drink and disrupt religious services. When Stephen had him "severely whipped," Cato drowned himself in a well afterward. Another of Stephen's slaves, Tom, also committed suicide by drowning. These suicides give the lie to the notion that northern slavery was somehow benign. For all of the Bijahs who were able to travel and fight, all throughout New England there were Catos and Toms whose situations were unbearable.

To piece together the last strands of Bijah's early story, Anthony drove down to the Springfield, Massachusetts, courthouse. Like most courthouses, the one on Court Square is not a particularly pleasant place. To get inside he needed to go through security and then find his way through the people waiting for criminal court sessions before arriving at the land records office on the fourth floor. He was looking for early land transactions in Deerfield and thought it was worth an afternoon rummaging through what Springfield might have kept. Early records like the ones he wanted are housed in the basement, so the clerk picked up her walkie-talkie to call down to alert them that a visitor was arriving. As the elevator door opened in the basement—the public is not allowed to use the stairs—Anthony was met by Tony Diaz, a short, muscular man who worked as the clerk and greeted him with a cheerful "Welcome, señor!" He walked Anthony down the cinder-block hallway to the large room that contained all the early documents, bound into large volumes, as well as a small desk and a photocopier. "Let me know if you need any copies," Tony told Anthony, and he sat down at his desk. It was an unpleasant institutional space. Facing the elevator was a stale-smelling lunchroom, with a wall of vending machines, behind a glass wall. Though there was no hint of the forgotten history and lives documented there, Anthony was pleasantly surprised. In heavy old books, on shelves covered with steel rollers, the old met the new in the unpromising space.

Anthony met me at the train station after his long day in the courthouse basement. I emerged from the station late that afternoon into darkness and drenching rain. Anthony looked tired and perplexed, so I got behind the wheel of the car. Hunched over, with my eyes fixed on the road as we headed up Interstate 91 in bare visibility, I asked how his day had gone. He was quiet for a moment.

"If you could dream of finding anything, what would it be?" he finally asked.

"A diary? Boxes of letters? Depositions from Lucy's court cases?" I rattled off my list of impossible wishes.

"Try again."

COURTHOUSE COPY OF ABIJAH PRINCE'S MANUMISSION PAPER.
Courtesy of Donald E. Ashe, Register of Deeds, Hampden County.

He held a piece of paper under the dimness of the map light. His voice trembled as he began to read out loud.

"Know all men by these Presents that I Aaron Burt of Northfield in the County of Hampshire and Province of the Massachusetts Bay in new England Weaver for Sundry good considerations me hereunto moving Have Manumitted Released and forever Discharged my Negroman Servant or Slave named Abijah alias Prince from any further Service or Servitude of any kind or nature whatsoever to me or my Heirs or assigns or to any Person or Persons Claiming Right to his Service."

The driving rain poured down over the windshield, the wipers going double time, as we crossed the border into Vermont in stunned silence. Anthony had found Bijah's manumission, the document that made him a free man, buried amid land records and indexed only by his first name.

But it wasn't Benjamin Doolittle or even Elijah Williams who had freed him. It was an Aaron Burt. Who was he, and what was his connection to Bijah?

CHAPTER FOUR

THE NEGRO NETWORK

All my hunches about Benjamin Doolittle proved correct: he neither freed his slave nor gave him land, though that is what most of those who have written about Bijah would have you believe. When Doolittle was in the midst of his struggles with the town of Northfield, he not only fought back to prove his theological soundness, but decided that he needed to rid himself of a liability. He hadn't freed Bijah at all—he had *sold* him.

Aaron Burt seems an unusual choice of slave owner—in middle age he would join the Shakers, a sect known for its antislavery stance—but a perfect choice to assist Bijah. Just thirty-four when he manumitted Bijah, Burt had known Doolittle for most of his life. Indeed, Doolittle had performed the marriage between Burt and his wife, Miriam Elmer, in 1740. But how did Bijah's manumission come about? I am convinced that he orchestrated his own sale as well as a series of important events that followed in rapid succession several years later, in the spring and summer of 1751.

Here is the sequence of events as I reconstruct them: Bijah went to Aaron Burt in 1747 and asked the young man to buy him, with the understanding that Bijah would eventually become free, either by agreement or by handing over his large military salary when his service ended. Burt agreed and settled with

Doolittle, who probably was glad to be rid of a professional liability and to have one less mouth to feed. Bijah left Northfield soon after with Burt's brother-in-law, Hezekiah Elmer, for Deerfield, where they both enlisted with Elijah Williams and served together in his company. When their military service ended, Bijah and the white Northfield teenager named Pedajah Field stayed on to work for Williams, even moving with him as he pursued treatment for his wife. Then, just as they were all moving back to Deerfield a few years later, Bijah learned that his little hometown of Northfield was about to allot land in several new divisions, but that a new law was going to be voted on in August: the only ones eligible to acquire some of this land would be legal residents, that is, those who were taxpayers on the town rolls for that year. Bijah needed to do three seemingly impossible things in quick succession: gain his freedom, become a registered taxpayer, and get his name onto the list of proprietors. ("Proprietors" can be thought of as the owners of a town, each having a "right" entitling him to an equal portion of all the land in that town.) It was time for Burt to free him.

Burt took his mission extremely seriously and wanted no legal slip-ups. He visited Seth Field, a Northfield justice of the peace, and asked him to write down the proper legal wording for a manumission, and then he took it home and practiced writing one himself, using Field's outline as a template for the document. On May 9 he went down to Deerfield, where he met with Asahel Sexton, who had worked with him in Elijah's Enfield shop, and Deerfield resident Ebenezer Barnard, who signed and witnessed the deed. Within a couple of months, someone traveled many miles down to Springfield to have the manumission officially recorded by the registrar.

I would love to know how Bijah celebrated, for celebrate he

must have done before leaving town. When Olaudah Equiano, the famous eighteenth-century slave who traveled the world and wrote a best-selling memoir, purchased his freedom, he bought a blue suit and threw a party. Perhaps Elijah poured rum for all and they lifted a glass. However he celebrated, Bijah didn't stay in Deerfield long and may even have ridden back with Burt to Northfield, where he perhaps went to live with Doolittle's son Lucious, now a shopkeeper, to reestablish his residency. Two days after the new residency rule was voted in, "Abijah Negro" was assessed one poll on the Northfield tax list. He had been a slave there for more than forty years; now he was a taxpayer with a proprietor's rights in the same town. One of only a couple of African Americans in the tiny outpost, Bijah was about to become its first black landowner. Within weeks he was on the list of proprietors, but the town was moving slowly in actually distributing land.

More legwork finally led us to an account book in the New England Historic and Genealogical Society and the descendants of Aaron Burt.

"It is so fantastic to learn that Aaron Burt freed a slave!" Susan Burt e-mailed me as soon as she got my letter. She promised to send her family's genealogy.

Bijah stayed in Northfield for less than a year, probably working for the younger Doolittle as well as doing odd jobs for others, while he made sure of his residency and his land. When he left town without actual property, he did so knowing that he was assured of receiving land when the divisions were finally made. He wanted to make a new life for himself, one that would give him something he craved and hadn't had for most of his life: black friends and community. By moving to Northampton, Massachusetts, a larger and far livelier town than either Northfield or

Deerfield, Bijah was joining what Anthony dubbed the "Negro network," a set of contacts and close relationships with other black people, mostly free men, who had found a way to establish position and property for themselves in western Massachusetts. Their numbers were very small, but they nevertheless formed a network of self-made African American men that existed smack in the middle of a bastion of time-honored slavery.

Today Northampton is the dynamic home of Smith College, part of the five-college consortium in the area that also includes Amherst, Mount Holyoke, Hampshire, and the University of Massachusetts. It is a liberal center of intellectual life, just the sort of place to be surprised and embarrassed by the discovery of its own slave history. Jonathan Edwards's servants represented just a drop in the regional bucket, for almost all the "river gods" and families whose names adorn streets and buildings in the region today owned slaves.

The Phelps family of Hadley owned a number of slaves and, like others of their class, felt responsible for their welfare. When the slaves were unwell, the mistresses sat by their sickbeds and administered medicines with their own hands. A letter from Sezor Phelps, a Phelps slave who served during the Revolutionary War, illustrates the ambiguous position of slaves in western Massachusetts. Literate and aware that war service was no guarantee of eventual freedom, he informed his master from Fort Ticonderoga that the captain refused to pay his wages. As a slave, he knew that his master was entitled to his earnings and had a vested interest in collecting what was owed. "I Want to know how all the Folks Do at home and I Desire yor Prayers for me While in the Sarves [service]," he wrote, "and if you Determine to Sel me I Want you Shoud Send me my Stock and Buckel." He signed himself "your Ever Faithful Slave," a closing that smacks of irony from a man who knew he needed to make plans while others decided his fate. Sezor's hope was to secure his belongings, if not his freedom, like other local African Americans. Eleazar Porter freed his servant Adam, and in 1767 Joseph Hubbard sold Adam nineteen acres of his farm for £26 on the condition that he keep it in his own hand for at least seven years; otherwise the deal was null and void.

Bijah was attracted to the Northampton and Hadley area because of the presence there of several free, landowning black men. Through them he learned not only the importance of owning land—a resource that was critical to all men at a time when land was cheap and necessary to survival—but also the art of legal self-defense. One of his most important early role models was a man named Ralph Way. When Samuel Porter of Hadley died in 1722, he left two servants: a fourteen-year-old girl named Sue, valued at £35, and Ralph, an indentured manservant who worked in Porter's kitchen. Ralph's remaining time of three years was valued by Porter's executors at £27. When the will was read, the Porter children were unanimous in freeing Ralph from the time owed the estate. A free man, he immediately set out to buy property and establish himself. By the time Bijah moved to the more cosmopolitan Northampton in 1752, Ralph Way had been a free black property owner and voter in Hadley (part of his property was in today's Amherst) for an astonishingly long period of thirty years.

In 1732, when Lucy was a child of seven and had not yet arrived in Deerfield, Way was already living in freedom and self-assurance as a farmer. He hired an attorney, the prominent Capt. Timothy Dwight, when he wanted to sue a white man, Nathan Dickinson, for a £50 debt. When Dickinson didn't show, the court awarded Way £28 plus costs. (Dickinson later showed up and appealed the judgment, and the case ended up in Superior Court.) Twelve years later Way was himself sued for debt and didn't show. Both he and his son, Ralph Jr., were in and out of court for years, both as plaintiffs and as defendants, usually trying to recover money owed to them or being sued for money they owed, as was common at the time. Ralph Way also set the record for the earliest known divorce in Hadley. In 1752—the same year Bijah moved to the area—Ralph divorced his wife, Lois, who had had an affair with a black man named Boston. This was no easy feat at a time when divorces were extremely hard for anyone to get in western Massachusetts. Only one other had been granted in Northampton, way back in 1695. Way later remarried and started a family. Clearly he was not a man to trifle with.

Eighteenth-century New Englanders made free use of the courts, but Way's cases are surprising because they show that free African Americans in this region had access to the judicial system from very early times. Some slaves even successfully sued for their freedom. For the most part, however, slaves in New England, like their southern brethren, remained slaves for life until individual states banned the institution. Even then the law was slow to be enforced in more remote areas. For example, sales of individual slaves in the Deerfield area took place for years after the practice was forbidden. Nevertheless, with Ralph Way's early example in front of him, Bijah saw possibilities for himself. Could he, like Way, become a landowner? More importantly, could he begin to dream of marrying, starting a family, and settling them, as Way had done, on his own property?

For two years, from 1752 to 1754, Bijah worked for Northampton hatter and church deacon Ebenezer Hunt. He moved in with the servant of Hunt's brother, a freed former slave named Amos

Hull, and Hull's wife, Bathsheba. Even though both Bijah and Amos had surnames, for some time others who dealt with them used sobriquets indicating the two men's race or status. Until they finally broke people of the habit, Abijah Prince and Amos Hull were referred to as Amos Negro, Abijah Negro, and, more encouragingly after his manumission, Abijah Freeman. Amos and the Hunts, along with a number of Burts, belonged to the First Church of Christ, but there is no evidence that Bijah, the former slave of a minister, ever joined a church, then or later, even when married to a deeply religious woman.

These years, ones we had thought of as the "lost years of Abijah Prince," took so long to piece together that we nearly tired of scouring the few records remaining from those towns in western Massachusetts. I began to think of them as Bijah's road trip and imagined him taking his newfound freedom on the road, riding the horse he surely had and visiting all the places where he'd been as a slave to see what they felt like when his movement was his own choice. That he settled down and worked at various jobs made more sense, of course, but what had his life been like?

As it turned out, Ebenezer Hunt kept a diary, last seen in his descendants' hands decades ago, in a town outside of Boston; it was worth trying to track it down. Rather than pick up the phone and try to explain the story, I sent a letter to the widow of one of the descendants, asking whether the diary might be in her hands and if she would be willing to show it to a researcher. Within days an excited elderly woman, related to both the Burts and the Hunts by marriage, called me up. "Your letter threw me into a tizzy," she said. She had cleared out her father-in-law's house a decade before, taking home with her a stack of old books. She didn't recall any manuscripts or papers that looked old. It was the dead of winter, so she couldn't face going out to the unheated porch where she kept them in an old chest. "That's all right," I tried to reassure her. "But if there is a break in the weather one day, would you mind just taking a quick look?"

Two days later, in the midst of a January thaw, she called back. We commiserated about frozen car locks and icy driveways before she said the words I wanted to hear. "I opened the chest this morning, and right on top there was a big envelope with this little book inside. It says, 'Ebenezer Hunt journal, 1738–1780.' I can't make out all the old handwriting—it's so hard to read—but he only seems to talk about little things like the weather." That, I told her, was great. We could read the writing. Did she mind letting us take a look?

Anthony couldn't bear to wait too long, and several days later he packed a sandwich and tore off to Boston. All day I imagined him looking through the journal, perhaps also finding the account book that was said to accompany it, and filling in the gaps of Bijah's missing years. That evening, however, he returned empty-handed. The journal was very short and added nothing to the story. His host had felt so bad for him, hovering about and offering lunch and trying to think of the names of other deceased relatives who might have the account books. "But," she said sadly as she saw him off, "I wouldn't be surprised if someone just threw it away years ago." Another closed door, another dead end.

The records suggest that Bijah stayed in Northampton for two years as a taxpayer, and employee of Hunt's, until about the time his roommates Amos and Bathsheba had their first baby in September 1754. Babies came to them every two or three years after that, and this gave Bijah, a middle-aged man without close familial ties, a strong and possibly brand-new notion of family. Sharing a house with a man his own age who was creating a family of his own and who by 1756 was renting a farm and had some live-stock made a lifelong impossibility now look entirely possible. African American women of marriageable age were rare in the area, however, let alone free black women.

It was small wonder that his thoughts turned to Lucy, who had grown up right before him in his travels in and out of her town. Now about twenty-five, she captivated nearly everyone who lived or passed through Deerfield. For a couple of years her owners, Ebenezer and Abigail Wells, ran a tavern in the parlor of their home, where farmhands paused for a midday meal and thirsty soldiers stopped for tankards of cider or shots of rum in the evenings. Lucy tossed lively rejoinders to them over her shoulder as she set down their drinks and plates, drawing them all in with her voice and wit. It's easy to see Bijah, the grizzled and gritty middle-aged man and war veteran, stopping in his tracks in the doorway at the sight of a young black woman handling them all with such comfort and ease, so witty and entertaining and so self-possessed.

He wanted to marry Lucy, but for this he needed to come to an agreement with Lucy's master and mistress. If they married, their children would follow Lucy's condition and be enslaved, unless the love and goodwill the Wellses bore her translated into an actual manumission. Free or not, he wanted her.

Let us go now to meet Lucy, the young woman he loved and with whom he hoped to build a new life. During the years Bijah first lived with Rev. Doolittle, then obtained his freedom, and finally moved from place to place, she had arrived in Deerfield, a young survivor of the horrific middle passage and New England slavery, and she had grown into a fascinating woman.

PART TWO

Lucy

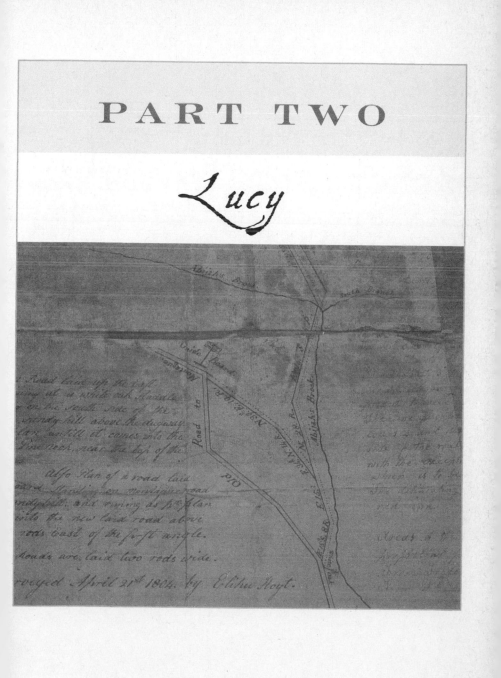

CHAPTER FIVE

LUCY ENTERS

The Schomburg Center for Research in Black Culture is located in a new brick building on Malcolm X Boulevard at the upper end of Manhattan. In Lucy's day this was a remote Dutch settlement, but today it is in the bustling center of Harlem, only a few blocks from 125th Street and the Apollo Theater. An extension of the New York Public Library, today the Schomburg houses one of the world's finest collections of books, manuscripts, magazines, rare newspapers, photographs, and art of Africa and the African diaspora. Here one can find the original manuscript of Richard Wright's novel *Native Son*, sound recordings of social activists Booker T. Washington and Marcus Garvey, and murals and paintings from the Harlem Renaissance. Poet Langston Hughes's ashes are buried beneath a mosaic on the ground floor.

I went to the Schomburg because I wanted to track down the truth about Lucy Terry, and I knew that previous researchers' notes were housed there. Perhaps they could shed light on the young woman who so fascinated Abijah Prince that he stopped his solitary wanderings when he fell in love and built his life around her. Who was she?

Lucy's legend was first set down in the nineteenth century by an old Deerfield resident and historian, George Sheldon, who wore a white beard nearly to his waist and delighted in posing for photographs in old period clothes. His ancestors had been original settlers of the town, and he grew up in a cattle-raising family, living among some of the elderly slaves who had known Lucy so long before. He threw himself into the task of recording the history of the place and thought nothing of climbing into his neighbors' attics while they were in church, making off with the old account books, papers, and ledgers stored there and forgotten.

Calling it a love story for all time, in 1896 Sheldon wrote to a number of people whose families had known the Princes and set down the story of Lucy—whom he referred to as "Luce Bijah," a name she never used—and Abijah Prince. His telling is the source for every subsequent retelling of their lives. It told how, after their marriage, they settled in Deerfield on a piece of land that became known as "Bijah's Brook" and started filling it with their babies. "She was a great story teller," he wrote, "and hers was a place of resort for the young people" of Deerfield. Most importantly, he wrote, she "comes down to us as a poet."

I went to New York to follow the trail of Bernard Katz, who in the 1960s had become so intrigued with Sheldon's story that he decided to write a young adult novel about Lucy Terry. Born in 1901, Katz was a jazz buff with an interest in African American history. At his death in 1970, he left behind boxes of notes and letters detailing his search, as well as an unfinished manuscript, all of which was donated by the family to the Schomburg.

I submitted my reader's ticket on the lower level of the library, collected several boxes of microfilm, and began to make my way through the hundreds of pages that both men, along with a Massachusetts researcher named Mary Adams Ball, had left behind. Beginning in 1968, Ball had spent three years scouring town history books, probate records, and historical societies from Deerfield, Massachusetts, to Guilford, Vermont, and in western Vermont from Bennington to Sunderland. Ball wrote Bernard Katz every two weeks from her home in western Massachusetts to his in Greenwich Village, outlining her searches and discoveries and dead ends.

Meanwhile, increasingly ill and confined to his home, Katz typed letters to every state court, federal court, records office, and library that might keep relevant records, seeking information on Lucy's two court cases, the Williams College admissions attempt and the Revolutionary War military service of the Prince sons, Caesar and Festus. The same responses always came back to him: there was no official record of any Supreme Court case. The government files contained no further information on the Princes. The college archives showed no evidence of any meeting between Lucy and the trustees. "I still have no evidence that Lucy's case in the U.S. Supreme Court against Col. Bronson, her neighbor in Sunderland, Vt., ever took place," Katz worried. "Can't find where they got the story. Also no confirmation of Lucy pleading for hours before the trustees of Williams College to get her son in. Also no proof that her son Caesar Prince served in the Revolutionary Army. These are still my most important problems—they're the ones I was expecting to find the answers to."

Every forward step was matched by two steps back. Together Katz and Ball compiled lists of slaves all over western New England and took handwritten notes from the papers of state officials from Maryland to Massachusetts. They drew timelines and charts. In the days before *Roots* and the burgeoning of amateur genealogy that it spawned, before the Internet and CD-ROMs, their work was slow and frustrating. Without finding most of what he sought, Katz began to write his book anyway, filling in the blanks with imagined drama and conjecture. Then one day a bereft Phyllis Katz wrote to inform Mary Ball of her husband's sudden death.

With that sad event, Jonathan Katz, Bernard's son, took up his father's task and finished the book in the way his father had begun it. *Black Woman: A Fictionalized Biography of Lucy Terry Prince* by Bernard and Jonathan Katz was published in 1973. For years this fictionalized account, with its conjectures mingled with facts, was taken as truth, even by scholars who assumed that the authors had discovered all there was to know and that everything they wrote was true—some of the Schomburg's biographical information on Lucy comes directly from this novel rather than from facts.

I hit the Print button with every murky microfilmed page that seemed to contain valuable questions or information, until finally the machine ran out of toner. "You've made a *lot* of copies," the dreadlocked technician grumbled when I asked for help in replacing it at the end of the day. I shuffled my papers, paid at the desk for my too many copies, and walked out of the library and into the autumn evening with more questions than answers, little wiser than I had been when I arrived in the morning. If Katz's and Ball's years of tenacious research left so many important facts uncorroborated, how could I expect to do better? In their novel about Lucy, the Katzes resorted to inventing her arrival in America. Perhaps, with luck, my work, and Anthony's determination, we could discover the truth.

The starting point was her obituary, which said she arrived in Bristol, Rhode Island, from Africa around 1730. That seemed to make sense, because Rhode Island had a thriving and direct slave trade, sending fast sloops back and forth across the ocean and bypassing the slower British trade. But nothing we could find linked her to this port, mainly because such detailed records were never kept.

HUGH HALL, BOSTON SLAVE MERCHANT. *Courtesy of Purchase, Estate of George Strichman and Sandra Strichman gifts; bequest of Vera Ruth Miller, in memory of her father, Henry Miller, bequest of Josephine N. Hopper, John Stewart Kennedy Fund, and gifts of Yvonne Moën Cumerford, Berry B. Tracy, and Mr. and Mrs. Jeremiah Milbank, by exchange; Mr. and Mrs. Leonard L. Milberg gift, and funds from various donors, 1996 (1996.279). Image © by The Metropolitan Museum of Art.*

The only other clue was her last name: so few slaves had surnames that hers must have come from a member of the prolific Terry family. The 1730 death of the prominent citizen Samuel Terry of Enfield, Massachusetts, seemed promising, since he was a long-standing legislator who spent considerable time in the Boston area and bought and sold so much land that his probate took seven years to untangle. Ultimately, however, Lucy's trail led not to him but to his son, also named Samuel.

It was a chance mention in a card catalog that led us to the Massachusetts Historical Society and the little account book of a Boston merchant named Hugh Hall. Son of a Barbados gentleman and a Boston mother who died when he was a small child, Hall showed great interest in religion, copying out sermons as a boy and hoping to become a minister. However, when he took his Harvard degree, his father settled him in a business career instead. He was only about twenty-four and on a visit to London to look after his father's affairs when he struck a deal for Guinea slaves to be shipped to Barbados. By the time of Lucy's arrival twelve years later, Hall was a broker in mortgages and property. His accounts and newspaper advertisements show that by far the bulk of his dealings were in slaves, largely in Boston, where his buyers included that city's most prominent ministers, but he also had many customers in the Connecticut River Valley area, where Lucy was to live.

Hall traveled between Boston, Barbados, and London, eventually setting up a warehouse in Boston on Pitt's Wharf, where Faneuil Hall stands today, and serving as the middleman, or New England retail broker, for several Barbados slave dealers. Ironically, Faneuil Hall is known today as "the Cradle of Liberty" because, even though its wealthy namesake, Peter Faneuil, inherited his money from an uncle in the slave trade, it was also the site of the beginnings of the Revolution (and also the place where "the first steps of slave emancipation in Boston were taken"). There Hall received shiploads of African men, women, and children; cleaned them up; gave them names like Quaco, Prince, Abba, Juba, and Bess; and advertised them in the newspapers, selling them for between £60 and £70 each. Yet he also believed in slaves' humanity and was committed to their conversion to Christianity.

Everything fell into place when we realized that Hugh Hall, Stephen Williams, and the younger Samuel Terry had all been classmates at Harvard and that as adults the three men kept up with each other. Williams and Terry both transacted business with Hall. Terry, who desired a career in the ministry, married a minister's widow from an established Nantucket family and probably desired the minister's status symbol of a slave. He had

HUGH HALL SLAVE ADVERTISEMENT FROM THE *NEW ENGLAND WEEKLY JOURNAL.* Courtesy of Early American Newspapers, *Series 1: 1690–1876, an Archive of Americana collection, published by Readex, (Readex.com) a division of NewsBank, in cooperation with the American Antiquarian Society.*

already bought an impressive property in Mendon in central Massachusetts, midway between Boston and Deerfield, consisting of over six hundred acres and a "mansion house."

On October 7, 1728, Hall advertised an upcoming sale of Negro boys and girls. Sometime between that date and January 1729, Samuel Terry entered Hall's wharfside warehouse and wrote out a bond for £70—the very price of a slave. Stephen Williams, as well as another acquaintance from Hadley, near Deerfield, did the same. Just as Lucy's obituary claimed, Terry had once lived in Bristol. Lucy probably arrived from Africa, via Barbados, a year or so before 1730, traveling in the hold of a pestilent slave ship, washing up on a foreign shore and into the hands of a man who was never able to retain the ministerial position he sought and who was in constant financial trouble.

In the years just before Lucy first appears in the Deerfield records, Terry was involved in a series of enormous debts, shady deals, social embarrassments, and legal cases. He was living beyond his means, for he was taken to court several times for massive debts. With their father's death in 1731, Terry's brothers were forced to liquidate the elder Terry's estate to pay off creditors, leaving Samuel with no inheritance. He took out a huge loan of £700 from Hall, using his Mendon property—the cleared land, big house, sawmill, and ironworks—as security, and when he couldn't pay, the merchant and slave dealer put the property up for sale. Terry began selling off his other property and borrowing even more money.

It was a help when the town of Mendon contracted with him to run their school, but just a month later he was hauled into court for a case of public drunkenness in which two women—neither of them his wife—allegedly put him to bed. Two men testified against him, and in January 1734 he accused them of defaming his character. They were cleared of this charge, and the town fired him from the teaching job, having earlier turned down his offer to preach for no salary. He left Mendon for the newly formed nearby town of Union, Connecticut, in October 1734, where he once again offered his services as minister and once again was rejected. He and his brothers, who had tried to help him out by co-signing one of his debts, were sued in early 1735 when he didn't pay. Desperate, he had been unloading property in any way he could. These efforts probably included Lucy.

It may have been that Stephen Williams, Elijah's brother, stepped in to help his old friend by arranging to sell the girl to Ebenezer and Abigail Wells, who lived across the street from his brother in Deerfield. A few years earlier the minister had contemplated going into the slave-trading business with two fellow clergymen. Or it may have been that Hall himself arranged the sale. However it happened, only months after Terry was again in court for debt and needed to raise money, Lucy Terry appears in Deerfield's official records for the first time when she was baptized, some six years after Terry bought a slave from Hall.

CHAPTER SIX

LUCY GROWS UP

When Lucy got to Deerfield, probably through a private sale arranged by Samuel Terry through Hugh Hall or Stephen Williams, she entered the home of Ebenezer and Abigail Wells, a childless couple. She was about ten years old, and an English speaker. She joined another slave, a young man named Caesar. Together the four of them worked, and together, though in separate seating areas, they attended services across the road at the meetinghouse. Lucy slept in front of the fire or up in the attic.

When the three Wells brothers and cousins took their Negro servants to the front of the church on June 15, 1735, Lucy and Caesar were not the only slaves being baptized. They stood with Pompey from Justice Jonathan Wells's house and Adam and Peter from Justice Thomas Wells's house. This was the time of the Great Awakening, when Jonathan Edwards and others were preaching a return to the old religious values, and Deerfield's minister, Jonathan Ashley, was anxious to add as many people as possible to his congregation. That year alone he added seventy-eight people to the Deerfield church, including a number of slaves. Ashley, himself a slave owner, marked all of them down as "children" who "entered into the covenant" even though at least one of them was an adult. After their baptisms, the five servants returned upstairs to the Negro and Indian gallery, where they sat separated from the whites.

In some respects, Lucy's early life in Deerfield in the 1730s and 1740s was much like Bijah's in Northfield, some fifteen miles northeast of Deerfield. After the peace that ran from the mid-1720s to the mid-1740s, soldiers with muskets were sequestered with local families. They ate many of their meals in the tavern that the Wellses operated for a time in their house, where Lucy lived and served; like her, many of the soldiers slept on the floor or in the attic. Men and boys worked in the fields at the edges of the colony. Women and younger girls hoed and weeded the kitchen gardens next to their houses and sweltered over the open hearths.

There were important differences in Bijah's and Lucy's lives, however, during these years. Unlike Bijah's more racially isolated youth and adulthood in Northfield, Lucy grew up in daily contact with other black people. There were many more of them, we now know, than had been previously understood to live there, for Deerfield, although a little place, was full of slaves. This network of black people, whose lives are little documented, were spread among the houses that lined the main street and also lived in the more outlying areas. In Deerfield, Lucy grew up with a clear understanding of her low position, yet in this same place she also became the confident and talkative woman I'd been searching for, the one whom people sought out for the tales she'd tell and poems she composed. On the street and in the tavern, soldiers bantered with the charismatic young woman, children begged her for stories, and Bijah fell in love with her. We had to go see where this had happened.

When we entered the Wells-Thorn house in Historic Deerfield, I had the feeling of looking for a spirit guide in an unoccupied museum. It is one of a dozen beautifully preserved houses in the village. Many remain private residences, but several are open to the public and staffed by enthusiastic guides who can tell you about the architecture, furniture, and original inhabitants. On that initial visit our guide, Peter King, showed us around enthusiastically, even allowing a usually forbidden visit to the attic, where Lucy and Caesar may have slept.

Today the house presents an odd combination, for in 1751, five years before Lucy and Bijah married, Wells began to build an addition that now is decorated as the Victorian inhabitants would have known it. The original dark colonial house is attached to the blue addition, whose large, white, airy rooms Lucy occupied for only a few years. It was in the older part of the house that I looked for clues of Lucy's early life, especially in the fireplace with its brick oven on one side, a structure large enough to hold an adult, where she cooked and kept the fire going day and night in all seasons, holding her skirts back as she stepped in and out. The kitchen windows were placed high to keep out intruders, and in Lucy's day they were covered with oiled skins that let in only the weakest of light. A rifle stood in the corner by the door at all times, and the door was bolted at night.

In the narrow buttery, two steps up from the small kitchen, Lucy and Abigail Wells churned butter and made cheeses by salting and turning them every day on their wooden shelves. Peter King showed us where they cleaned and stored the dishes. In the largest room, with its curtained rope bed where Ebenezer and Abigail slept, stood a table and chairs, a walking spinning wheel, and a highboy. This room later served as the tavern where Lucy was such a hit with the customers. "Her volubility was exceeded by none," someone later wrote, "and in general the fluency of her speech captivated all around her, and was not destitute of instruction and edification." She was, those who knew her believed, "a prodigy in conversation."

There is something confounding about standing in the houses left behind by those we wish we could have met. I looked out the window that Lucy had looked out; I touched the chair she had sat in. In the hundreds of years between us, passing hands had rubbed the doorways smooth, Lucy's fingerprints obliterated by centuries of housekeeping. I longed to know what had happened in these rooms between her theft and her freedom, to catch an echo of her voice, but the rooms did not speak to me. There were so many things I wanted to know. Who in this household combed Lucy's African hair? Or was it perhaps cut short and hidden by her cap? Who taught Lucy to read and converted her to the Christian faith that she kept throughout her long life? Did she play with other children?

When George Sheldon began writing the history of Deerfield, he could recall people who had heard Lucy's voice. Descended from one of the town's oldest families, cattle farmers whose house still stands at the end of the street, he himself had known one or two of the former slaves when he was a child and they were elderly, and he regretted that his own family had been among Deerfield's many slaveholding families. He found it so shameful a history that he felt compelled to publish it twice, once in his two-volume history of Deerfield and again as a separate magazine article. Despite his work, Lucy somehow gets presented as the sole African American resident of Deerfield, and for years the town embraced her story at the expense of the many other black people who lived there over the years.

None of this sat right with Bob Romer, a retired Amherst College physics professor who spent time as a guide to Rev. Jonathan Ashley's house and became obsessed with recovering the town's black history. Romer knew that Ashley had owned three slaves, and he was particularly incensed at the silence surrounding Jenny

Cole and her son Cato. Ashley brought them back from Boston in 1739 as a teenager with her baby, and though they lived and died in his house, not even a stone marks their burial places. It was these two whose story propelled him into a passionate quest to honor the forgotten others. Today Deerfield honors its black forebears with plaques and a website.

When the teenage Jenny and her baby arrived in Deerfield, Lucy had been there for about four years and was fluent in the English language and the American way of life. Both girls were from Africa, and both had known the crowded slave ship with its stench and death, the landing on an American shore full of white barbarians, and the experience of being sold. Jenny, however, became a mother at an early age—no one knows by whom—and it was doubtless with great pride that Ashley presented the adolescent slave and her baby to his wife, Dorothy, who had just lost her own firstborn infant. As had been the case for Abigail Wells a few years earlier, there was suddenly a black girl to fill a void in a childless household, even though Dorothy went on to fill her house with children for whom Jenny was forced to care.

With each new baby the Ashleys produced, Jenny saw her work increase. Years later, when the Ashleys' grandchildren began to appear, she raised them too. Although her son Cato was baptized into the church when they arrived, she never accepted the religion of her captors. To the end of her long life she prepared for a return to her original home across the ocean. She neither forgot nor forgave her abduction and always recalled, as though it had just occurred, the white men who seized her and a group of other children playing near a well, not far from the home of her royal father, when she was twelve. Now the two stolen girls occupied houses at opposite ends of the street. Jenny prepared for her future in an increasingly crowded household by "gathering as treasures to take back to her mother land," as Sheldon put it, "all kinds of odds and ends, colored rags, bits of finery, worn out candlesticks, fragments of crockery or glassware, peculiar shaped stones, shells, buttons, beads, cones—anything she could string." And she taught Cato too to prepare as well for his "return" to Guinea—which, of course, he had never seen—whenever it might happen, before or after his death. America was not, she told him, his home.

Every time Romer walked tourists through the Ashley house, he saw where Jenny and Cato had worked, and every time he walked through the adjoining graveyard he noted their absence. The discrepancy rankled so much that he began combing the accounts and vital records to find evidence of the other African Americans whose lives had slipped into the fog of Deerfield history. There was a lively and extensive group of Deerfield descendants who prided themselves on their ancestry and held reunions. Why were they all white? he wondered. Where were the African American and Native American Deerfield descendants of slaves? Over a period of several years he constructed a map of the street as it existed in 1753, showing where on the half-mile slaves had lived. Within a year or two he had found nearly two dozen slave and free African Americans, almost completely blended into the tiny white community in terms of numbers, if not in status or treatment.

Lucy lived, Romer discovered, amid a surprisingly sizable black community for such a small place. Like Lucy, the other slaves lived in ones and twos with white families, in the same houses, an arrangement associated more with urban than rural slavery. Black and white had accounts in the same small shops and taverns that came and went on the street over the years, and town slaves got to know others who came to Deerfield from the surrounding areas with their masters to visit the shops and taverns. Among these must have been Bijah, nearly thirty years old when his future wife arrived in Deerfield as a child.

Later on, as I read more in the town accounts, it became clear just how many slaves there were and how often new slaves arrived. Joseph Barnard, a prominent store and tavern owner, kept accounts of Pompey's work for others and for himself, sending him out for long days to cut wood or take grain to the mill. Timothy Childs bought a little girl named Phyllis for £100 when her owner, a minister in Westfield, died. By 1741 there were several Caesars in town. By 1746 there were at least sixteen slaves on the street alone, with more to come. There was indeed a black community in this unlikely place.

Just about all of them had accounts at the local shops, and one way to tell slave from free African American is to look at what they bought. With no land to cultivate or family to provide for, those deprived of freedom spent their money on small things to cheer themselves. Free blacks who had to support themselves bought necessities. In August 1742, Peter, like so many other slaves who managed to scrape together a bit of money, bought gloves, a snuff box and snuff, and strings of beads. He paid for some of these things by his hunting and trapping, using mink and other furs to get credit at the shops. Prince got store credit in exchange for fox skins and by pawning his violin. Others bought shoe buckles, vest buttons, tobacco and pipes. But they all, slave and free, bought gunpowder and flint and shot both for their own hunting and to defend the town. This would have been unthinkable away from the frontier, and five hundred miles farther south, this kind of slave—armed but not free—was almost unimaginable, but it was still slavery nonetheless, with people condemned to a lifetime of servitude and subject to sale.

I thought I knew a great deal about American slavery, but other things about life in Deerfield surprised me. In the South, laws were passed throughout the eighteenth century to keep the small white population secure from the large slave population. Slaves could not marry, learn to read or write, enter into written contracts, or testify against whites in court. In New England, there were no such restrictions, and at some point in their lives many black people held a quill dipped in ink, even if only to sign with an X. And as we know from Bijah and Lucy's story, they sometimes appeared in court. Even though alcohol flowed freely in the taverns of these towns and most homes had their own supplies of rum, cider, and other stimulating drinks, in Connecticut laws barred taverns from serving blacks and Indians.

Free blacks in Deerfield were not subject to such legislated restrictions but still led restricted lives. Peter, who may have arrived with Lucy, was a young man deprived of women and pleasure, and he often tried to break out of his confining life. On at least one occasion, in 1738, he broke into someone's supply of spirits and indulged in late-night revelry with his friends. The now-twenty-nine-year-old Peter was forced by Ashley to come forward in the meetinghouse and confess to theft, drunkenness, and lewdness. The church held in check what the law did not legislate.

Deerfield presented a picture of slavery that went against so much of what we think we know about American slavery, for we tend to think of northerners as abolitionists rather than as slaveholders who were comfortable in that role. In these smaller northern areas, race in and of itself wasn't necessarily a discriminatory factor. A free black person could buy property, and his children might even attend school. Slaves shopped in the local stores. Literacy was not forbidden. When there were wars, both blacks and whites were armed. Yet we have to guard against thinking that forced servitude was somehow benign simply because in these northern towns blacks dwelled cheek by jowl with whites. Sometimes on remote farms in the early days master and slave even ate together, but Lucy and Caesar did not share the Wellses' table. Long after the deaths of Ebenezer and Abigail Wells, when she herself was an old woman who went back to visit Deerfield, Lucy refused an offer to join a family meal. "No, Missy, no, I know my place," she is reported to have said, something that either shows that the social deference of her childhood ran deep or that she was capable of deep irony. The law recognized the rights of free blacks but also upheld the institution of slavery. Here, just as in the South, black children were bought and sold away from their parents, even while they were forced to go to church. In church, black and white alike were reminded that they were unseparated but also unequal. On southern plantations, men were hired to hunt, whip, and control slaves. However, just as in Charleston and Atlanta and New Orleans, auction blocks in cities like Boston and Philadelphia and New York reminded slaves that they could be sold at any moment.

To the modern mind it seems a kind of moral schizophrenia, but to eighteenth-century whites it was the natural order.

Even though Lucy arrived during a lull that, except for minor skirmishes, lasted from the mid-1720s until the 1740s, everyone, including the black newcomers, knew about the troubled origins of Deerfield and the decades of warfare that formed an often-repeated part of a living history. Lucy knew that slaves not only had been there from the beginning but had been among the first to suffer in its struggles. The February 29, 1704, raid on Deerfield still defines the historic village, and Lucy and the other

Deerfield slaves knew the story about it as well as their masters and mistresses. In kitchens and fields they heard how the snow glistened in the moonlight on that leap year day, rising up the sides of the stockade that surrounded many of the houses as the settlers slept secure in the feeling that winter and bare trees protected them from any stalking danger. The sentry, lulled by the cold and the quiet, drifted off to sleep and didn't hear the raiders as they discarded their snowshoes and mounted the stockade walls on stairs of snow. Once inside, the Canadian Abenaki attackers, directed by their French officers, split into groups and went to separate houses, dashing babies' brains out against hearths, ransacking trunks, and tomahawking and clubbing forty-one resisters. Elijah's father, the Rev. John Williams, only survived because the gun he raised toward them from his bed misfired and he and his remaining family were taken captive in a group of 111 villagers. The weak and slow were killed, and the rest subjected to a long winter march to Quebec, to be held for ransom. Some of the children, including Williams's daughter Eunice, were given to Indian families to raise. Eunice never returned to live in Deerfield; instead, she converted to Catholicism and married an Indian, refusing to go back to her original family. (Her descendants still visit Deerfield and have worked hard to reeducate the public about their culture and history and to rewrite the one-sided story of bloodthirsty natives versus innocent settlers.) The first to be cut down in the raid was Parthena, an enslaved black woman standing in the Williams's door; her husband, Frank, was captured and later tortured to death.

Deerfield still bears the scars of this raid. The original house is gone, but the "Indian House" front door is preserved in the Memorial Museum, covered with the marks of tomahawks that forced entry into John Sheldon's house. In the mid-twentieth century, the Deerfield occupants ransacked their family trunks, painted their faces, and began reenacting the raid, stopping from time to time to photograph each other in their costumes. The pseudo–Native Americans were straight out of 1950s television, with their inaccurate costumes and language.

Lucy, like many of the people living in Deerfield, had never known war. Peace between the English and French (with their allies the Abenakis from Canada and New England, assisted by the Hurons and the Iroquois of the Mountain) had followed Grey Lock's War, which ended in 1727, although much of the fighting ended two years earlier. For nearly twenty years, until 1744, the peace reigned between the English and the French, and there were no raids on the New England frontier.

Consequently, when there was another raid on Deerfield on August 25, 1746, "the English colonists were woefully unprepared to war." Fifty of the French commander Vaudreuil's Abenaki men moved quietly toward the village on a Sunday afternoon, hoping to take captives for ransom. They looked for a good place from which to launch an attack and finally settled on the Bars, a meadow with two deserted houses and a field of corn and vegetables. Hiding themselves among the alder trees and behind stacks of freshly mown hay, they waited for the Amsden and Allen families to return from their hiding place to work their fields on the quiet Monday morning. Knowing of attacks in other villages, the Amsdens and the Allens preferred not to expose themselves, but knew that without a crop they would starve in the winter and spring.

When Eleazar Hawks, a neighbor, went out bird hunting and came unsuspectingly close to the raiders, they shot and scalped him, and at the noise everyone within earshot in the town screamed and ran in chaos toward a mill. A boy, Simeon Amsden, was caught, killed, and scalped. Racing toward the Deerfield River, Samuel Allen, John Sadler, and Adonijah Gillet turned around at the bank and began firing. Only young Sadler escaped across the river; the other two were killed. The noise alerted the soldiers assigned to protect the town, and they and the other men threw down their work and raced to the Bars. By then Oliver Amsden was fighting a losing battle for his life. Young Eunice, Samuel, and Caleb Allen all raced in another direction. Eunice tripped over her long skirts and was tomahawked, yet somehow survived. Caleb got away by hiding among the cornstalks, but his brother Samuel was captured. It was a fast and desperate fight. By the time the would-be rescuers arrived it was over. Around them lay the bodies of five slain men, three of them scalped and the other two decapitated. Eunice, bleeding profusely from her head wound, was still breathing. Two natives lay dead in the meadow. John Sadler and Samuel Allen were nowhere to be found, and the raiders, though pursued, had disappeared. In despair, the Deerfield men carried the dead and wounded back into the village as the horrified residents, black and white, gathered in shock on the street.

It was twenty-one-year-old Lucy who put the experience into words for everyone. By this time they all knew of her way with words. No other poems of hers survive, yet her acknowledged facility with language and her ability to mesmerize her listeners with stories suggest that this wasn't a one-off composition. Using the singsong ballad form so common at the time throughout England and the colonies, Lucy's "Bars Fight" was picked up and repeated far and wide for more than a century, making her the first known African American poet. (Another ballad, "Springfield Mountain," composed a few years later about an event in that nearby town, uses nearly the same rhythm and structure, showing just how much the music and poetry of the time fol-

lowed the English tradition and how much Lucy now was im-
bued with that culture.)

August 'twas the twenty fifth
Seventeen hundred forty-six
The Indians did in ambush lay
Some very valiant men to slay
The names of whom I'll not leave out
Samuel Allen like a hero fought
And though he was so brave and bold
His face no more shall we behold.
Eleazer Hawks was killed outright
Before he had time to fight
Before he did the Indians see
Was shot and killed immediately.
Oliver Amsden he was slain
Which caused his friends much grief and pain.
Samuel Amsden they found dead
Not many rods off from his head.
Adonijah Gillet we do hear
Did lose his life which was so dear.
John Saddler fled across the water
And so escaped the dreadful slaughter.
Eunice Allen saw the Indians coming
And hoped to save herself by running
And had not her petticoats stopped her
The awful creatures had not catched her
And tommyhawked her on the head
And left her on the ground for dead.
Young Samuel Allen, Oh! lack a-day
Was taken and carried to Canada.

The poem used a structure meant for easy memorization, so that young and old could remember the fight through Lucy's words, but someone wrote it down in the meantime. Paper was scarce and expensive, certainly for a young enslaved woman. She may have written it down, but it wasn't published until one hundred years later on the front page of the *Springfield Daily Republican*, thirty-three years after Lucy's death.

There is another way to read Lucy's poem, which has often been dismissed as hardly worth attention. Sharon Harris, in her book *Executing Race: Early American Women's Narratives of Race, Society, and the Law*, argues that it needs to be understood as a cultural text that mocks the traditional captivity narrative, like John Williams's *The Redeemed Captive*. Harris places "Bars Fight" against the background of the region, where the Pocumtuck Indians were wrongly blamed by Sheldon and other early writers for all the strife against the white settlers, when in fact they were trying to hold on to rights granted to them decades earlier. Calling Lucy's poem a satire, Harris is certain that Lucy could not listen to the repeated stories of Deerfield's past captives without recognizing the irony of her own similar situation. Seen this way, "Bars Fight" is an act of resistance, a "satire" of whites' "lamentations about Indian captivity." Harris also points out that the folk ballads of Africa would have given Lucy a long familiarity with the form. Given her reputation for eloquence, coupled with the fact that she sometimes purchased paper, it's impossible to believe that she didn't write other poems, lost to us today.

Standing in Lucy's house or outside in the garden on the quiet street, I began to see how life rolled on for her in Deerfield. Week after week, twice every Sunday, Lucy and the other slaves sat in their separate gallery of the meetinghouse and attended services. (She was admitted to the fellowship of the church—full communion—on August 19, 1744, when she was about nineteen.) After the lull that ceased with the Bars fight, war resumed, yet another in the European wars of succession that spilled over to North America. For two years, from 1747 to 1749, Wells kept a tavern in his large front room, and Lucy waited on tables and poured drinks for soldiers and visitors in addition to her work in the household and garden. From December to the following April, sixty-two soldiers were housed in the town at varying times, and it was left to the town's servants to cook for them and clean up after them. The extra work may have been the reason Lucy had to be treated by the doctor by the end of the year, but when peace was declared the men went home, leaving quiet in their wake but perhaps also uneasiness about safety. Meanwhile, some of the male slaves had served in these wars, and they returned from action to find their domestic situations unchanged.

By January 1749, after the war had ended, Rev. Ashley sensed some frisson of discontent spreading among Deerfield's "servants" and instructed Jenny and Cato to ready his house for a special service for the slaves. All the servants obediently but reluctantly trooped there on the evening of January 23. Ashley took as his text 1 Corinthians 7:22: "For he that is called in the Lord, being a servant is the Lord's freeman. . . . Likewise also he that is called being free is the servant." He wanted to remind them to accept their station in life and to remember that servitude was fundamentally Christian. Servants, he told them, achieve freedom in the Lord, and to be the Lord's freeman is a privilege and an advantage; he could show them how to achieve this. After prayers he sent them home, assuming he had given them sufficient reason to accept their condition, but of course none of them believed that freedom in heaven was sufficient reward for slavery in life.

Jenny and Cato retired to their corner of the kitchen, still hoping to return to Africa in this life or the next, while Lucy returned to the Wells house unconvinced by his words. She remained a devoted Christian throughout her life and memorized much of the Bible, but never for a moment did she believe that Christianity negated the need for freedom on earth.

Neither did a slave named Prince, now owned by Joseph Barnard, accept this sermon. In September he decided that another sort of freedom was far more desirable. He put his fiddle under his arm, made up a bundle of heavy clothes—an old brown coat, "a double-breasted blue coat with a cape," a brown overcoat with cuffs and a cape, a new jacket and new leather breeches, stockings, and pumps—took up a rifle in his other hand, and tiptoed out of town. Barnard immediately advertised in the *Boston Weekly Post-Boy* and got him back. After that, Prince decided that the enslaved life was no life at all. The last we hear of him, only about a year and a half later, is when Barnard paid £2 for Prince's coffin.

As Lucy's years in Deerfield passed, slaves departed and others arrived. Rev. Ashley bought a third man, Titus, in 1750 for £56. Caleb Sharp, a mixed-race (black and Indian) slave back from military service, was purchased by Oliver Partridge, who turned around and sold him to Samuel Dickinson, but only three months later Sharp was somehow freed. Over in Hatfield, Ephraim Williams sold a little boy named Prince to Israel Williams for £225 in old currency, or $100. As Deerfield settled into peace and prosperity, the black population, slave and free, continued to increase.

One resident's story is particularly fascinating and differs radically from the usual experiences of black people in early Deerfield. In 1722 Heber and his first wife, Hagar, were freed and given ten acres of land by their mistress, Elizabeth Pratt, a widow living in Easton, south of Boston. From then on, Heber was known as Heber Honesty or Honestman. In 1737 he bought land in Huntstown, today Ashfield, Massachusetts, near Deerfield, where he was one of the original settlers, moving there with his second wife, Susannah, and the white Thomas and Elizabeth Phillips of Easton. Mrs. Phillips died, leaving behind a new baby, Phillip, whom Heber and Susannah raised. During the French and Indian Wars, everyone in Ashfield, which was unfortified, picked up and moved for several years to Deerfield, where Heber and Susannah knew Lucy and Bijah. Later in life Heber gave Phillip Phillips some of the land in Ashfield "in consideration of the love & affection I bear to my well beloved Friend Phillip Phillips." The feeling between the older black couple and the young white man was reciprocated, for Phillip Phillips took care of Heber and Susannah in their old age.

Deerfield has one foot in the past and one in the present, and people still live, work, and are educated here. Students at Deerfield Academy greeted our tour guide at the Wells-Thorn house as we stood in the doorway saying our farewells, and Peter King told me that an apartment on an upper floor of the house is rented out to local residents. For a moment I imagined renting this place, hoping that some apparition of Lucy might walk into the room, but then the vision faded. Lucy's house lives on, but I realized that she no longer lives there. It wasn't until much later that I discovered why: Lucy did not grow up in this house.

After a lag of a few years, I went back to see the house again. A friendly young intern was acting as the guide that day, explaining colonial domestic life to a woman and her two young daughters. She led them in, saying, "This house was built in 1747." It

EBENEZER AND ABIGAIL WELLS'S HOUSE (NOW THE WELLS-THORN HOUSE). *Photograph courtesy of the Pocumtuck Valley Memorial Association, Memorial Hall Museum, Deerfield, Massachusetts.*

took a moment to click. "Wait a minute," I said when she paused. "Lucy Terry arrived here about twelve years before that to live with the Wellses. Do you mean the house wasn't here yet?"

The answer is yes and no. There had been a house on the Wells lot for many years; apparently it burned down sometime between 1716 and 1726, and another house was built before Lucy's arrival. It turns out that the current house is not that house. Dendrochronology, the science of tree-ring dating of buildings that discloses the last year the lumber grew, has recently proved that the house standing there today—both the original and the presumed addition—were built in 1747, the year after her "Bars Fight" poem was composed. A different house stood on the same property when Lucy was young.

I left the house after my first visit wondering if perhaps the reason that no one had been able to fill in more of her story was that they couldn't get past the layers of false and revised histories. The story of Bijah and Lucy always began and ended with Lucy, and rather than looking in the house of someone who had claimed to own her, I needed to look in her own home, where she lived with her husband and her children.

CHAPTER SEVEN

COURTSHIP AND MARRIAGE

Bijah may have been watching Lucy for a while, wondering if he could convince her to give up the home she'd known for so many years—a home where she worked hard but was well cared for—and throw in her lot with a much older man and a hardscrabble life. But what did age matter to her in a time when older men often married younger women? In her eyes, he was an unhoped-for joy: a free black man who loved her and who wanted to marry her and set her up in her own home and who would work to make her free.

Had Lucy been a privileged white girl like Elizabeth Porter Phelps of Northampton, she would have kept a daily journal describing her beau's visits to her house, the sewing of her trousseau, the financial agreement struck between father and fiancé, the conversations with her female friends, and serious consideration of the dangers of inevitable childbirths. But of course I found none of these for Lucy, even though discussions clearly took place between Bijah and Ebenezer Wells, between Lucy and Abigail Wells, and among the Deerfield slaves.

Even if she had kept such a journal, serious events kept everyone too busy for frivolous occupations. The last, and most famous, of the French and Indian Wars broke out in 1754. Seven years after his military service, Bijah was now nearly fifty, on the verge of being too old to fight, but other men commissioned long ago suddenly found themselves elderly officers on active duty. Deerfield once again saw soldiers stationed everywhere, and servants like Lucy found their workloads increased in the taverns, inns, and private houses where they were billeted. Ebenezer Wells, once again Ensign Wells, was wounded and underwent a painful operation and series of not very successful treatments. Lucy and Abigail had to tend to him. Slaves found themselves pressed into active military service, often as the replacements for those who didn't wish to go. This was the time when Jonathan Ashley's slave Titus served. He may well have been glad to exchange his life under his severe master for a more dangerous and exciting time.

In order to be closer to Lucy, Bijah left the Hulls and Northampton and took laborer's jobs closer to Deerfield. He worked there during the summer and then went to work nearby in Sunderland, Massachusetts, where his old "Negro network" friend Ralph Way, the strong-willed man who owned land in Hadley, also owned some property, but he was warned out of town late that fall because he wasn't a legal resident. He made sure to take work that kept him close to Deerfield and Lucy.

Even without a journal or letters, from my table at the library in Historic Deerfield I slowly pieced together their courtship and preparations for their life together from local merchants' accounts. I saw how Lucy, so financially cautious, suddenly began to act differently. Unlike the other servants, who so often spent their small occasional earnings on nonessentials from stores such as Elijah Williams's, Lucy rarely bought anything for herself over the years. But almost immediately after Bijah gained his freedom, she began to shop. She bought a fan. She bought pins and chocolate. Abigail Wells gave her permission to work for Ebenezer Hinsdale at his store, and she used part of her earnings to buy

ELIJAH WILLIAMS'S STORE C. 1870. *Photograph courtesy of the Pocumtuck Valley Memorial Association, Memorial Hall Museum, Deerfield, Massachusetts.*

five yards of checked cloth. She bought a bit of expensive cambric, enough to make a handkerchief. The following January she had saved up enough to buy seven shillings' worth of imported linen. A bit more cambric. Ribbons. A double-stranded white necklace. More ribbon. A string of beads. A skein of silk thread. A thimble. A mug. Buttons. Five yards of galoon, a narrow gold or silver trimming for clothes. A sheet of drawing paper. She was putting together a trousseau and a hope chest. She bought almost nothing for herself in the twenty years that she'd lived in Deerfield, but now she kept dashing across the street to Elijah Williams's shop. The purchase that delighted me the most, that said the most about who she was, occurred in December 1751 when she bought herself three sheets of paper.

In 1756 Bijah began to make small purchases as well: he bought a knife for himself, and he sometimes stopped in at Elijah's tavern at the end of a day's work to refresh himself with a mug of cider. When he couldn't find work, he went fishing, earning an impressive seven shillings—the equivalent of more than three days' paid labor—for four large salmon. In April he too began to spruce himself up, buying five and a half yards of shirting fabric that Lucy perhaps sewed up, using her new thimble, and a few weeks later a pair of hose. Men in those days dressed in breeches that fastened just below the knee, with stockings—often striped—over their calves; working men wore long shirts and often wore pewter buckles on their shoes. He too was putting together a new outfit.

This may well have been the first wedding between black people in Deerfield since the time of Parthena and Frank, the couple killed in Elijah's father's house in the 1704 raid, and it caused real excitement and anticipation among the other Deerfield African Americans. You could sense the eagerness and seriousness with which some of the other Deerfield slaves treated an event that they had never experienced. Lucy was one of their favorite people, and at about thirty, she was marrying a free and respected man who had links to other free blacks in the region. It was the closest the frontier slaves would ever get to celebrity among their own people, and they wished to honor it as best they could. Titus, who could sew, bought sewing supplies and a pair of shoe buckles. Ishmael bought a pair of gloves. Caesar, who lived in the Ebenezer Wells house with Lucy, bought a psalm book, more evidence that both he and Lucy had been taught to read and that he, like her, took his religion seriously.

Weddings in those days were quite different from what we might expect from today's elaborate affairs. Brides rarely wore white until the twentieth century, and weddings took place in homes rather than in churches. Ministers performed some marriages, but not most. Saturday wasn't the accepted wedding day, and evening weddings were common. Of African American weddings on the northern frontier we know little, simply because so few ever took place. In the South, where such weddings were largely outside of the law, couples and communities relied on African traditions handed down through generations or kept alive with the importation of new slaves, or they devised their own traditions, such as jumping together over a broom. In Toni Morrison's novel *Beloved*, Sethe's mid-nineteenth-century Kentucky mistress is amused to hear that her slave wishes to have any ceremony at all; she feels that her permission to let them be a couple is sufficient. In Lucy and Bijah's eighteenth-century Deerfield, steeped as it was in a Puritan-descended ethic, such a partnership would have meant living in sin, so those who wished to live together married.

Bijah and Lucy were married on Monday, May 17, 1756. Elijah Williams, now also justice of the peace, gladly performed the ceremony, forgoing all fees as a gift to the couple. He had been present at Bijah's military service, his manumission, and now his wedding. Beyond those simple facts recorded in the Deerfield town records, we can only imagine the details of an event that marked a colossal shift in their lives. Bijah had already achieved, in less than ten years, everything he could have dreamed during those long Northfield years of lonely servitude. At an age when many men's lives are set and unchanging, his was about to change completely. He was about to go from being a fifty-year-old bachelor to a married man soon to be the father of six. Lucy, still a slave surrounded by slaves, most of them older than she and with no hope of gaining their freedom, was about to move into her own house with autonomy, her own belongings, and her own determination of her future. She also faced thirteen years of regular childbearing.

The ceremony itself probably took place in the Wells house. Since there are no letters, I can only imagine it. A fragrant spring day. Lucy in her trimmed frock and cap, Bijah in his new shirt. In front of them, Elijah Williams in his uniform and, like all the other men of his class, armed to the teeth because of the war. Abigail and Ebenezer Wells, sitting down because, at sixty-four years old, he was not well and only had, in fact, another two years to live. Standing at the back of the room, Lucy and Bijah's friends: Titus in his new shoe buckles, Ishmael in his new gloves, and, standing seriously to one side, Caesar clasping the psalm book. I knew that I was reading sentimentality into bare facts gleaned from prosaic purchases, but as I sat at the table taking notes on a similar day, I wanted it to have happened that way, even though Elijah indicated on the marriage certificate that Lucy still belonged to Ebenezer Wells. Yet a year later almost to the day, when Ebenezer Wells wrote his will, neither Lucy nor Caesar was listed among the property that he was leaving to Abigail and his nephews. Why had he freed them?

By 1756, when Bijah and Lucy married, the French and Indian War was in full swing. Ensign Ebenezer Wells squeezed back into uniform as a clerk but was soon wounded. Elijah Williams, going deaf, reopened the commissary as he reorganized the ranks. As the French sought to expand their American holdings by building a series of forts southward from Canada, a young George Washington had already been sent out to engage them in 1754. Battles spread between the French (and their native allies) and the English from as far north as Crown Point, at the tip of Lake Champlain, down to Virginia. By mid-1755, Elijah—now Major Williams—had been getting disturbing news of sightings of native scouting parties in the region, and the word from Albany was that not only were groups gathering there, but that at least one of them had its sights on Deerfield. The town needed guards and a militia, but it was July—how could they get all the crops in if the men were sent away? The ranks of available men were already depleted by the demands of the provincial army. Only four weeks later natives were discovered preparing an ambush. With the number of adult men in Deerfield down to just seventy, the choice seemed to be death by attack or slower death by starvation of people and livestock. Williams responded by having four forts built around the town and organizing militias.

Massachusetts men were reluctant to join until Governor William Shirley promised that they "would serve only under their own officers, that they would be subject to provincial and not regular discipline, and that they would be employed only in an area east of Schenectady and north of Albany." In other words, they would be relatively close to home and would not be subject to the harsh British punishments of severe and often deadly whippings.

Deerfield's solution to the manpower problem was direct and simple, though it was one that would later shock Washington when he was sent up to Massachusetts during the Revolution: all able-bodied men between sixteen and sixty enlisted, and this meant all the black men as well as the whites. Among all the familiar names of Deerfield men who joined up, including fathers and sons, were the names of slave and free. We found the names of Titus Ashley, Caleb Sharp, Cato Ashley, Cesar Ashley, Caesar Hinsdale, Caesar Hoyt, Peter, and Abijah Prince. A month after his wedding, fifty-year-old Abijah Prince had re-upped: he walked into Elijah Williams's store, which was now once again a commissary, and fitted himself out for service. He left with gunpowder, lead, flints, sharpening stones, and a drum rim to make himself

NINETEENTH-CENTURY MAP SHOWING ABIJAH'S BROOK.
Courtesy Town of Deerfield, Massachusetts.

a drum—a new source of income. Perhaps he could make enough, when his service ended, to buy his wife's freedom.

Soldiering wasn't the only way a black man could serve in Deerfield's military: drummers were respected and important members of militias, and the role was open to any man with a drum and an ability to play it. Their staccato rhythms woke soldiers up and sent them to bed, told them when to eat and when to assemble. Drummers led the others into battle and regulated their marches. In towns and garrisons they sounded alarms and gathered soldiers. When in October the town decided to build four garrisons, it was probably Bijah who marched down the street with his drum to gather everyone, then regulated their days within one of the four forts. With Bijah at the head of their formation, the Deerfield militia prepared to meet the French—and he may have gone as far as Crown Point in this latest service.

When his military days at last came to an end Bijah could, at long last, turn to what he'd dreamed of for so long: working a farm alongside a beloved wife and making a family. He returned from service with a salary and perhaps with the ability to free his pregnant wife as they settled down on several acres that they rented from Ebenezer Wells, behind his property on the street. Wells had several parcels of land that he rented out to farmers, a practice that Abigail kept up after his death. Bijah and Lucy bought a New Testament and set up housekeeping "at the foot of the hill, south of the burying ground," on what is now part of a farm across the road that now leads to Greenfield. An 1804 map shows "Abijah's Brook" running north and south. Long after they moved away from Deerfield, and long after his death, Bijah's name lived on in Deerfield lore.

Only eight months, almost to the day, after their wedding, Lucy gave birth to their son Caesar. A few eyebrows may have been raised at the timing, but a month later the Princes stood proudly at the front of the meetinghouse as Rev. Ashley baptized the first freeborn black in Deerfield.

CHAPTER EIGHT

DAILY LIFE

It's a beautiful Saturday in July, one of the very few in an unusual summer of heavy humidity and heat. I'm sitting on a bench with Martha Noblick and Bob Romer in the kitchen of the Hall Tavern in Deerfield, watching two women in period costumes prepare a typical eighteenth-century meal. The tavern is not one that Lucy and Bijah knew—it was moved here from Charlemont, Massachusetts, in the 1950s—but it is of a period, style, and location they would have recognized.

"People ate seasonally and really well here," the two cooks assure me as one slices cucumbers for a salad and the other lifts the lid of a hanging cast-iron pot holding a large chicken surrounded by vegetables. "Everyone had meats, corn and grain, and vegetables from the garden in summer and from the root cellar in other seasons." They made stews and fricassees, fish and roasts, sauces and puddings, cheeses and butter. They ate rice and beans and flapjacks. Beer, rum, and cider were considered essential food and important parts of a daily diet. Although white flour was a luxury, I'm still surprised to learn today that they rarely baked loaf bread of any kind in the summer. "Too hot," I'm told, for it took hours just to get the fireplace's brick oven up to temperature. In the winter, with the fireplace going round the clock, it made more sense to bake this way. They raised their bread dough with beer "emptins"—what was left at the bottom of a beer barrel—instead of with yeast. After building an oven fire, they tested the temperature the old-fashioned way—by putting their hand inside. But in all seasons they used the fireplace itself as an oven. Later this afternoon the cook in period costume will bank a bed of coals and set a covered dish on it, topping it off with more coals, to bake a blueberry pie. She and her companion are tickled to hear something I read in a two-hundred-year-old Deerfield cookbook, *The Pocumtuck Housewife*: in the winter some housewives kept a fish frozen in a bucket of water outside the kitchen door. When they wanted to make a fish stew, they simply went outside and sawed off a couple of slices.

Anthony and Bob wander off while the rest of us trade recipes, and I begin to feel that I am one of Lucy's neighbors who has stopped by for a chat on a summer afternoon while the men are out working. If it weren't for my jeans and the cell phone in my pocket, I could believe us all to be in the eighteenth century. By now Deerfield feels like home, and I am beginning to see and understand Lucy's daily life in the house on Abijah's Brook. Over the past few years I have gotten a handle on the way people lived then, the foods they ate, the clothes they wore, the always surprising fact of widespread slavery, the waves of warfare.

Even so, there were things about Lucy's and Bijah's lives that startled me and made me rethink what I thought I knew about how they lived. Until then part of me still saw their lives as a costume drama—almost real, romanticized, nearly authentic, but ultimately performed like this wonderful demonstration by people who would get into cars and drive home at the end of the performance to watch television, leaving behind the ghosts of earlier inhabitants who had spent their evenings at the tavern or at home knitting, sewing, trading stories, reading the Bible, or playing music. Wealthier families treated themselves to balls and parties. George Sheldon, Deerfield's nineteenth-century historian, wrote that Lucy's house drew as to a magnet the children of Deerfield, who found her home and company too appealing to stay away. Throughout the day they came, singly and in little groups, to listen to her talk as she went about her work. She must have put them to work, not letting them get their entertainment for nothing, trading their armloads of firewood or turns taken at the roasting spit for recitations of the "Bars Fight" poem and dramatic descriptions of that terrifying day, Bible stories, or invented tales.

Bijah too had much work to do, but I had not anticipated his surprising relationship to the other slaves. I knew that he divided his time between working his rented farm in Deerfield and working for others as an experienced laborer, taking on a variety of skilled and unskilled jobs, doing everything from masonry work to field labor to well digging in order to make ends meet. In fact, on the very day I was chatting with the women at Hall Tavern about cooking, an archaeological dig was going on down the street, led by a University of Massachusetts professor named Bob Paynter, who had put up an educational sign that read WHO WAS ABIJAH PRINCE? He and his graduate students had unearthed a well that Bijah dug for Deerfield merchant Joseph Barnard.

Although Bijah worked for men like Barnard, in these early years of his marriage he found himself more regularly on Rev. Jonathan Ashley's land, working alongside Ashley's slaves Titus and Cato to cut brush or erect fences. They must have known each other for years, so I was stunned when I found Bijah's name on the debit side of the ledger, owing the minister for the work of the other two men. Alongside Bijah's use of his livestock, as though they were one and the same sort of transaction, Ashley had meticulously recorded in his minute script all the instances of Bijah's paying him for the use of his servants. "Cato & horse a day," he wrote, or, "Cato and 3 cattle a day," or, "Titus 1 day cutting wood," or, "Titus & Cato to How & a horse to harrow." Did this mean that Bijah tacitly accepted the slave system and now looked upon the two men as slaves whose labor was as available to him as it was to any white man with the price of their hire? Was there a class system at play among the black inhabitants of Deerfield that now put Bijah and Lucy on the other side of an impregnable wall called "freedom"?

On one level it seemed straightforward enough: Bijah needed help in his fields. In years to come his own children would do this work, but until then it was necessary for him to hire others. Because it was primarily a barter economy, he traded his own labor, and the surplus from his field, for Titus's and Cato's work. Thus, on some days he worked alongside them as a hired man and on other days he worked alongside them as their hirer. Yet I also came to another perspective: perhaps it seemed to them better to work for someone who understood and had shared their situation. Though younger than Bijah, they were also his friends, and they were trapped in a situation that he had recently escaped and for which he had great sympathy. They probably enjoyed an easy relationship, with Titus and Cato happier to work for him than for others, and certainly happier whenever they were away from the dour minister. During the days, Ashley sent them off to work for others while he pocketed the earnings; then in the evenings, he wrote carping letters to the town officials complaining of the high cost of keeping his large family and of entertaining visitors in the style to which they were accustomed. If they were forced to work for others—and this after Titus had served in the war—better it should be for Bijah, who knew them and understood the irony of their situation. It is not surprising that at the end of their days of labor Titus and Cato retired to the kitchen fire with Jenny and their pipes and rum, unable to anticipate a day of emancipation that Ashley would in fact never grant them.

Bijah did just about any kind of work that needed doing in order to make money. But more than just a laborer-for-hire, he showed himself to be every bit the entrepreneur. He had his own maple sugar works—buckets and taps—and a sugarbush outside of the growing town where he tapped trees and boiled sap. He cleared land for Elijah Williams and dismantled a beaver dam for him. He hoed his own fields and those of Rev. Jonathan Ashley. He mended fences and cut wood for Ashley, mowed hay for Elijah, then hired Titus and Cato to help him with his maple sugaring. Together they dressed flax by first beating it with a hard wooden block and then "hetcheling" (combing) it through a bed of nails or needles to turn it into soft threads ready for spinning into linen and tow cloth. He hoed and harrowed his land as spring came in and it was time to plant crops. Lucy spun flax and wool for the doctor, Thomas Williams.

All of this hard work proved they were like the majority of working-class Deerfielders and well accepted in the community as they settled down to an ordinary life. It reminded me of my father, who grew up in one of the only black families in a tiny Michigan town and yet encountered little racial trouble in his youth. When outsiders came to town and began to hassle him and his many brothers, the other kids came to their defense. "Them's *our* coloreds," they'd say, as though it was all right to go back home and bother *theirs*.

Lucy and Bijah were naturally mindful of race, but they expected to be more than some of Deerfield's few free blacks: they intended to live exactly as the others of their class did. Their labor enabled them to buy things they needed for the kitchen and farm, and they wanted to run things efficiently. As soon as they could, they purchased a secretary's guide—an all-purpose reference book that showed them how to handle business letters, accounting, and the necessary methods of keeping track of their work and finances. As free people, they needed to use the proper forms for all their dealings, and this book contained instructions for correct spelling, letter writing for all occasions, business arithmetic, bookkeeping and accounting, weights, measurements (including measuring land), and writing deeds, leases, and indentures. Some reference books of this kind even included instructions on planting, tree grafting, and wine and cider making. No illiterate person could use one, and a year later the middle-aged Bijah bought not only a pair of spectacles to read his volume better but also sealing wax to mark legal documents with a personal imprint and to seal letters. Although certainly not common among slaves throughout America, the Princes' literacy may not have been entirely unusual where they lived. Caesar, over at the Billings house, walked into Elijah's store in August and emerged with sleeve buttons, garters, a snuff box, and a parrot in a cage. Yet he went back two weeks later to buy an inkpot.

A literate couple, hardworking and ambitious, Bijah and Lucy hired slaves but also worked alongside them as hired labor. We began to believe that we were already learning more than had been known about any other African American family from that time. Like archaeologists, we were slowly unearthing the details of daily life that shed so much light on how people like Bijah and Lucy actually lived. They were a couple who had never written their own narrative, and whose family papers were lodged in no library, yet every detail we found said something not just about the Princes but about black people all over New England. Was there more to discover?

Early on in my Deerfield research I read through Dr. Thomas Williams's accounts. A relative of Elijah's, he had an honorary degree from Yale and served for twenty years as the province's official physician for the line of forts running from the bottom of present-day Vermont to western Massachusetts, and like Bijah he had been at Fort Massachusetts. He also had treated Lucy when she still served the Wellses. Thomas Williams was Deerfield's first properly trained doctor and had an extensive medical library and a penchant for experimenting with the latest exotic treatments. For really serious care, those who could afford to called on the services of Dr. Richard Crouch of Hadley, the British-born and Edinburgh-trained doctor who practiced all over that half of the state. Both doctors were available to those who could pay them, but while Crouch had to be paid in cash, Williams accepted barter in the form of goods and labor. He also made house calls as well as keeping office hours, mixed up treatments himself, and handed them out in little blue Delft pots that had to be cleaned and returned when empty.

When I read Williams's medical account book on microfilm—being much more careful these days to hit the Print button only when necessary—I was shocked to learn what this discovery could mean. Not only had Bijah and Lucy made numerous visits to the doctor, but here, in line after line, stood the entire medical history of the Prince family, parents and children, over a period of years. It needed decoding, but it might have been the only surviving medical history of an African American family of the mid-eighteenth century. It was certainly the only one I had ever seen.

I could not read it. Or rather, I could read it only enough to know that it gave prescriptions and costs but not diagnoses, and that it did so in abbreviations from the Latin, which I could not read even if Williams had written in whole words. But somehow, if the account book could be translated, it would give an entirely new outlook on their lives during these years. Anthony threw himself into deciphering this locked history, and over the months the story behind their Deerfield years slowly revealed itself. It would turn out that the Princes had several seriously close calls, and although they went to the doctor only when it was absolutely necessary, they were willing to work very long hours in order to afford treatment.

I was now teaching several days a week in Manhattan, and each day as I headed to my office Anthony headed to his: a table in the reading room at the New York Academy of Medicine, an imposing old building on Central Park on Manhattan's Upper East Side used largely for medical conventions and meetings. His table was in the academy's rare books library, renowned for its antiquarian medical texts, including the oldest medical manuscript in the world, from ancient Egypt. The room was elegant, lined with medical texts from over the centuries. In front of him were a Greek lexicon and a Latin dictionary, and the librarians retrieved the other books he needed: books on childbirth and herbalists, the *materia medica* of eighteenth-century England and America.

He found that within a year of their marriage Bijah was injured. For months Bijah was in and out of the doctor's office or was attended at their house on Abijah's Brook, and he came away from each visit with a different treatment. To pay the good doctor, Lucy spun, together they hoed Williams's garden, and Bijah brought in his hay and went to the mill for him. They did all this despite Lucy's second pregnancy. On June 1, 1758, their second child, a girl they named Duruxa and nicknamed Dack, was born, just a year and a half after Caesar. They were now following the normal pattern of having a baby every year or two; had Lucy been even younger, she could have expected to give birth to up to a dozen children, never using a doctor's services.

Williams, like most physicians of his day, believed strongly in removing infection and illness by purgatives, emetics, and bleeding, and the Princes submitted to all these cures. Williams bled from different areas of the body, using leeches, cups, or a spring-loaded knife. He raised blisters with plasters made from Spanish flies in order to pull internal infections to the surface and excise them by lancing. Whatever Bijah's wound was, as it began to heal he dried it out with a lead oxide astringent. These cures were ultimately effective, but the Princes were now deeply in the doctor's debt. Bijah sold a gun to Daniel Arms's shop, using part of the proceeds to pay his bills, but he also made enough between that and his savings to buy a mare on Christmas Day—in those times a business day like any other. He and Lucy now had more mobility and this was an important addition to their livestock. They kept pigs—Titus helped him to slaughter his hogs—and at least one cow, and they often rented an ox team for the really heavy work. But this was really subsistence farming, with some profit made from selling their butter and working for others. The death of Ebenezer Wells reminded them that they lived on and farmed rented land. His widow Abigail, who needed the income, had no intention of asking them to leave, but if she died they couldn't be sure that her heirs would let them stay. If they wanted to stay solvent—but more importantly, to get ahead—they needed other entrepreneurial and creative ways to make money.

Perhaps it was in his occasional stops at Elijah's tavern, where others sometimes bought him a drink at the end of the workday, or in his long conversations with Lucy that Bijah began to explore other business ventures. With Deerfield bounded by two rivers—the Deerfield River and the Connecticut River into which the Deerfield flowed—lots of people on the street had land on both banks and frequently needed access to their fields on the other side of the water. Cattle grazed across the river in the warmer months, and fields of rye, wheat, and Indian corn lay on the other side as well. With no bridges, the town kept a scow, or flat-bottomed boat steered by poles, for public use, but this wasn't always available when someone needed it. Farther down the Connecticut, water transportation was big business. Deerfield could support nothing on that scale, but there was still a little money to be had in a smaller operation. A few months before Lucy's second labor, Bijah, after being laid up with a respiratory or gastric problem, began ferrying workmen, livestock, and supplies.

Caleb Sharp (or Sharp Caleb—he went by both names), the mixed-race man who had served twice with Bijah in the military and who now was also free, set up a merchandising business with a man named Aaron Scott. Caleb had bigger things in mind, however, and quickly set up a mill in nearby Conway. With the French and Indian War still raging all around them, an easily accessible place to get wood sawn and grain milled was a godsend to Deerfield's merchants and farmers, who wasted no time giving him business. It wasn't long before Bijah was over in Conway helping Caleb at the mill and at boating, and in early August he came back from Caleb's with a hog, two hundred feet of boards, and a boat of his own. Now in business for himself, though continuing to work his own farm, he rose beyond laboring only for others.

There was no turning back. When Bijah had to see the doctor again in October 1758 for infected wounds and bad coughs, Thomas Williams entered the accounts in his book not under the name "Abijah Negro," which he had used up to now, but under the more respectful and appropriate name of "Abijah Prince." Any subsequent lapses from this occurred only when the doctor's assistant entered items into the account book.

Lucy and Bijah celebrated their third Christmas together by buying three pints of rum, perhaps to entertain a trickle of friends who dropped in for a drink and a slice of pie made from the apples and suet they had laid in earlier that month. Despite persistent illnesses, it had been a good year.

A year later Lucy became pregnant again, and this time things did not go smoothly. She suffered from morning sickness and headaches. She had no reason to expect a difficult delivery, in spite of the dangers that women always faced in childbirth. However, on Thursday, August 7, 1760, when Lucy delivered her third child, a daughter named Drucilla, nicknamed Cill, something went wrong. The baby was fine, but Lucy was not. The next morning Bijah rushed to Elijah Williams's shop to buy three quarts of rum and a pound of currants, probably to steep a recognized strengthening postnatal infusion to feed to Lucy by delicate spoonfuls. He waited another day, but when she didn't improve he finally called in the doctor and was probably treated to a scolding for the remedy he'd given Lucy. Like other medical men of his time, Williams believed that "hot irritating things" like strong liquors—as opposed to the "coolness" of wine and ale—could be disastrous to women who had just delivered babies.

He examined Lucy, but she had sunk even lower by the next day when he returned. From his prescriptions we began to piece together what had happened: a probable tear, causing interior and exterior inflammation. He felt her pulse, examined her thoroughly, applied a soothing and healing combination of lard and rosewater, and warned Bijah not to try to move her. By Sunday she had developed a fever, one of the worst danger signs, and he treated her for a sudden weak pulse and malignant fever and bled her. He returned the same afternoon to see if she fared any better. She was near death.

As Lucy lay in such a precarious state, Bijah seemed likely to lose the person with whom he had entered into a new and inevitably rewarding phase of life. Still, he had to pry himself from her bedside several times to ferry the doctor across the river and to keep up the work on his own farm. While he was out, Abigail Wells no doubt looked in on Lucy and sat by her bedside as she fought to recover; slave mistresses did no less for their servants, and she and Lucy had been together for twenty-five years now, first as mistress and servant, and now as landlady and tenant. Although baptisms normally took place on the Sunday between the first and second week after the birth, Lucy was in no condition to leave her bed, and Cill remained unbaptized as her mother inched her way back to life. Two weeks after giving birth, Lucy made her way slowly back to Dr. Williams's office, where he bled her again and dressed her injuries. A month after Cill was born she was finally baptized. Lucy and Bijah spent the rest of the year struggling back to health, but more serious injuries lay ahead.

These dramatic circumstances took place against a background of comings and goings in Deerfield, reminders to the Princes of the precarious position of black people even in a place like Deerfield, which accepted the Princes as free people with free children. At the beginning of January 1760, Rev. Ashley sold Titus, Bijah's longtime friend, co-laborer, and sometime hired hand, to a new owner in Stockbridge, Massachusetts. Six years later Thomas Dickinson, down the street, would sell his man Hartford to William Williams in Pittsfield. Accustomed all their lives to seeing black people bought and sold, saying good-bye to Titus and then to Hartford nonetheless would have been a blow.

The selling of Titus may have been the prompt that Bijah needed to firmly establish himself and his family on their own property, and may also explain his mysterious absence in the year of Cill's birth. He vanished from the record for the summer months of 1760, leaving Lucy and the children and returning only in time for Cill's birth. He did it again the following summer, only occasionally showing up to buy supplies or see the doctor, but not working for anyone else. The record showed that when Caesar was four years old Lucy began to instruct him from a primer, the second one they had owned, but it still provided no answer to Bijah's unexplained absences from the family that meant so much to him. As it turned out, the real drama, the one that would define their character, independence, and resolve, was already beginning.

PART THREE

Landowners

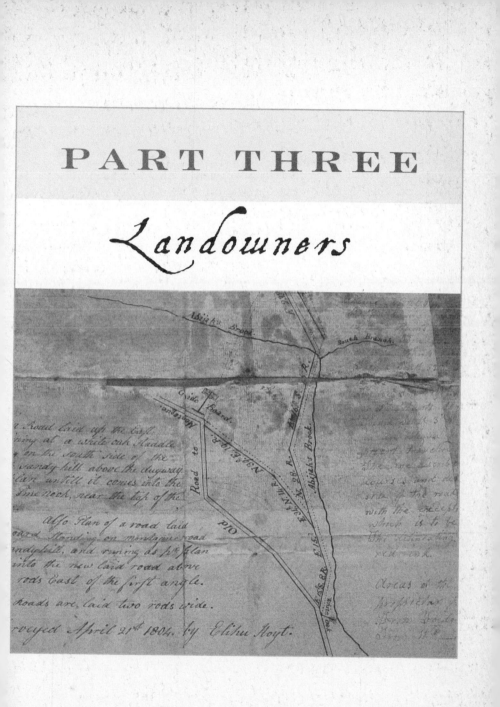

CHAPTER NINE

GETTING TO GUILFORD

Land—uncleared virgin forest as far as the imagination could stretch—was what everyone wanted, from the natives who were losing it in alarming quantities, to the numerous children of settlers, to Boston and Connecticut bigwigs, right up the chain to those in command of the most powerful European nations. Bijah and Lucy were no different. Like everyone else, they needed it to provide for their family, to pass on to their children, and as a wise investment. The only question they had was how to get it.

Two different situations began to unfold for them in the spring of 1760, both holding great excitement and promise. That spring Elijah Williams was buying up rights—the legal right to proprietorship in current and future land distribution for new towns—to as many lots as he could in Guilford, Vermont. Once roads were made, it would be less than a day's horse ride from Deerfield. Unwisely giddy in the climate of land speculation, he was adding these to the several lots he'd previously acquired in Guilford as one of the town founders when the first grants had been approved in 1754. The law required that five acres be cleared for every fifty granted. Because the original grant came through alongside the initial conflicts of the French and Indian War, which had made it too dangerous to settle in a remote place, six years later only one or two men had gone up to begin the required work of cutting down acres of old-growth maples, oaks, and chestnuts, pulling up roots, and making a livable and arable space and building a house.

Busy men like Elijah, who bought on speculation, contracted with someone else to do this backbreaking work. That's also what David Field, a Deerfield merchant whose land speculations eventually outpaced his ability to hang on to them, was doing. He agreed to give Moses Brooks one-third of the crops and the use of the property if he would settle temporarily on his Winchester land for five years, clearing and planting it and building a small house. Even modestly situated men like Benjamin Doolittle were caught up in speculating, as was Rev. Jonathan Ashley, who amassed many hundreds of acres in various parcels that he disposed of as easily as he sold his slaves during financial hard times. Getting permission to found a new town was fairly easy. For formal approval, all it took was someone enterprising enough to petition the governor and enough people to add their names to the petition—often neither knowing nor caring about which town they were signing up for. Men did it to either establish a family inheritance or realize a quick turnaround on an investment that cost next to nothing.

The process sounded simple enough, but the system was rife with exploitation. For one thing, the governors of both New Hampshire and New York claimed royal jurisdiction over the land between the Hudson and Connecticut Rivers, and both freely handed out grants—often to the same property—to petitioners. In New Hampshire, Benning Wentworth was particularly happy when King George II appointed him governor, for he was a bankrupt who now found himself enjoying a good salary. With every town he approved he personally gained considerable property. The immediate result was a feverish land grab that

BENNING WENTWORTH, ROYAL GOVERNOR OF NEW HAMPSHIRE.
Courtesy of the New Hampshire Historical Society.

attracted speculators from all over New England and the mid-Atlantic region.

With joyful and generally illegal abandon, Wentworth established 138 towns, many of them later challenged, and added some 65,000 illegal acres, many of them within New York's territory, into his personal holdings. No one complained until he chartered Bennington, named after himself. For years afterward, grantees found themselves battling their neighbors over disputed property rights. In these early years no one the Princes knew seemed particularly worried about the legal ramifications of competing grants; that wouldn't happen until the Revolutionary War forced grantees, under the fiery pressure of Ethan Allen, to choose sides: New Hampshire, New York, or the newly named state of Vermont.

Wentworth, something of a rogue from his early days, had supporters as well as detractors. As a Harvard student, he set the record "for fines and broken windows." His main business interests, importing wine and selling lumber and munitions, were in Cadiz and England, and he made frequent trips there. He was in Spain when New Hampshire's governor offered him the lieutenant governorship, and Wentworth reportedly "behav'd with a great deal of insolence & ill manners" toward the governor when he returned. His enemies mocked his business travels, calling him "Toby, the Cadix pedlar," and later, when he fell on hard times, the "Spanish bankrupt." His creditors and friends joined together to come up with the £300 commission needed to secure him the governorship of New Hampshire, which proved his financial making. He amassed a fortune through the land grants he handed out and built a forty-room mansion in Portsmouth on the New Hampshire coast as well as a large lakeside summer home, but he finally fell out of favor and left office under a cloud of corruption, scandal, and greed. None of this was helped when, after his wife died in 1755, he married his housekeeper, starting a round of crude gossip that was in fact unfair to the bride, who was a respectable woman from a good family. When he died in 1770, he was one of the richest men in New England, having become so on the backs of men desperate or equally greedy for land.

With four small children and living on rented land in Deerfield, Bijah and Lucy couldn't hope to get ahead, let alone gain the sort of independence that the self-confident Ralph Way of "the Negro network" was already well on his way to achieving over in Hadley. Although Bijah was still laboring for others, doing his own farming, and establishing his small business ventures, none of it was on the scale that could allow them to prosper the way that Way did. Within ten years, Way would be living, along with his son's family, in two houses on his own land, with a barn, producing sixty-five bushels of grain and twelve tons of high-quality hay a year, as well as taxable barrels of cider. His prosperity was remarkable for a black man and his family at that time. That is why the Princes blessed their good fortune when, one day in 1760, a man named Isaac Searles approached Bijah with an offer to go in on a petition for a land grant in Sunderland, Vermont, near Bennington. Bijah promptly agreed to add his name to a list that included some of the most prominent New Englanders of his time.

Almost nothing is known about Searles, except that he was a Northampton shoemaker. Though later in life he was well off, and a successful politician representing Williamstown in the Massachusetts legislature, no portrait was painted; he made it into no reminiscences or diaries or family genealogies. Our research, however, proved that he was a calculating man who knew how to work the system and was always on the make. He made his living by buying and selling, and land was only one of his speculations. He knew the ins and outs of acquiring property and counted on taking advantage of a town's ability to confiscate and auction off property from proprietors who hadn't paid land taxes. He owned numerous lots in what would become southwestern Vermont: in Arlington, Hubbarton, Pownal, Salisbury, Stamford, Stratton, Sudbury, and Wilmington, originating petitions for most of these towns, even though he lived over the line in Williamstown, Massachusetts, where Bijah had served in 1747. For several years, on and off, Searles and Bijah had been neighbors in Northampton. Searles did some business with Elijah Williams, and it is even possible that Bijah acted as a deliveryman for some of Elijah's purchases from Searles and others in Northampton.

Perhaps Bijah didn't realize that Searles was a well-known hothead and schemer. At the time when a newly married Bijah rejoined the military, Searles was living in Hoosick (later to become Williamstown), fomenting difficulties between the townspeople and the military personnel. Initially dismissed by Col. Israel Williams as a low person not worth regarding, the officer changed his mind when Searles presented a petition "filled with insults and accusations" against him to the General Court, having forged the names of twenty other complainants. In a letter that July, Williams pointed out that Searles and several others "have supposed their success depended upon ye men's distruction of others, and have spared no pains to obtain their designs." The court investigated and forced Searles to sign a self-condemning confession—no doubt composed by Williams—admitting that he had vilified Williams's character, accused him of lying to the courts about the operations of the fort, and "wickedly contrivd of my own malice to Injure him in his good name . . . and had said things that were not true—for all which I am heartily sorry and ask his forgiveness . . . and Promise for the future I will behave myself towards him and all others as I ought to do." He begged Williams to withdraw punishment. He was contrite, but unaltered by the episode.

On November 17, 1760, about the time the Sunderland petition was going forward, Matthew Thornton, a prominent Boston physician and politician, wrote to the Governor's Council of New Hampshire to complain that a man named "Searls" was claiming to have a grant for the same land that Thornton and others were given. Thornton correctly feared that the governor was reneging on their grant, for Searles did indeed manage to take it over.

Today Sunderland has a quaint, picture-book village center. Just twenty miles from Bennington, it is reached by major roads, but Anthony was surprised to find that the clerk's office is a few miles away, housed in a one-room addition built onto the clerk's house and only open part of the week, for half-days. Besides issuing the usual dog licenses and taking care of other small-town business, Rose Keough, a petite blonde, preserves and stands guard over the heavy old volumes that constitute the town's history. She clearly respects them, preserving as an archivist would the minutes of old town meetings, the charter finally declaring Vermont a state, and the records tucked away in the many ancient books, but she also treats them as living objects rather than museum artifacts. There, often out of order and always in the fading old script that we'd now come to know so well, sits the story of Sunderland's origins in 1761.

I went with Anthony on his second visit to take a look at the charter for the town that had lasted all these years. We didn't realize it until later, but the sixty or so proprietors' names break down into several groups. A number of them were prominent New Hampshire and Massachusetts politicians, including: William Brattle, who served for many years in the Massachusetts legislature, was a witness to the peace treaty between the commonwealth and the Penobscot Indians in 1754, and gave his name to a well-known street near Harvard; John Downing, a member of the New Hampshire Council and a proprietor in about thirty other Vermont towns; Thomas Hubbard, former speaker of the Massachusetts House; and of course, Benning

Wentworth himself. Another group consisted of well-connected Connecticut people, including Thomas Clap, a slave-owning minister and president of Yale, and Francis Bernard, governor of New Jersey until 1760, when he became governor of Massachusetts. A handful of others were Dutch descendants and major property owners from around Troy in eastern New York State. A good number of the rest were Northampton men, among them a batch of Searles's presumed relatives. Had all these men actually met together for the required proprietors' meeting, Bijah, the only free black man on the list, would have been in some of the most august company of the region. But, like Searles, Bijah would never himself live in Sunderland.

In the 1750s and 1760s, even though both Guilford and Sunderland eventually got off the ground around the same time, Elijah Williams was in danger of losing all the Guilford properties he had amassed. He and a number of Deerfield and Northampton men had received a New Hampshire grant for Guilford back in 1754, but nothing really had been done by way of development owing to the wars. A couple of men went ahead and made their clearings, but despite extensions, so little was done that the entire grant was likely to be forfeited for lack of property development. The war extensions would run out soon. If work didn't begin on the settlements, all their speculation and hope of a quick turnaround and profit might be lost.

As it turned out, Searles also had his eye on that neighborhood. Like an ambulance chaser, he was scouring all the petitions and grants to see if there were any in jeopardy because of noncompliance with the terms of the charter. Sometimes it worked. Around the time Elijah was fretting about his grants and getting deeply involved in the French and Indian War, Searles sniffed out a languishing 1751 grant for the town of Wilmington, close by

Guilford. He wrote to Governor Wentworth to "humbly pray" that he and his unnamed petitioners could take over the property "heretofore granted upwards of Ten years Since & nothing done by the grantees thereon." Wentworth, with the king's permission, gave it to them.

Searles's luck continued, for Wentworth granted the Sunderland petition in 1761. Bijah, along with all the others named in the petition, now had the legal right to one hundred acres there, with more to come whenever the rest of the land was divided.

By now, at least on paper, Bijah was well on his way to becoming prosperous, if landownership by itself could indicate prosperity. He had the right to five acres in Northfield, Massachusetts, and the promise of more there in the future, and the right to one hundred acres, and eventually more, in Sunderland, Vermont. Now he was working toward ownership of one of Elijah's hundred-acre lots in Guilford, Vermont. None of these properties was a gift; all of them came from his own efforts. So much of what I'd read— so much of the myth of Bijah—assumed that he owned what he acquired through the goodness of whites who had known him when he was a slave. Instead, we were discovering that, like his freedom, Bijah got everything he owned through his own ingenuity. He acquired the Northfield right to land through his own astuteness, and the Sunderland land by adding his name to a legal petition. Now he was using his own backbreaking work to get the Guilford property, a place where he could permanently settle his growing family. Unlike the other property acquisitions, which were straightforward, this one would take time and a complex series of transactions before he became the legal owner. The hard part was figuring out how it happened.

Four years into the quest, the facts we had unearthed about

Lucy and her husband were mounting. Some biographers tack streams of paper around their study walls, writing flow charts on them with colored pens. I started making lists of everything I could find on the Princes. The lists evolved into databases, charts, and calendars. I painstakingly filled in Excel cells and rows with dates and events, from the minutest purchase of pins to the most momentous discoveries of manumission and marriage. Our sense of the importance of the story also grew as we put together an unprecedented picture of how slavery, freedom, and race worked in complicated ways in the second half of eighteenth-century America.

As the seasons passed, we fired up the woodstove and spent our weekends entering data into a chronology that we could sort to look for patterns. Month by month I downloaded calendars for most of the individual months of the eighteenth century, typing in colored-coded events like the Princes' work for others, their payment of taxes, or their settling of debts in the local shops. By now I could sort through a year and calculate everything they had bought, from half-bushels of grain, to drinks in the tavern, to major purchases like the boat, and see how things began to fit into the flow of their lives. I could flip through the months and see where they were and what they were doing and where the blanks fell. Every week or two they appeared in the various store and private accounts, working for someone, paying taxes, buying supplies.

For the spring of 1760, a big gap appeared in the calendar and there was silence. Neither Prince bought anything, worked for anyone, or appeared in any record. Just as the prime planting and working season was under way, when Bijah usually would be haying in others' fields, "hetcheling" flax, or hiring Titus or Cato to help out in his own, nothing. But where could he have gone? It was unlikely he was in Northfield. The Northfield property was theoretical: if divisions were made, he'd get his promised acreage, but so far, apparently, nothing had been done there. A winter gap could mean simply that they were lying low in the fallow season, but a summer silence probably indicated absence rather than lack of activity. The calendar showed something else: this absence coincided with Elijah's purchase of the land they would come to own.

With the pressure on to clear land or forfeit the grant, a likely scenario was this: Elijah now owned ten 100-acre lots and one 50-acre lot in Guilford, and all the able-bodied men he knew were tied up with the war. If Bijah went to Guilford and began clearing the requisite five acres of each lot, his labor would pay toward the mortgage for one of the lots. The Princes would get their hundred acres, and Elijah would preserve his investment. With Lucy once again pregnant and caring for three children aged three and under, it was nearly impossible for her to travel to the wilderness with him. In August she went into labor with Drusilla's difficult birth, and the silence ended abruptly when Bijah fetched the doctor to save his wife's life.

From there, different patterns began to form. There was one pattern of the Princes in Deerfield, very much a part of the community, their family growing and the work unending, but secure in the knowledge of their Sunderland property. Now another pattern emerged: Bijah came and went, dividing the rhythm of each year between his Deerfield life and what appeared to be regular sojourns in Guilford.

In September 1761, a month after Bijah returned, presumably from Guilford, the Sunderland charter was granted. Bijah became an original proprietor, with five initial acres and the right to up to another hundred in each future division. With this property right secured, the Princes began a cycle of staying away from Deerfield for longer and longer stretches, sometimes even in the winter. They disappear from the record for much of the winter of 1761–62, all of the following spring, and part of the next autumn.

When the New England spring, with its muddy roads and slow greening, returned in 1763, the Princes disappear for two months, yet the domestic hum of their lives goes on as before. When they come back into the picture, Lucy knows that she is again pregnant, and that her repeated lying-ins have become harder and harder. When she gave birth to Festus, their second son, at the end of 1763, she had given birth four times in six years, although this time the birth went well enough for her not to need a doctor. Only seventeen months after Festus's birth, a fifth child and third son, Tatnai, arrived on June 2, 1765. Lucy had been pregnant for eighteen months out of the last twenty-six, in the constant round of childbirth, breast-feeding, and gestation that came to most women who married. The miracle was that, unlike so many others, Lucy survived her fertile years.

On the last day of October, the day before enactment of the Stamp Act (passed in Britain to raise money for the British troops stationed in America, the Stamp Act levied a tax on anything written down on paper, from playing cards to licenses to almanacs), Bijah went to the doctor and paid ten shillings—the equivalent of five days' work—to officially register the births of the five children. It was not necessary at that time to register births; indeed, it wasn't commonplace to do so until long after the Civil War. Yet Bijah knew that wherever they went in life, in an unsettled and often unsafe America, registration would give them proof that his children were born free.

Having learned so much about the Princes, we could almost

see them in Deerfield as their children played with other children on the grass outside their houses in the waning summer evenings, while Bijah and Lucy rested in their chairs, sharing a glass of rum with other parents. We knew that they recognized class differences, probably calling Elijah "Mr. Williams" and never aspiring to a place at his table. They were secure in their own rank and well liked. We knew that Bijah sometimes stopped into a tavern at the end of a tiring day, that others often stood him a drink, and that a game of skittles or quoits sometimes followed.

While we had pieced together a story about the Princes—in many respects a story they didn't even know themselves—there was still much that we didn't know. We did not, for example, know what a single member of the family looked like. We did not know how they spent their winter evenings, or anything about the conversations they had with their neighbors as they met on the street while running errands. An early historian commented that they were well educated. Even though their firstborn, Caesar, later wrote his name with a shaky hand, this did not mean, at a time when reading and writing were taught as separate arts, that they could not read or do sums or memorize. Several of the Princes received letters in the post office in later years. One of them, probably one of the girls, learned to write a decent hand and keep accounts. Bijah, as head of the only free black family in town, paid his taxes regularly, and the children felt entirely at home in Deerfield. Lucy possibly taught them at home: the summer of 1764 finds them not only farming but buying a third primer. Bijah bought a spelling book just two years later, perhaps to take with them to Guilford, for they disappear from the records again shortly afterward.

When Caesar turned ten, they had him indentured—service in exchange for learning a trade and room and board—with formal documents, perhaps to Ralph Way, the black landowner in Hadley. It was pretty clear that Bijah and Lucy, while preparing for their children's future, were also steadily planning out their own during these years. They were still renters in Deerfield, but now Bijah began buying building and domestic supplies, seemingly for a home of their own. As his periodic absences continued with regularity, they seemed to concentrate their efforts on the slow creation of a home that belonged only to them.

Anthony and I spent an hour or two talking at the end of each day, either in person or on the phone if I was away working, about what he had managed to locate and how it fit into the emerging picture of their lives. In New York he made his way meticulously through the medical records of Elijah's cousin, Dr. Thomas Williams. The Deerfield physician's ledgers, housed in the *New-York Historical Society*, were slow going. Written with quill pen like all the others, they were even harder to read because they were Latin abbreviations for medications, not diagnoses. Like an archaeologist, Anthony moved backward through the coded information.

He discovered that something was critically wrong with Bijah. Now sixty-two years old, comfortably making the day's ride between what is now Vermont and Massachusetts, he had seemed as strong and active as ever. He could expect to live, like many other Deerfield men in times of peace, another thirty years. He was not, however, immune to injury, and in the spring when Caesar was sent away to work, disaster struck. Some part of his body—a shoulder? a hip? a leg?—became dislocated. Perhaps Bijah was working with a team of oxen in his field and the enormous animals pulled away from him too fast. Perhaps he was thrown from his horse, or a tree he was felling crashed down the wrong way. Perhaps he lay unconscious in a road or field, his dogs raising a howl to bring Lucy and the children or a neighbor to his rescue. Whatever happened, it was serious.

Bijah was hurt in April, but resisted getting the doctor for several days, probably because of the cost. There had been a lot of visits to the doctor in recent years, and as their debt stagnated, the doctor added interest to it. By the time the doctor was finally sent for, Bijah was fevered and delirious. Dr. Williams sedated him and went about the painful resetting of the bones, bleeding him afterward to try to bring down the fever and infection and dressing the wound. It was so bad that the doctor had to come back each day for several days that week to dress the injury himself, rather than leaving it to Lucy, returning periodically for several weeks afterward. Injured and fevered, if he survived, Bijah could be crippled, and if he did not survive he would leave a widow and five small children.

Fate favored him. He mended slowly, visiting the doctor himself a few weeks later, but he was unable to work for some time; a short trip he made in mid-May required hiring a man and horse to transport him. A month later he was back at work haying for the doctor to pay off what they owed; in the meantime, Lucy spun flax for the doctor to try to defray the hefty but necessary bill. By the end of the year Bijah was fairly fit again, but the aches and pain recurring after a major injury surely plagued him for the rest of his life.

As Bijah got back on his feet, he worked nearly as hard as before. His sugar works were transported in March 1768 to Conway, where he set out his buckets and spouts and tapped a stand of maple trees. Some progress was made in turning Guilford into a settled place: the land had finally been surveyed and divided into lots, and a couple of Deerfield people the Princes knew, Henry Hicks and Charles Coates, had moved the more than twenty miles up there. They kept their accounts at Elijah's store since the new "town" was so sparsely settled.

Then, just as we thought we understood their lives, the Princes surprised us again. As Bijah slowly recovered from his injury, another black man, Darby, moved to Guilford, practically next door to the property that the Princes were clearing and where Bijah seemed to be spending part of each year. Darby contracted with Salah Barnard to clear and plant the land, and in 1768 he moved up from Wallingford, Connecticut—where Bijah was born and grew up—with his wife. Darby often passed through Deerfield for medical care and supplies. His family and the Princes must have known each other in Wallingford, in Deerfield, and now in Guilford. This could not be coincidence. Were they related? Did Darby work for the Princes? The "Negro network" was taking on new meaning as its roots were revealed to extend further into the past than we had imagined.

With this discovery, another door opened, but onto a corridor of closed doors. We had gotten accustomed to thinking of Bijah and Lucy as people without pasts, since we could find nothing about their youth and didn't know the stories of their early lives that they certainly recounted to their children at the kitchen table and in front of the evening fire. But Darby's entry into their lives, an evocation of their past, offered the tantalizing suggestion that Bijah had other family or other friends that he maintained from an earlier life. Lucy's family may have remained in Africa, but Bijah's perhaps lived down the road.

We couldn't know their pasts, but we did know what was in store for Elijah Williams. Just as Darby moved to Guilford, Stephen Williams wrote in his journal that he heard that his brother was "greatly in debt . . . his creditors come upon him & he is like to have his Estate torn in pieces." Elijah had been aggressively buying and improving his property. Indeed, Bijah had worked for him a few years earlier when the prosperous man was making improvements to his house and outbuildings, seemingly untouchable in terms of his accumulating wealth and property. He spent a fortune on furnishings. His work as commissary in two wars had given him great influence and power, and his Tory leanings allowed him to serve as an intermediary between the politicians and businessmen in Boston and those in the west. With the end of the French and Indian War, however, and with the first stirrings against the monarch occasioned by the friction over the Stamp Act and its repeal, he was no longer in the strong position he'd been in before. Overextended and overoptimistic, Elijah Williams was going bankrupt as accounts and payments he couldn't meet were called in. Frantically he began selling off his land holdings in the hope of salvaging what he could. The river god, Bijah's mentor, was going down fast, but his downfall provided an opportunity for Bijah.

Elijah's brother Stephen and several others put together a plan to rescue the overextended businessman in 1769, and his superfluous properties began to be sold off. A consortium of Boston buyers, which included the famous patriot John Hancock, banded together to pay £526 for all of Elijah's Guilford lots, including the lot that the Princes were in the process of settling on. We cannot know Elijah's exact arrangement with Bijah. If it was only a handshake, Bijah's claim could have been in jeopardy. His name appears in no surviving document of the several transactions that rapidly followed when, only a year later, Elijah was dead at the age of fifty-eight, leaving his lands in the hands of his creditors. Eventually, however, Bijah's lot was legally his, free and clear. The Princes now needed to decide whether to live full-time on their own beautiful land in Guilford, or whether to stay in

Deerfield on rented land, among the friends they and their children had made over the years.

If the Princes wavered in their decision to move from Deerfield as the country moved once again toward war, a horrifying rumor concerning Rev. Ashley was circulating through Deerfield about this time and may have provided the final impetus they needed. In 1770 the minister's family included his wife Dorothy, three daughters ranging in age from thirteen to twenty-seven, and three sons. A series of white servant girls came and went over the years, usually on contracts of several months. In addition, there were black slaves, including Lucy's friend Jenny Cole, who had arrived so many years before with a baby in her arms and a dream of returning to Africa, and two black men. Ashley had sold Titus several years earlier. The other man, Jenny's grown son Cato, Ashley reportedly had castrated.

I read the chilling accusation that Ashley had had his slave "cut"—a term used for gelding animals—as I sat in the Deerfield library. I had not yet met Bob Romer, the Deerfield guide who was putting together the list of slaves in Deerfield, but thanks to librarian Martha Noblick, I was on the phone with him within minutes. He corroborated the sordid rumor and promised to put some documents about it in the mail, but neither of us could tell how much of it was politically motivated and how much was true. Throughout 1770, the merchant Samuel Barnard went about telling people "this scandalous story" about Cato's castration, which was popularly believed even though the church discounted it. Three years later it was part of the written charges against the minister, who was by now an enormously unpopular man and whose own wife had tried to kill herself twice during their marriage.

Even if the story proved untrue, the minister certainly had opportunity—Dr. Thomas Williams, the Princes' doctor, lived right down the street and was related to him by marriage—and with a household of teenage girls, he may have even decided he had cause. The rumor about Cato wouldn't die no matter how hard the church authorities tried to dispel it. Perhaps it was in response to this rumor that Bijah stopped working for Ashley, going to the minister's house only to pay his taxes when Ashley served as the local middleman who took promissory notes for groups of local people and paid the taxes as a lump sum to the collector, getting reimbursed by the individuals, no doubt with interest. Bijah never became a full member of Ashley's church or any other, although Lucy was devout and no doubt hustled him out the door with the children on Sundays; times were more relaxed now, and it may have been that nonattendance was no longer punishable by fines and lectures, especially when imposed by a man whom no one obeyed any longer.

Whether or not anyone thought to ask or examine Cato himself is not clear. But Cato's life was absolutely a restricted one, and he was psychologically affected by his experiences. Like his mother Jenny, he collected so many items like copper buttons to use in his "return" to Africa that people in the town began to use the term "Cato's money." He never married. His mother, privy to so many of the household's secrets, lived to be eighty-five and after the minister's death spent twenty-eight years in greater ease with his widow. A few days before Jenny died, a visitor to the Ashley house found Jenny Cole and Dorothy Ashley happily chattering like old friends while they sewed. They died only three weeks apart after Jenny fell down a flight of basement stairs and broke her neck. She was, Cato said, "dead as a hammer."

Those years together after the minister's death were, someone later commented, the happiest years of the two women's lives.

Revolution was in the air, but family concerns grew as well. Another son, Abijah Jr., had been born to Lucy and Bijah in 1769. Clearly they needed more space. Meanwhile, down in Northampton their friend Scipio Smith was arrested and sentenced for attempted rape. More tragically, something inexplicable and unrecorded happened to their eldest daughter. Duruxa, fondly known as Dack, was merely a teen in 1773 when an illness or other calamity befell her. For nearly the rest of her life she would be known as insane. If ever there was a time for a black family to want to leave town and start over, this was it.

With war again in the air, and growing discomfort about Deerfield, Bijah and Lucy packed up the last of their belongings and headed for their hundred acres in Guilford to begin the next chapter of their lives.

CHAPTER TEN

BATTLES
ON THE HOME FRONT

It's a cold February day, and I'm having lunch with Craig Wilder in Hanover, New Hampshire, across the bridge that connects that town to Norwich, Vermont. Craig is a Dartmouth professor who specializes in early African American history. I've been thinking about the Prince children lately and wondering what the move to Guilford must have been like for them. In the early years of the research I imagined them as being their own company, too busy with everyday work to have a social life and content with the joys of the country, to regret what they left behind in Deerfield. Recently I've been wondering if I had gotten it wrong. Why didn't Caesar come home when his parents surely could have used his help on the farm? Why did Festus enlist so quickly in the military? Was Guilford really such a pleasant place for them to live? Then I realized that I knew little about their childhoods at all.

I tell Craig about the research, and we chat a bit about what western Massachusetts was like in those days. A former professor at Williams College, he knows the region well. At first I had envisioned the Prince children almost as Deerfield mascots, anomalous free black children in a town where the other black youths were enslaved. As I combed through my chronology and saw how long they lived there, it seemed unimaginable that they hadn't had friends, that Deerfield hadn't truly been their *home*. A reluctance to uproot their children would go a long way toward explaining Bijah and Lucy's slow, decade-long move into Guilford.

"Would the children have gone to school with the white children in Deerfield?" I asked Craig. "At first I thought no, but now I think they must have. Lucy and Bijah bought several primers and spelling books."

"I'd be more surprised if they did not than if they did," he responded. "The racism that mandated that kind of segregation didn't kick in until the nineteenth century in those little out-of-the-way places. It was a local matter, not one of state or national policy, and people just did what was most comfortable for them and their way of life."

"So you think they went to school?"

"Yes, sure."

"And what about Caesar and Festus serving in the military during the American Revolution—would they and the other black soldiers have been treated differently from the white soldiers?"

"I imagine that they'd be treated just like any another soldiers. There were certainly large numbers of African American men fighting in the Revolution."

Lots of men tried to get out of the war. In rural areas, whole communities desperately needed them at home to plant and reap. Enlistments tended to be short, often just a few months at a time, to allow them to get back to the agricultural work they had to do in order to survive. In towns, more well-to-do men hired others to serve in their stead.

For black men, however, the Revolutionary War offered opportunity, hope, and excitement. African American patriots like

Boston's Crispus Attucks, among the first to fall in the war's opening shots, embraced American independence. Southern slaves left their masters in droves when the British promised freedom in exchange for service on the loyalist side. Even the resolution by the Massachusetts House of Representatives the following year to exempt "Quakers, Indians, Negroes and Mulattoes," along with ministers, teachers, and Harvard faculty and students, from conscription did little to stem the flow of black enlistees, much to the consternation of southerner George Washington, who was shocked to find black and white soldiers amicably drilling together on the Lexington Green.

Over in Stockbridge, Agrippa Hull, the son of Amos and Bathsheba, with whom Bijah had lived in Northampton after gaining his freedom, enlisted in the Revolutionary Militia in January 1777. He quickly gained access to influential men when he was assigned to Gen. John Patterson as an orderly, and when he held the same position later in the war under the famous Thaddeus Kosciusko, who had arrived in America from Poland the previous year to aid the American war effort in Saratoga, at West Point, and along the Hudson River. With his long face, hooded eyes, and dark skin, Agrippa would become a striking figure in old age. The seventeen-year-old volunteer served throughout the war. Six months later on July 11, 1777, Caesar Prince, now twenty, enlisted for an expedition in the legendary northern campaign.

On June 17, less than a month before Caesar signed up, Maj. Gen. John Burgoyne began moving his substantial British troops down from Canada and through Lake Champlain. There were eight or nine thousand of them—nearly half of them Germans, along with a number of Canadians and natives—and the company included "extensive artillery and dozens of baggage wagons."

The British took Fort Ticonderoga on July 6 when American forces retreated, and then they continued on, settling down in mid-August near Saratoga, where the famous Battle of Saratoga would later occur. Caesar, like others, was reimbursed for a total of 120 miles of travel in addition to his pay, but his service was sandwiched between major battles. Part of a relief effort, he was in one of the militias put together after the fall of Fort Ticonderoga to aid American soldiers. His company went to reinforce the northern army retreating from Burgoyne's troops. There were a number of skirmishes and battles, one of the most important being that of Oriskany Creek on August 6, a week before Caesar's hitch was up, with heavy losses of both British and Americans. When the two thousand Massachusetts militia men returned home together, the harvest season was upon them, and "it seemed as if no large force could be permanently maintained."

Military encounters took place up and down the American colonies, and although the Revolutionary War action would largely skirt Guilford, the town the Princes arrived in was far from quiet. Still, it was a beautiful place, and when they made the permanent move in 1775, the year before war was declared, Bijah and Lucy were proud to be on their own land. By today's standards, their house was small but typical of a family farmhouse in the eighteenth century: about twenty feet by thirty feet, it was most likely a typical one-and-a-half-story cape with a ground floor and sleeping loft under the sloped roof, an el extension or porch, a central brick chimney with a fireplace in each of the two ground-floor rooms (the heat rising up through the sleeping loft in cold weather), and a root cellar to store food. A big maple tree offered shade and beauty on one side, and behind it a long stone wall protected them from the road. They put up a barn and other outbuildings not far from the house, made stone fence enclosures for the farm animals, dug a well, and built a privy. Most importantly, they got in their crops of grain, corn, and vegetables to feed themselves and their livestock through the next year.

The house that John Noyes, who would organize the attack on the Princes, was building across the road dwarfed their comfortable settler's house. The locals found it pretentious and well suited to a newcomer who immediately tried to insinuate himself into local politics, running for just about every office, but not, in the early years, successfully. In one election the only vote he got was the one he cast for himself. He had money, however, and patience, and with time he would break into the positions he desired. For the time being he worked on enhancing his property and scowling each time he looked out and saw the Princes obstructing his view. Their land was better than his: their open meadowland was backed by low mountains, whereas his barns rose on hills that were difficult to plow. The two houses stood in silent opposition to each other, separated only by the dirt road and several hundred feet. They weren't close enough to see into each other's windows, but they were close enough to hear each other, to see each other's land, fences, gates, and livestock, and to have their children able to confront each other. Noyes's biggest objection seems to have been that his neighbors, the people he saw every day from his fields and house, were black. The big maples lining the road were not enough of a barrier for him, and the more he saw them the more his resentment grew.

Was Noyes's hostility the reason why Festus, the Princes' second son, left home so young? Or was it that the lure of adventure was stronger than a quiet country life? Festus seems to have moved to Stockbridge, Massachusetts, as an adolescent, perhaps living with Agrippa Hull and his mother. There, at fifteen, he joined the militia on July 8, 1779, and was later mustered into the Continental Army. He initially signed up in the same Stockbridge, Massachusetts, company in which Agrippa Hull had served. As a teenager without a family to support or crops to get in, Festus was a good catch for the recruiter, who didn't question his age and probably collected a bounty. Since so few men agreed to join for longer than a few months, Stockbridge paid a premium to those who committed to a nine-month term. Festus would spend the bulk of the next four years—until the end of the war—in the military. Now himself part of the "Negro network," Festus's brother Caesar reenlisted that autumn, serving alongside Ralph Way Jr. under a Hadley captain; Agrippa's brother Amos also joined a Hadley company, showing that the "Negro network" had moved into a second generation.

Anthony was tireless in tracking down records of Caesar's and Festus's military service. He read muster rolls in Boston and New York, West Point records in Manhattan and Albany. His travels finally took him to Stockbridge itself, a quintessential Berkshire town made famous by Norman Rockwell. He hoped to find at the Stockbridge Library Association the answer to our question about why Festus, a boy from Deerfield who had moved to Vermont, enlisted in this town, and whether he had even stayed on there afterward. Agrippa remained in Stockbridge for the rest of his life, setting himself up as a successful butler at the parties of the Stockbridge elite, and at a time when Festus was making his living as a musician, we found a catering bill Agrippa submitted in which he charged the hosts for "musick." His wife, Peggy Hull, became known for her wedding cakes, but Agrippa became famous for a war story he laughingly repeated about himself. One evening while working for Kosciusko at West Point, when the great man had left for a few days, Agrippa decked himself out in the general's clothes—all the way from the gold buttons to the ostrich feathers in the hat—and threw a party. Kosciusko unexpectedly returned that evening and took it all in immediately. Saluting the faux general, he introduced him at headquarters "as an African prince come to fight for the cause of freedom." Agrippa never lived it down.

Anthony entered the Stockbridge Library Association and went down to its spacious historical collections on the lower level. In looking around the room at the displays of antique furniture and glass cases of domestic objects, he felt someone watching him and turned around. There on the wall was a large portrait of Agrippa in old age, staring down from its prominent perch on the wall. This was the man, now balding and tired-looking but still regal, who in his youth had played with and served alongside Festus in the American Revolution. It was one of the few portraits Anthony had ever seen of someone who had known the Princes—and the *only* one of a black person who had known them.

Festus, with his musical talents, was a great addition to his unit. As the children were growing up, Bijah had bought a Jew's harp to amuse them, but he and Lucy knew that their second son was unusually talented, blessed with a natural ability to play any instrument he put his hands on. To encourage Festus to develop his talent, Bijah traded an old horse, with a saddle and bridle, for a violin. After the war Festus listed his occupation as fiddler. He was put to work as a fifer in the Tenth Regiment Colonial Company, under Capt. Warner, gathering men for daily duties and inspiring them in battle. Later in the war he was a drummer in the Third Regiment of the Continental Artillery. Drummers did more than supply a beat that could be heard for miles: they also administered corporal punishment, worked with surgeons to evacuate casualties, and maintained the guardroom. Fifers and

AGRIPPA AND MARGARET HULL IN OLD AGE. *Left: Historical Collection of Stockbridge Library. Right: Massachusetts Historical Society.*

drummers were paid well, at the same rate as corporals, and field music sometimes expanded—as Festus's group did when he later served in 1781—into full musical bands. In July 1780 he was in Peekskill, New York, and the next month they crossed the Hudson River, marched down Rockland County, and crossed over to Camp Totoway in New Jersey, where they stayed until early November, when they marched back to West Point. When his stint was up, Festus waited only a few months before reenlisting, this time moving to the center of the action at West Point.

It was a heady time in the progress of the war. The young Marquis de Lafayette had just returned from France to rejoin the Revolution. Because the series of forts that formed West Point was a crucial line of defense in the war along the Hudson River, discipline was tight and the rules stringent. The men couldn't bathe in the river during the day, sell rum, or skip church services. Festus and the other men spent more than eight hours a day drilling or on fatigue duty (collecting wood, mending fortifications or buildings, airing bedding) or guard duty, which was as much about keeping deserters in as enemies out. Although there were certainly battles that involved American-style fighting, the men were taught to march in formation and to fire in volleys from straight lines, as the British did. The civilians—many of whom were women engaged in support duties like laundry—were tightly controlled too. If their hogs ran wild or attacked soldiers, the animals were confiscated. If anyone sold liquor or entertained soldiers after the evening drums, their liquor was confiscated. As at home, drinking was part of the leisure hours and had to be restricted, but it was not prohibited. Like the others, the young Festus probably spent much of his free time writing letters home, reading the Bible, playing ball games, and mending his uniform.

On August 3, 1780, when Festus had been at West Point for only a few weeks, a new commander arrived: Benedict Arnold. Disappointed at being passed over for promotions, and annoyed at being reprimanded for his extravagant spending, Arnold turned traitor to the American cause. He had made a secret and treasonous offer to the British to "sell" West Point for £20,000, and by the time Arnold was sent by Washington from Philadelphia to West Point, the plan was already in motion. In his neat, educated script, he wrote out a list of the men and fortifications there. There were, he wrote down, more than three thousand men. He described each fort, the best approaches to them, and their strengths and weaknesses. Then he handed the list over to British Maj. John André, who tucked it into his boot and made for the British lines. Lucky to escape with his life, Arnold fled to New

York City and became a brigadier general in the British army, eventually overseeing the burning of Richmond, Virginia, and New London, Connecticut. André only got as far as Tarrytown, New York, before being captured; he was eventually tried and hanged. Five years earlier Arnold had fought alongside Ethan Allen at Fort Ticonderoga. Now he was fighting against his own country, while Allen was traveling around Vermont, including Guilford, to battle on two fronts with his Green Mountain Boys. Festus was at West Point during all this excitement.

While the Princes were at home on a prospering farm, Festus was where the rations were short, pay was in inflated paper promissory notes, and winters were bitter. Benedict Arnold's successor, Maj. Gen. Alexander McDougall, wrote repeatedly that the West Point soldiers suffered under "distressing circumstances," owing to lack of meat and wages. One day the sergeants confronted him "in a body, requesting to know when they should be clothed, fed and paid. They painted to me in lively colours their distress, some of them from passion and temper." The overcrowded huts and barracks they lived in often lacked "Doors, Floors, & Roofs," their clothing consisted of deplorable rags, and some went without shoes, stockings, winter coats, or blankets in the frigid winter. Despite the deprivations, men were required to present a neat appearance, with braided hair if it was long.

When his stint ended at the end of that year, Festus went home for only eight months before enlisting for another three years. This time he was more directly involved. As a mattross, he was in an artillery unit, working alongside riflemen to reload their muskets as they learned in eight-hour sessions to load and shoot smoothly, three times a minute. He was also reported to have been in the horse guard, some of whom were elite riders who accompanied dignitaries and high-ranking officers like Lafayette, under whom Festus probably served. And once again his musical skills were called upon; like his father before him, he served as a drummer during these years. Present during the greatest act of betrayal of the war, sixteen-year-old Festus gained a new perspective on the pettier disagreements between Vermonters and Yorkers going on back home. Now a whole nation, not just a nascent state, was at stake. After these formative years at the heart of the battle for America, he would never really call Guilford, or even any particular town, home.

One by one his siblings began peeling off to find their own way in the world. Bijah and Lucy sent one of their boys, probably Tatnai, away to work in the shop of a cooper (maker of wooden barrels) in Massachusetts. Still at home were Duruxa, Drucilla, and Abijah Jr. Duruxa, of course, could not leave, owing to her illness, but Cill, now an independent woman of twenty-two — and reputed to be, like her mother, a poet with a strong wit— decided to leave too. By the summer of 1782 she had moved back to Deerfield and taken a job in David Hoyt's Deerfield tavern, with its banter and the society of everyday life in an established town. There among her old schoolmates she walked down the street among familiar faces and spent her days working alongside another woman, Hannah Thomas. She put money aside but also began treating herself to little luxuries, and made enough to provide for her own needs. Purchasing stockings, a snuff box, an apron, shoe repair, cloth for a petticoat and for someone to sew it for her, a pair of cloth shoes, and bushels of corn for her family gave her a sense of self-sufficiency as well as the welcome routine of an everyday life in a thriving town.

She made short visits home, and when Festus and Agrippa

were released from service, her brother came to Deerfield for a short time to work for Zadock Hawks, the shoemaker. In December her parents had a nice town visit themselves. She treated her father to drinks in Hoyt's tavern and paid part of her salary over to him; she also paid the bill for Lucy's keep at Hoyt's and for stabling Lucy's horse while she was there. It was a happy time, and she knew that she owed it to the goodwill and respect that her parents enjoyed after such a long residence in the town. When Dr. Ebenezer Barnard, the grandson of one of the witnesses at Bijah's manumission, came in one day, she bought him a mug of flip. She stayed for fourteen months, which may well have been the happiest year of her life.

Anthony and I at first assumed that Drucilla, an outgoing young woman, simply found Guilford boring and had no social life in the country. Then we began to bump up against facts and realizations that made us understand why Bijah and Lucy might actually have sent their children away. For one thing, although the American Revolution had been going on since 1776, a virtual civil war was taking place practically on their doorstep. As early as the town meeting of 1775, the moderator had to open with a plea for civility and unity. He wasn't referring to the war for independence—most Guilford people were staunch patriots—but to the smaller local war over the emerging state of Vermont itself, whose central battles took place in this very town.

Vermont was in a state of civil war at the same time that the Revolution was being fought, all because both New York and New Hampshire had granted the same lands to settlers. "Vermonters," who had received their lands from New Hampshire, wanted to form a new state. "Yorkers," who were in charge, wanted to remain part of that state. Now the Vermonters, led by Ethan Allen and his Green Mountain Boys, rebelled and set up an alternative government. There were two sets of governments and town meetings, two sets of books, and violent confrontations. Just as in the national Civil War a century later, neighbor faced off against neighbor as Vermonters and Yorkers kidnapped, jailed, and shot at each other. Guilford, which set up its own Vermonter sheriff and constable and levied taxes for the Vermont cause, was the hotbed of these battles, some of which took place almost literally in the Princes' backyard. There is no evidence that either Bijah or Lucy took sides in the violent dispute—or indeed in politics at all—but as beneficiaries of New Hampshire grants, they may well have sided with Vermont. Still, the location of their house, so near to the gathering place at the Packer's Corner tavern and to Leyden with its shop, meant that many of the combatants passed right by their property, at all hours of the day and night.

With all this going on around their doorstep, it was no wonder that Caesar did not move from Hadley to Guilford and that the other children began to look for ways out too. Yet somehow that didn't explain how the Princes themselves became targets of violence. Did it have simply to do with race? That was a conclusion that Anthony resisted, since we had no evidence for it. Then one day he made a discovery that forced us to rethink, for the rest of that summer, everything we had imagined about their life in the new town.

In the summer, Anthony drove out to the probate court in Brattleboro, a newly constructed, tiny building of three offices, to see if he could find any will that Bijah may have left behind. The clerk looked up Bijah in a card catalog, which led to a book, which showed that he had died intestate, with no will recorded, although there was a record of Lucy and Festus becoming the administrators of his estate. Still, she said, there should have been a listing of possessions and debts and an accounting of the estate, but apparently no one had provided one. Since this was just information copied into a ledger, Anthony went on to the official probate clerk to ask about the originals, but he was told that all the original probate documents were in storage in Newfane and unavailable to the public. A call to the Superior Court clerk confirmed that they were public records, so he arranged an appointment.

Larry Robinson proved to be a real Vermonter: efficient, but short on words. The old Newfane courthouse was also classic New England, a white clapboard building with pillars and a tall belfry, facing the village green. It had a very impressive courtroom with a gallery, large windows on two sides, and oil portraits between them of all the famous Windham County jurists. Since there was no trial going on, Anthony was offered a seat in one of the jury rooms, where he went through a loose-leaf binder of inventories of all the court records by type and date and location.

The records were stored across the street in the sheriff's office, and once again, as he had done so often in these years of searching, Anthony went through security doors. However, this was the first time that he had seen old jail cells, complete with bars and toilets, used for storage. He passed a second floor with a meeting room, walked down a corridor, and climbed up to a hot, airless attic. It was a maze of archival boxes, neatly numbered and stacked nearly six feet high, forming narrow passages in the large room, a labyrinth arranged in numerical order. He moved the boxes one by one until he found the numbers he'd written down on a piece of paper, then struggled to lift out the correct ones and maneuver them through the slender maze into the small break room, moving aside jigsaw puzzles on the table to set it down. The eighteenth-century probate records, folded in three and tied with bits of thread around the packets, had decedents' names

HOUGHTON'S TAVERN, WHERE BIJAH WENT TO COURT IN GUILFORD.
Courtesy of the Vermont Historical Society.

written in browned ink on the outside edges. They were neatly placed in the box but not organized, so he had to go through them all, one by one; still he found nothing. On a whim, he decided to look at other boxes from the same time period.

His exact words to me when he got home that evening were ones I'd never heard him use: "Lo and behold!" He had opened a box of densely packed justice records and, selecting among the sometimes mouse-nibbled documents, picked one up at random. The neatly written words on the upper edge read, "Tateny Prince vs. Joseph Stanton." He picked the next one up; it said "Abijah Prince Jr. vs. Joseph Stanton." Why were Bijah and Lucy's teenage sons taking this man to court? The answer was heartbreaking.

On April 9, 1782, constable Abel Joy stood outside of Joseph Stanton's house, a summons in his hand. Unable to hand it to Stanton, he called out its contents within Stanton's hearing: Stanton was to appear before William Bullock, Justice of the Peace of Guilford, on April 30 to answer to charges brought against him

concerning the youngest sons of Abijah Prince. Three years earlier, just ten days before Festus first enlisted in the army, a Guilford man, Joseph Stanton, had assaulted the two youngest Prince
children, Tatnai and Abijah, beating them with "Staves Sticks
&c." until their lives were "greatly Despaired of." They were only
fourteen and ten at the time. Stanton was a close relative of the
Princes' neighbor John Noyes. The attack on the boys was the
opening volley in a highly personal war that would come to em-
ploy a variety of people and means to drive Bijah and Lucy off
their land. It isn't clear why Bijah waited three years to bring
Stanton to court. He undoubtedly had words with Stanton, but
when a pattern of abuse later developed, he gathered everything
together into a series of lawsuits.

It wasn't his first time in court. Two years earlier he had sued
Abner Turner, the cooper for whom his son had worked. The boy
moved in for six months and fulfilled his end of the contract, but
Turner never paid the promised wages. Every time Bijah tried to
collect, Turner put him off, so Bijah finally hired a lawyer from
Hadley and filed charges in 1780. After Turner's third no-show,
the judge ruled in Bijah's favor, ordering that Turner's shop and
its contents be seized if he didn't pay. From that moment on, the
Princes went into court with stunning regularity.

The day after delivering the summons to Stanton, Constable
Joy left another summons for John Noyes, ordering him to answer to Abijah Prince's charge that the previous May, Noyes had
broken through their gates and cut down a dozen of the Princes'
old-growth trees and set loose cows and pigs to destroy the Princes'
crops of corn, flax, potatoes, and grass. Bijah demanded compensation, but he hadn't waited for the law to intervene. With Abijah
Jr., he had broken into Noyes's property and set his own livestock
on all the crops growing there; somehow they stayed for over a

month. When Noyes countersued, Bijah freely admitted in court that he had done it and agreed to have an independent appraiser assess the damage and fix the costs, but he never paid them. Like a pendulum, they went back and forth in the court for two years, with charges, countercharges, and retaliations.

With these cases pending, Bijah turned his attention back to Northfield. For some reason, he had paid no further attention to the property he should have acquired there, never even returning in the nearly thirty intervening years. Perhaps it was as simple as his taking for granted that when proprietors' meetings were "warned" or advertised, as required by law, he would naturally hear of this in Deerfield, a mere fifteen miles away. Back in 1753, however, Northfield had made its fourth division; he never knew about it, but his name had been assigned to a lot. The next year, when a further division was made, his name was again entered on the list as a proprietor, then for some unknown reason crossed out, and no land was assigned to him. He never heard of this either. When he heard nothing (and we too were unable to locate any newspaper warnings of meetings), he must have assumed that no meetings or divisions ever took place. Finally, in 1782, around the time Abijah and Tatnai sued Stanton, Bijah decided to look into his proprietorship. Perhaps he wanted to set up one or more of his sons on the property, as he and Lucy may have felt that things were getting too difficult for them in Guilford. But when he went down to Northfield, he discovered that he had no land, even though on paper a lot had been was assigned to him.

He demanded that this injustice be addressed in the next meeting, to be held in June. It was clear that others were in the same situation and had never received land due to them. On June 12 the third item on the agenda was to discuss whether they would "grant & lay out to Abijah Negro" and several others their due acreage. Bijah attended this meeting, and when the item was read out he firmly requested a correction. His name was not, he reminded them, "Abijah Negro"; it was "Abijah Prince." Accepting the correction and the rebuke, they chose a committee to negotiate with him, eventually agreeing to a cash settlement of £5 (several hundred dollars in today's money). Using a boilerplate deed, he changed the language to make it clear that this was land "which I ought to have had laid out & assigned to me." He signed his name to the amended deed in front of witnesses the day after the meeting, making his imprint in the sealing wax. Not all the land in Northfield had been divided up yet, and he did not relinquish his right to more land when that happened. He received about an acre in 1785, which he chose to sell, recording the sale the next year.

We still couldn't prove that race was the reason for the difficulties with Noyes and others, but slowly we began to eliminate other possibilities. Did the two families take opposite sides in the Revolutionary War or the Vermont war? Was it simply a feud, like the Hatfields and McCoys? Might religious differences account for it?

Guilford by then had about one thousand residents, most of them spread over many square miles. There was a congregational church in the town center, and it was so well attended that during the warm months the attendees spilled out over the lawn because the sanctuary could not hold them all. This would have been the Princes' church; although the earliest membership list is lost, it's hard to imagine that Lucy, whose obituary comments that she memorized most of the Bible, did not see to it that her family attended services. Indeed, she chose to record Bijah's death there rather than with the town.

The Noyeses were Baptists, a large and growing sect. In the early nineteenth century, there would be four Baptist churches in Guilford alone, but the Noyes family brought a different sensibility to the practice of their faith. They held services in their new house, and some of them, including John, were known to see angels and have visions. One of the youngest sons, Nathan, recalled a night of a full moon when several of his brothers and other friends were sleeping in a neighbor's barn and saw an old man they knew to be on his deathbed rise up in front of the house, wearing a white cravat and a coverlet, then float away. At the time of Nathan's conversion, he saw a white throne "and one seated upon it clothed in white," surrounded by twenty-four elders singing his praises and casting golden crowns at his feet. Nathan once had a vision that could well describe the differences between the two families. Having by this time left home, he "saw two houses, one on each side of the road, standing on the side of a hill, decending [sic] to the West; it came to my mind to put up for the night, at one of these houses; and as I drew near, saw both houses had their front doors open." In one house he "saw quite a number of people dancing, and carousing; a thought struck my mind, that I had rather lie in the street than stay in that house." The people in the other house were kneeling in prayer, in preparation for his baptism. Could this be a dream about the Prince house across the road from the self-righteous Noyeses?

We always imagined Guilford as a paradise, but it played rough in those years, and we began to understand more clearly what it was really like for the Princes. From 1779 on, Noyes often arranged for others to attack the Princes or to take Bijah to court, paying the costs for those who couldn't afford to sue, putting up bonds, and sometimes acting as their lawyer, bombarding his neighbors from all directions and throwing at them whatever charges he could: debt, trespass, destruction of property. Whenever Bijah went before a justice or a magistrate, either Lucy or one of their sons, or both, accompanied him to act as witnesses. The Princes made sure that their children learned never to back down, never to let a provocation go unanswered, no matter what the cost.

It was toward the end of that summer, as the field across from our own Guilford house was being hayed for the last time of the season, that Anthony came home in great excitement with a copy of a page that came out of yet another court case, but this was something new and remarkable. For the first time he held something that Bijah and Lucy had actually owned. The page showed that Bijah and Lucy had sued James Burrows, a Guilford man, for not paying money Burrows owed them. Bijah and Lucy went to court prepared with a list of witnesses to call. Then Bijah pulled his account book from his pocket and read out a list of what Burrows owed him, alleging that Burrows refused in the past "and still doth refuse" to pay what he owed. Even though Burrows paid a bit on account, he owed the bulk, and here was the proof.

Bijah told the justice and the witnesses that Burrows had "my horses [for a] jorney fifty miles." Over the course of 1783, Burrows had "four days works with the boy and team" and "eight days more with the boy and team." He had eight pounds of salt

PAGE FROM ABIJAH PRINCE'S ACCOUNT BOOK.
Courtesy of the Windham County Superior Court.

shad, a hat, a "peck of beens" and "half a Cake of Chocolate," half a pound of brimstone, a pair of shoes, coffee. In addition to these items, Burrows owed Bijah for "braking an ox yoke" and "damage to braking a brake." Then, after itemizing the costs, Bijah handed over the page and entered it as evidence.

He was more than just an elderly farmer; true to his entrepreneurial spirit, he was running a little business of his own, a smaller version of Elijah's shop so many years before. Here was more proof of his ability to navigate a white-controlled world, despite a hostile neighbor who resented his presence. It went against our assumptions that race controlled all aspects of life at the same time that Noyes and his henchmen reinforced the truth that racism was a fact of life. Just like other small businessmen, Bijah kept accounts of debits and credits, expecting his white customers to pay their bills on time. He hired out his own team of oxen, his own horses, and his own wagon. Apparently he took orders from his neighbors for items to pick up on his trips to Leyden and Deerfield. The magistrate, impressed by the Princes' orderly presentation of the case, asked to see Burrows's own accounts and told both parties to return a month later. Then, based upon "a strict sarch [search] and Examination of the accounts of both Parties," he ruled in the Princes' favor and ordered Burrows to pay. When he did not, the magistrate issued a warrant for Burrows's arrest and ordered the sheriff to seize his property. There was another suit, this time by another Burrows, William, who appeared in court in January with legal representation: none other than John Noyes. The Princes were ready for him and had their own lawyer, Samuel Knight. In another blow to Noyes and his friends, Edward Harris, justice of the peace, decided for Bijah once again.

Despite their successes in court, the Princes were becoming weary of the constant battles. Lucy was now sixty years old, her husband eighty. Their oldest sons were living on their own. Cill, who had returned from working in Deerfield, may well have left again. Only Duruxa and Abijah Jr. were living at home. It was during these troubled times that the Princes, feeling the need for another man's presence, brought in Scipio Smith, a middle-aged mulatto from Northampton, to work for them.

Aging parents, children who were women or minors, a hired man—to Noyes and the gang he assembled to run them off, the Princes must have seemed completely vulnerable. Soon after, John Noyes's brother Amos broke into the Princes' property again, setting his livestock upon the crops. At this rate they would have no food for themselves and no feed for their livestock; they would be destitute—which, of course, was part of Noyes's plan to drive them away.

The Princes' tenacity undoubtedly surprised Noyes, who came from a state with a long history of slavery and racism. He hadn't reckoned on the resolve of two elderly former slaves who not only showed no subservience to whites but repeatedly asserted their rights. This was a different New England from the place where he had grown up with a sense of familial and racial privilege. Bijah and Lucy were accustomed to living among white people who accepted their freedom and their equal standing under the law. In a way they were quintessential Vermonters: independent, staunch, and uncowed by social status. They were probably unlike any black people Noyes had ever seen, and because of that they threatened his familiar world by resisting all his aggressions and assumptions of superiority.

It may well be that it was the Princes' lawyer, Samuel Knight, who suggested the next, most drastic step. He was a member of Vermont's General Assembly and therefore a colleague of some of the most important people in the state, including Gov. Thomas Chittenden and Ira Allen, brother of Ethan. The Governor and Council, the state's supreme executive body, was not a court, but aggrieved citizens could go before them at the annual meeting and petition their help to enforce laws and remedy wrongs. Lucy, with her reputation for eloquence, was a natural to appear before such a body. Leaving behind her husband of more than four score years with the remaining children and Scipio, she traveled up to Norwich to plead their case against Noyes in front of the highest governing body of Vermont. If they were to be run off their land, it wouldn't be without a fight.

CHAPTER ELEVEN

LUCY GOES TO COURT

Norwich, Vermont, lies across the river from Hanover, New Hampshire, where Dartmouth College is today. Perhaps Lucy traveled there with Knight himself, since he had to attend the sessions. But where would a black woman who was not a servant have stayed in such a town in 1785? Even if she had the money and they would admit her, the taverns and inn would be filled with visiting dignitaries and their entourages, come for the sessions. Chances are that she had the name of a local black family with whom she could stay.

On Thursday, June 2, 1785, she watched the grand procession of the governor, lieutenant governor, and others as they entered Norwich with a cavalry escort, met by members of the militia under the command of a Col. Paul Brigham, heading for the house of a lawyer, Daniel Buck, near the meetinghouse in the old town center, farther north than it is today, where the Council was to meet. She was prepared to speak this day, despite the natural awe of such an imposing spectacle, but there were not enough members of the Council present to constitute a quorum. Disappointed, she went to her lodgings to rest and prepare for the following day. Once again there was no quorum.

On Saturday morning, the members gathered once more, and again they did not make up a quorum and the session was adjourned to the following Monday, June 6, at 9:00 A.M. She had the weekend to look around, but Norwich was not a major town. On Sunday she might have attended church services and prayed for her family and for her success.

By Monday the business before the Council was backed up because of all the delays. In appointing Benjamin Olds of Marlboro to be a justice of the peace for Windham County, they were getting closer to her home, but no closer to her petition, for they adjourned to eight o'clock the next morning without hearing her. She'd now been in Norwich for at least five days, and away from home for a week, but she was no closer to redress than she had been the week before.

Her fortune changed the next morning, Tuesday, when at last she stood to address Gov. Chittenden and the rest of the members of the Council. John and Amos Noyes, she told them, were harassing and endangering her family. She recounted the offenses over the years: cheating them out of money due to them, beating her sons, tearing down their fences, destroying their crops, committing violent and frightening assaults. She begged the governor to intercede and to offer protection, to make the persecution stop. Witnesses corroborated her story, either in person or in writing. Also present, and probably in the room when Lucy spoke, were two influential men—Stephen Row Bradley and Isaac Tichenor—who figured importantly not only in the state and federal governments but also in the legend of Lucy Prince.

This was an unusual situation, and probably the first time a black person, let alone an African woman, had addressed the highest officials in the state. After deliberating, they responded firmly in Lucy's favor, declaring that John and Amos Noyes had been "greatly oppressing" them and that the Princes were "much injured." They found that the situation was so bad that if Guilford didn't take steps to protect "Abijah, Lucy & family in the enjoyment of their possession, they must soon unavoidably fall upon the Charity of the Town." The Council instructed the governor to write to Guilford's selectmen and tell them to watch over the Princes and sort things out. Vindicated, and with relief, Lucy returned home, perhaps carrying with her the written and sealed version of this order of protection, ready to face the case against Amos Noyes.

It was an enormous public humiliation for John Noyes. For a politically ambitious man to have his actions condemned by the very body that he wished to join, to have been so disparagingly painted by Lucy in front of the highest officials of the state, and in front of the audience gathered to hear them, and then to have the governor write to Guilford's selectmen on behalf of the Princes, had to have infuriated him.

When the case against his brother Amos came before the justice, John Noyes acted as Amos's lawyer, again facing off against the Princes' lawyer Samuel Knight, who called a series of witnesses in Bijah's case against Amos for breaking into the Princes' property. Noyes tried to act the soul of reason. It wasn't Amos's fault, he began, because the fence was already broken, and Amos had spoken to Bijah about the two of them repairing it together, but Bijah refused, so Amos went ahead and repaired half of it himself. He also asserted that the fence was covered with frost and snow, making it hard to see and easy to break—although this was the first of May, a highly unlikely time for snow. It went to trial, and on August 2 the court found Amos guilty of trespass and told him to pay Bijah for damages and the court for costs.

That should have been the end, yet on October 4, months after Lucy had returned from Norwich with the Governor and Council's letter that her family must be protected, Noyes's mob of hired thugs broke into the fenced land known as Abijah's

Close. The attackers were poor men, many of them with a startling combination of criminal records. Even when sober, they were an intimidating lot, hot-tempered and quick to use their fists. Rufus Fisk was a blacksmith with formidable arms and fists who was often before the courts. Ezekiel Foster, a big man also in his thirties, had a "giant frame and a countenance that bespoke authority," a polite way of saying that he was a bully with a history of assault. Oliver Waters was also a large, volatile man in his late thirties who had been arrested two years earlier for beating up a genteel and well-liked sawmill owner and convicted for impregnating a young woman he'd never met before, on a Sunday afternoon at Joseph Martin's house.

Martin himself, a farmer, had been paid to beat up a black man named Robert who lived with his wife, Quaw, and their daughter, Sally, in Colrain, Massachusetts, just a few miles from Guilford. In January 1784, Robert's family was assaulted and abducted by Elijah Fobes, a doctor living in Colrain, and his brother Walter of Norwich. They held the three for two months, perhaps forcing them to work. When the family finally escaped, they pressed charges. But before the case resumed, astoundingly, Robert was kidnapped again, this time by Joseph Martin, who held him for two days before he got away. The next month Elijah Fobes was convicted and ordered to pay Robert damages of £145—an enormous sum of money. His brother went free. Martin too was eventually convicted after not one but two jailers were hired to guard him. Martin pleaded no contest and sold his property in order to pay the huge fine, then moved to Guilford. In hiring Martin a year later to assault the Princes, Noyes knew that he could count on his antipathy to black people.

The four men apparently fired themselves up at William Packer's tavern, an eating and drinking establishment a short way down the road from the Princes' farm. Half a dozen witnesses, including Packer, saw them head out and later testified against them. Daniel Edwards and William Burrows joined the others as they broke down the Princes' door and attacked Scipio Smith, the Princes' hired man. He was beaten so badly that his "life was Greatly dispaired of," but Bijah, Lucy, and their teenage son escaped injury, and it may be that they ultimately drove off the men. As the rioters fled for Leyden, they set fire to the Princes' hayrick, fortunately doing little damage. As far as the attackers were concerned, the Princes and their farm and business were history. Their hayricks burning, their crops destroyed, the ruling against them be damned: the Princes were now left nearly destitute.

Our lingering reluctance to attribute these predations against the Princes to race evaporated. While in some ways Noyes and the attackers were acting like simple thugs, there was no longer any denying the role that racism played in their attacks. These men seemed, however, to differ from the other people the Princes lived among, and they complicated the picture of a state that wrote antislavery into its first constitution. The Princes were generally accepted in the community and the church, and there was for the most part a live-and-let-live attitude in this part of early Vermont. Noyes was able to call upon the disaffected, poor men with few opportunities to attack black people who had more than they did.

At the end of that summer, we made a research trip to the University of Vermont library in search of information pertaining to Lucy's later life. Instead, as the special collections librarians rolled out box after box of materials from the Stephen Row Bradley collection, we found a letter from a Guilford selectman named Bigelow. He wrote to Bradley, who was then state's attorney (similar to today's district attorney), to plead for mercy for a repentant William Burrows, part of the mob that had attacked the Princes.

Bigelow's letter told of the mob breaking into the Princes' land and house, but also told of a changed Guilford in which "they are all cooled down and I find a disposition in the people in that neighbourhood enclined to peace." Burrows, he wrote, not only acknowledged that he was at fault but was racked with guilt for taking part in the riot "and has been friendly to the Negros [sic] in helping discover [reveal] the abuse done them in destroying their hay." Because Burrows was poor and had made it up to the Princes, Bigelow asked that the dispute be allowed to die quietly. Burrows was nevertheless found guilty and remained jailed until his fine was paid. Another attacker, Joseph Martin, never went to trial, but Rufus Fisk was convicted. He never paid his court costs, so Noyes bailed him out.

It was the first we'd heard of this major case brought by the state of Vermont—rather than the town of Guilford—on the Princes' behalf, and the first we'd heard of Burrows's involvement. Armed with this new information, Anthony went back to the Newfane courthouse to track down the other rioters, only to discover that since he'd last been there the attic where all these invaluable old court dockets were stored had been condemned by Vermont OSHA (Occupational Safety and Health Administration). The air in the stifling attic was considered dangerous. They refused to let him in, but eventually Sheila Prue, the new Windham County sheriff, agreed that he could go in for a few moments at a time to retrieve boxes and look through them on the second floor.

There, armed with a state case and Burrows's name, the whole sordid story came together. He learned about the state prosecuting the rioters, about Scipio's savage beating, about the hayrick burning and the flight to Leyden. He learned that all of the men had been arrested and indicted by a grand jury; that Scipio, Lucy, Bijah, and Abijah Jr. were all called as witnesses; that there was a series of trials; that the men were found guilty. In an astonishing coincidence, one of the judges turned out to be the nephew of Aaron Burt, the man who had freed Bijah and had undoubtedly known Bijah all his life.

Why Noyes, a man with money, should care so much was more of a puzzle. To solve it I had a conversation with Connecticut anthropology professor Warren Perry, who was excavating slave plantations in Connecticut as well as the recently discovered African burial ground in lower Manhattan. When I told Perry about Noyes he said, "That's not surprising at all! If Noyes was originally from Stonington, Connecticut, he came straight from slave plantation country." While 95 percent of Connecticut residents didn't own slaves, the better-off citizens were more likely to: most wealthy merchants owned slaves, as did half of wealthy farmers, professionals, and clergy. We weren't able to locate any African American slaves in the Noyes family but did discover that Noyes's grandfather "owned" at least one Indian. The sight of free blacks working such fine land must have been too much for a man who saw the subjugation of people of color as perfectly natural.

This was not a widely shared opinion among southern Vermonters in the late eighteenth century. All the representatives of the law whom the Princes encountered—from the local sheriff all the way up to the governor—took their right to equal protection under the law seriously. Now that a justice of the peace had ruled against him, the county court had convicted nearly all his accomplices, and the Governor and Council had taken him to task, Noyes had no choice but to accept the situation and calm down, but the damage had been done. The Princes were just about ruined, but Noyes would go on to law-abiding success, helped to that position by Vermont's U.S. congressman, who later referred to Noyes as a "villain" who stabbed him in the back in order to get ahead politically. In the meantime, Bijah and Lucy concentrated on recouping their losses and settling their children.

CHAPTER TWELVE

BIJAH'S LAST YEARS

Caesar's marriage to Sally Larnard in Hadley was a happy event for them the following January, and the couple quickly—perhaps too quickly—were expecting a baby. In the continuing saga of bad fortune, the baby died in June. Ralph Way paid for its tiny coffin.

Festus was working as a musician and had begun the postwar travels that would mark his wanderlust. Tatnai, at twenty, was working in Northfield, where he was reported to have been working for Samuel Hunt, who had a farm and a tavern. One hundred years later, a local historian whose family had known Tatnai claimed that his peculiar weakness was for raw eggs, which he could catch in his mouth when tossed to him. Inevitably one of the local teens, Dick, tricked Tatnai by deliberately tossing a rotten egg, which he threw up. Tat was no abject servant, however, and for two weeks afterward Dick stayed in at night to avoid a beating. Finally a mutual friend acted as mediator and the two made up, Dick offering an apology and a quart of rum. In this perhaps apocryphal story, we see the beginnings of Tatnai's life-long residence in towns, working regularly alongside whites.

Bijah and Lucy's last years in Guilford were quiet ones. Bijah was eighty-one when crops began to fail all around Vermont in 1787, leading to near-famine a couple of years later. A black farmer, Jeffrey Brace, who lived in Poultney—his story of harassment by a neighbor uncannily resembles Noyes's treatment of the Princes, down to the livestock set on his crops, the destroyed fences, and the legal cases—resorted to carrying iron on his back across the mountains to exchange for grain in Manchester, "a distance of about 30 miles," in order to support his family during these difficult times. The crop failure and Bijah's advanced age probably prompted what previously had seemed unthinkable: he sold the Guilford land to Augustus Beldon for just £15 (about $1,500 today). Bijah, Lucy, and their daughters retained the right to remain on half an acre for another eight years, with the right to gather wood for fires and fencing. This was a standard accommodation made to widows and the elderly. Bijah signed over the deed, believing that he was not leaving his family homeless because he retained for them land across the state in Sunderland, Vermont, land that he was owed as a result of being on Searles's successful petition.

It must have been around this time that—if it really happened as the legend around her implies—Lucy attempted to get one of her sons admitted to Williams College. The college was in the planning stages around 1790 as it made its shift from a free school to one of higher education. There is no evidence of this in any college archives or the Williams family papers, but the story is nevertheless a plausible one. Sitting on the college's board was none other than John Williams, Elijah's son, still living in Deerfield, and Lucy's daughter Cill was once again living there that year. As I imagine it, Lucy went to Deerfield—not Williamstown—and asked for a meeting, which Williams surely would have granted her. George Sheldon, Deerfield's chronicler, wrote that she lectured the trustees, ultimately unsuccessfully, for three hours, quoting chapter and verse of the Bible. Nevertheless, for the first time in the long years of the Prince family's dealings with the Williams family, they were turned down because of race.

The fact is that their sons were now too old to attend college in any case. The older sons, Caesar and Festus, were grown men and long gone from home, as was Tatnai. Their youngest son, Abijah Jr., was by now gone as well, or about to be settled elsewhere. Instead of going to college, young Abijah made his way to Glastonbury, Connecticut, where, away from the disasters that had formed his youth, he set out to reinvent himself. In the late 1780s, he fell in love with a young African American woman named Anna Harris from Coventry. Going way past his budget and earnings, he did everything he could to erase the look of a country farm lad as he prepared for his wedding, ordering up a custom-made wardrobe of breeches, jacket, knee buckles, hose, and shoes, and buying a psalm book. He and Anna married in November 1789, but the Princes' luck kept lurching downward. The next year Abijah Jr. and Anna's baby died. Just three years later, Abijah Jr. himself died. We never discovered how.

During that summer of searching, Anthony and I became sadder and sadder as these last years of Bijah's life unfolded before us. We had believed that after Lucy's triumphant return from Norwich and after all the successes in the courts, they settled back proudly on their land, masters of all they surveyed, ignoring their vanquished neighbor. Instead, we were piecing together a story of losses. One by one the things they had worked so hard for were being taken away. The farm was gone, two grandchildren were dead, and now their youngest son had passed away. Lucy remained at Bijah's side, as did his daughters, but only two years away from his ninetieth birthday he must have felt that he had had enough. In 1794, on an unseasonably warm and sunny Sunday during the January thaw, and behind a door that no research will ever open, Bijah died. He was buried—but perhaps not until spring when the ground had softened—on his farm. An inscribed slate headstone was placed at his grave, somewhere near the road that ran along the edge of the farm. One hundred years later, in the late 1800s, a farmer tossed it aside and plowed the field, only to be told later by indignant neighbors that he had destroyed the grave of one of Guilford's most important early residents. The road has shifted, and no one today knows exactly where Bijah rests.

Three months after Bijah's death, the Guilford community was shocked at the arrest of John Noyes's son for desecrating graves. Over a period of fifteen months he had regularly broken into a burying ground, "injuring the graves of certain deceased persons—and disturbing the remains of the deceased—and committing other enormities." At first we were horrified to think that he disturbed Bijah's grave, but the attacks took place in a cemetery in another part of town. Ironically, the Noyes burial sites must themselves have been disturbed: the headstone for John Noyes's father was recovered from someone's house foundation and now rests unceremoniously in the Guilford Historical Society.

The Noyes family did not easily escape reminders of the man who had fought so hard to retain his property and protect his family against his neighbors. Shortly after Bijah's death, Noyes's daughter Betsy was riding her horse home just as it turned dark. At the hollow containing a spring, "there suddenly appeared a fearsome apparition, so close and so startling that both horse and rider were tremendously frightened." The horse bolted, and she hung on as best she could as they tore past Bijah's grave and up to her house. Everyone swore that it was Bijah's ghost, come to avenge his family.

Bijah continued to be sighted up to modern times. One spring soon after I had learned about Bijah and Lucy and thought I might like to write about them, Anthony and I drove out to where we thought their land was. Spring in Vermont is a messy affair known as mud season. The dirt roads begin to thaw and heave, leaving ruts, ditches, and ripples that can make them impassable, especially old, unmaintained roads. Without our truck, we went as far as we could, then stopped and got out. The stillness was eerie. Not a bird sang, not a squirrel rustled through the dead leaves on the ground, not a chipmunk scampered across the mossy stone walls that meandered through the woods.

Then I saw them. Bijah was in front, mopping his face with a bandanna as he made his way down the hill. He was tall and looked tired. Lucy walked behind him, for some reason with her hands folded in front of her apron.

"It's all right," I heard Bijah say. "Go tell our story."

Then they faded away, as silently as they arrived. I had no idea then that far back in my own family history was a connection between Bijah's family and mine. I got back into the car immediately, and when Anthony came back from his look-around I told him I wanted to go home. For weeks I didn't say a word about what I had seen.

A year or two later, Anthony went back, and as he walked around a man came up to him and asked what he was looking for. Anthony told him we were searching for the Princes, and the man broke into a smile. He told Anthony that he lived by the Prince property and that people around there were mighty proud of Abijah. In fact, he went on, a number of people had seen him over the years. The first was a woman who looked out of her kitchen window and saw a black man sitting up in a cherry tree, smiling down at her. He was tall and looked very friendly, she said. There were several other sightings, mostly from people who'd moved away and lost touch.

Noyes, perhaps rehabilitated, or perhaps considerably wiser politically, became an upstanding citizen, holding nearly every public office in town, sitting for thirteen years in the state legislature, and helping to reelect Thomas Jefferson. Yet the writers of Guilford's history still remembered him as "Squire Noyes," with "one of the most pretentious of the ancient Guilford homesteads," while they recalled Bijah as the "old colored pioneer." Noyes and his wife died just days apart, in 1827. In a final irony, he did eventually purchase Bijah's farm, via Rufus Fisk, after the family had departed. We don't know if it brought him any happiness.

With Bijah's death, Lucy and her daughters, along with Festus and Caesar and his wife, Sally, decided to consolidate and finally settle on the Sunderland land. Caesar and Sally went ahead of the rest of the family, moving into nearby Manchester, but Sally didn't last that long. By November 1794, she had left her husband, and he put an ad in the newspaper, disclaiming any responsibility for her debts. In a departure from the usual boilerplate for such ads, Caesar revealed both his bitterness and his eloquence when he instead wrote, "Whereas, my wife Sally has eloped from my bed and board, and I am suspicious may run me in debt, this notifies whom it may concern, that if they trust her it must be at their peril, as I shall not pay any debt of her contracting after the date hereof." The family shrank a little more after her defection.

With only a year left to remain on the Guilford lot, Lucy and Festus went to Brattleboro in the fall of 1795 to file the paperwork that would establish them as Bijah's legal heirs and the administrators of his estate, taking this important document with them. He had shown them the value of legal documents. His life also illustrated to his family that hard work and determination, the Puritan strivings that were all around them in their youth, finally weren't enough to arm them against ruthlessness, even in New England, a region whose association with liberty turned out to be exaggerated.

According to the laws of the time, Lucy and Festus, as Bijah's executors, should have returned to the court to provide an accounting of the estate. Instead, ignoring probate requirements, the remaining Princes packed up their belongings, and Festus drove his mother and sisters west to take up the most prolonged and difficult drama of their lives, looking back over their shoulders as they left behind the grave of a remarkable and deeply loved man. Lucy was still very much in the play, but it was time for her sons to become the lead actors.

PART FOUR

Sunderland

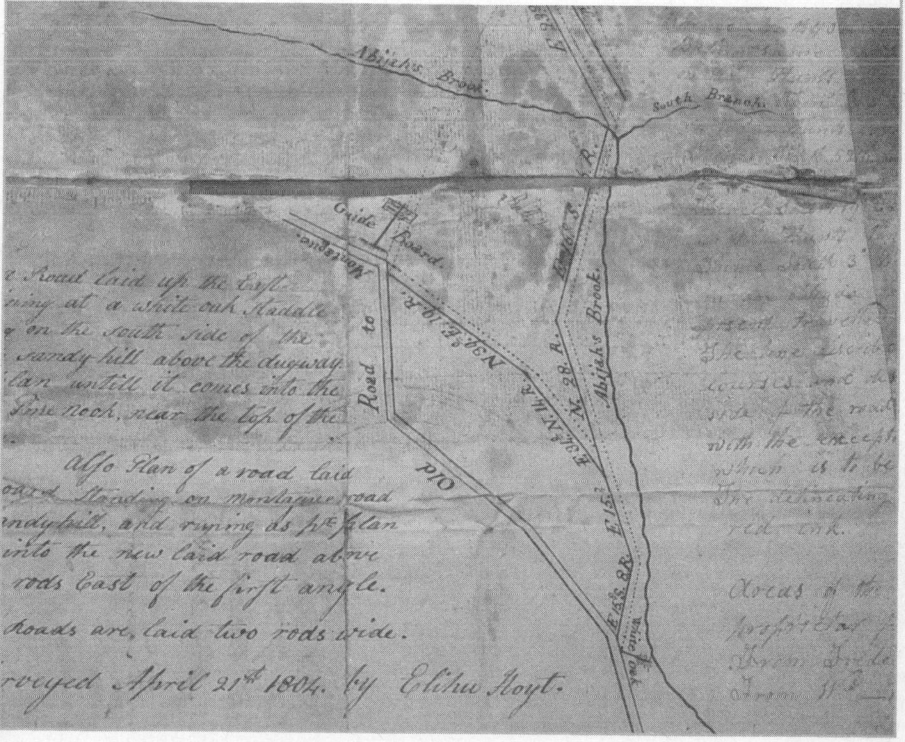

CHAPTER THIRTEEN

BETRAYED

We had come to love old papers. Letters, account books, ledgers, original censuses, muster rolls, military dispatches, tax lists, land records, court dockets, church records, probates, newspapers, sermons, petitions, journals: they all held the promise of new discoveries, of secrets about to be unlocked as we deciphered their crabbed or scrawling handwriting. Written with quill pens in eighteenth-century script, their capitalized nouns in the middle of sentences, "ye" for "the" and "ym" for "them," both *y*'s pronounced as *th*, long *f*-like *s*'s, the felicitous spelling—all delighted us. Sometimes the lines were written in one direction, then the paper had been turned sideways to write in another, in a tangible hatch work designed to save paper and postage. We sat like twins who shared a secret language as we pored over them, often with no luck, but sometimes unearthing nuggets of information that utterly changed the story of the Princes. When we worked apart, our first greeting in the evening was always, "Did you find anything today?" usually followed by, "Can you make out this word?"

Working together almost became a competition, but an unfair one because nowadays it was always Anthony who made the discovery. We would seat ourselves in a library, a stack of materials in front of us, and divide things up. Inevitably I handed him the very item that ended up containing the surprise. Or I would wave my hand toward a bookshelf and say, "There might be something in there," and he'd gaze for a moment, pick up a book seemingly at random, then open to the only page that held what we needed. I finally conceded that it was less a knack than some sort of research fairy that guided him, even when I slapped the table and asserted that it had been my turn to make a find.

So it was that on the day we spent at the University of Vermont Anthony asked the librarian if there were any other research collections concerning legal matters that we should see. She thought for a moment and said we might want to look at the Park McCullough collection, stored in their annex. A glance at the finding aid showed that it was promising, but the collection was mostly uncataloged and only open on certain hours on certain days. Luckily today was one of those days, but the librarian who staffed it wouldn't be going over until two o'clock. Anthony tried charming her into opening it early, and she laughingly refused. We went to lunch and then drove over to the annex, arriving exactly at the opening time. We had a long drive home and needed every minute until they closed.

We were hoping to find court records concerning the last, and most famous, aspect of the legend: that Lucy had argued a case in front of the U.S. Supreme Court to establish her ownership of the Sunderland, Vermont, property against a man who claimed it was his. Anthony had spent a year trying to find anything at all on this. We knew that years ago the Katzes, who had researched and written about the Princes, had come up empty when they searched. Everywhere we went, people urged us to give up on it. I e-mailed the regional office of the National Archives and Records Administration (NARA) in Waltham, Massachusetts, where all the national court records are housed. They looked and though they found nothing, I urged them to look again. Nothing. The

NARA clerk dutifully followed every dead-end lead I requested. Finally, coming to the end of the road, the clerk wrote in no uncertain terms that there had been no Supreme Court case. Their records were meticulously preserved, and none of those having to do with the judges of the legend that the Katzes had pursued (Samuel Chase of Maryland was most often cited as the judge before whom Lucy argued) were relevant, nor was there any case with someone named Prince. There was, he said, metaphorically slamming the book shut in a final e-mail, no U.S. Supreme Court case involving Lucy Prince.

Anthony went to the Vermont State Archives in Montpelier and met with state archivist Gregory Sanford, whom one person described as "a cross between Jerry Garcia and Bigfoot," and Christy Carter, assistant state archivist, who worked hard for several months to help us find a lead. Finally Greg suggested getting in touch with Tanya Marshall, then coordinator for the Vermont Judicial Records Program, who had recently been hired to locate and catalog all court records throughout the state. He did, and that began a long e-mail correspondence that kept them both on the trail. Tanya was indefatigable. Week after week she e-mailed lists, locations, and titles of collections. She was a night owl, and Anthony rushed to his computer the first thing every morning to see if she'd come up with anything during the night. Over and over the same answers kept coming up, always beginning with hope and ending in frustration.

Over and over we discovered that courthouse fires were the norm. This seemed to be a simple excuse for clerks to stop looking, but we found ourselves staring at scorched pages often enough to realize that it was in fact true. Old wooden buildings full of old papers seem to have gone up in flames with frightening regularity. In Bennington County the court records burned in the nineteenth century. Ditto Addison County. It began to look as though there were no trail to follow.

By the time we sat down in the annex we were the only ones, other than the librarians, working there. They had already wheeled out the relevant parts of the collection, leaving us to go to it, and we worked our way through the books and papers. With only fifteen minutes left before they closed, and two items in front of us, Anthony asked which one I wanted to look at.

"I'll take this one," I said, pulling one over, and pushing a little book toward him. "You take that one."

"Are you sure?"

"Yes."

Sure enough, only moments passed before Anthony smiled and said, "Here we are."

It was the notebook of a Bennington lawyer named David Fay, of an old, established family famous for owning the Catamount Tavern, then known as Fay's House, where Ethan Allen's Green Mountain Boys, who had fought for Vermont statehood, began. At the top of the page was the heading "Caesar and Festus Prince vs. Eli Brownson," and what followed was a list of lawsuits, continuations, and judgments.

"So it was the sons who brought a suit, not Lucy," I breathed.

And so it was that another door opened, but only enough to change the whole picture without giving the details. On two little pages in front of us lay the entire outline: the dates, the sessions, the courts, the decisions, the appeals. Like Charles Dickens's novel *Bleak House*, these back-and-forth cases were caught in an endless loop of continuations and appeals. The court met on a regular rotation, so when cases were continued, months passed between sessions. Because each county's court met only twice a year, and the state supreme court just once a year within each county, the Princes' cases began in 1797 but didn't get resolved until 1804. Even then, we discovered, that wasn't the end.

Nowhere were there any depositions, dockets, or details. Why exactly were they going to court? Where did they live? Who argued the cases? Did it really go to any supreme court? How did they support themselves as it ground on into a new century? What role did Lucy play, and what happened to her family while it was going on and on? With the librarians looking at their watches, we made photocopies and hurried to the car, the questions cascading out as we drove the three hours home.

The land they were fighting over was beautiful, even nicer than the Guilford land, in a town that still had fewer than six hundred residents. A visitor to Sunderland in 1797 described it as "a paradise, where Nature, with a profuse and liberal hand, has poured out every beauty, as well as blessing, that can fascinate the eye, or gladden the heart of man . . . on those majestic hills . . . what palaces, and what delightful villas are destined to rise."

It was left to Lucy and her children to discover that a series of behind-the-scenes maneuverings, perhaps preventable, now left them homeless in a place where they had hoped to prosper. It all began decades earlier in 1761, when an advertisement appeared in the *Boston Post-Boy* in September, calling a Sunderland grantees' meeting for that autumn in William Lyman's house in Northampton. Bijah, perhaps away in Guilford, either never saw it or thought it unimportant. He wasn't alone: only a few locals, the same ones who called the meeting, attended it.

In a rapid series of meetings, Searles, the conniving land speculator, and the others began to take control of the land, and the land-jobbing machinery had commenced. Over a series of months, then again over the next year or so, a very small group of men, led by Searles as tax collector—he was the only one of them with a legitimate claim to Sunderland land—approved a series of questionable practices. There is no evidence that a legal quorum of original proprietors was ever assembled; even so, they went on to levy taxes on the rights and then announced in the *Boston Post-Boy* that any Sunderland proprietor who didn't pay the newly levied tax by October 4 would have his land sold at "vendue." (The ad above this one offered a slave for sale.) Few, if any, of those whose land was at stake probably ever saw the ad. Searles and his associates hired someone to begin laying out roads, and offered extravagant payments for surveying, charging it all to the proprietors. Bijah, whether in Deerfield or Guilford, had no way of knowing about any meetings or taxes, and eventually, owing to his nonpayment of taxes, his land was sold. This underhanded practice was not unique to Sunderland: as late as the 1780s, many proprietors living outside of Vermont had never heard about taxes or tax sales before their land was sold. The sheriff of one town held public auctions at midnight, when only one purchaser's agent was present to make a bid.

It was a brazen scheme. Bijah, like others on the original petition, had gotten his right to Sunderland land when the governor approved the petition. He did this in good faith, with the understanding that his acres would always be there for him and his family. He never conceived that Searles, in his role as tax collector, might sell that same land for a pittance, for nonpayment of taxes, to a relative. A month later Searles bought it back, later selling it to Gideon Brownson of Salisbury, Connecticut, for an astonishing £35 and 5 shillings, a crucial sale that would profoundly affect Lucy and her children Caesar, Festus, Duruxa, and Drucilla decades later. Except for the governor of Massachusetts, the president of Yale, and a New Hampshire congressional delegate—all impolitic choices for swindle— most of the original proprietors, nearly all of them living outside the area, lost their original five-acre lots. Over the next few years Bijah and most of the other original proprietors would lose their rights to each subsequent division of land without ever hearing of it. Searles and his friends dealt out the rights to each other, selling them to those they knew, transactions not reflected in the two sets of minutes they seem to have kept. Gideon Brownson, a Connecticut man who would figure so prominently in Lucy's future, established the first settlement along with a number of others.

Eli Brownson must have been flabbergasted when an extended family of black people showed up and claimed that the land that his family had owned for thirty-five years was theirs. He had bought the land from his brother Gideon, and Abijah Prince's name was on the deed as the original proprietor. Could it be that these black people were this Abijah Prince's heirs? For he had never known that among the prestigious men who were the original proprietors was a black man.

Eli Brownson lived in nearby Manchester, not on the Sunderland land. Meanwhile, the Princes began gathering there. Caesar was living in Manchester, and it's not clear exactly when his mother, sisters, and Festus joined him, nor where they all lived when they arrived from Guilford. It wouldn't be long before Tatnai joined them. Until the land dispute was settled, they had to live in rented accommodations, or in exchange for work. A number of African American people lived in the region, so maybe they found rooms with some of them.

At the end of 1797 Caesar and Festus faced Brownson in county court. Brownson was an important citizen, with a deed to the property, and he certainly wasn't going to hand over some of the most fertile and desirable property this side of the Hudson River just on their say-so, no matter what documentation they brought, so he chose the best lawyer available. David Fay was a prominent attorney from a well-known family, with experience arguing before the state supreme court, and he later went on to be state's attorney for Bennington County. He had until June to prepare the case against Caesar and Festus, but in the meantime the Princes had to fend for themselves. When the case finally got to court, it was over quickly, with Brownson winning. Caesar and Festus immediately appealed to the state supreme court. However, the state supreme court, a traveling court like the others, wouldn't meet in their region for another eight months, not until February 1799.

As we tried to picture the grown sons of Bijah and Lucy fighting for their rightful inheritance, Anthony and I differed. He saw them as well-spoken and respectful, yet firm. I agreed, but put more attitude into my picture. Raised by two people who never backed down and who always went to the law to support their causes, they had to be strong-minded and self-assured. I cheered them on, thrilled to see them pick up where their father left off, and imagined them strutting into the courtroom, the proud sons of Abijah and Lucy Prince. "Strutting?" Anthony would have none of it, and he was probably correct. Proud and polite, yes; arrogant, no.

It was a long wait for them—and frustrating for us not to know how they passed this time. Except for these court dates, their actions and locations during these final years of the eighteenth century lapsed into silence. They couldn't have occupied the land or built upon it while the case was still making its way through the judicial system; the sons and perhaps Drucilla must have worked for someone.

When the state supreme court judges gathered in either Bennington or Manchester in February, they ran short of time and continued the case to their June adjourned term, four months later. The case finally was heard, perhaps with new evidence, and this time the Princes won. The battle was over by June 1799, but not the war.

Even though the judgment was against him, Brownson refused to be defeated. He turned around and began a suit of his own, against them. In the meantime, they may have considered the land theirs. Someone recalled that Festus built a log house on the property, and with no place for his mother and sisters to live, this might well be the time when he did it. With a couple of men working on it, a cabin could go up in under a week. Brownson's charges aren't clear; had they by now taken possession of land that he claimed was his? Did long possession trump original rights? The new suit went back to the county court in December, continued again until June—at which point the three men would have been locking horns for two years. It was to go on for another five.

Here's the picture we were able to pull together of the Princes in 1800. Tatnai is working in Manchester for a man who dies intestate and owes him a sizable amount in back wages. Then Caesar and Tatnai move one hundred miles away, to Vergennes, the oldest city in Vermont (although very small by other standards—today it has only about two thousand residents). The oldest and

ELI BROWNSON. *Courtesy of Special Collections, University of Vermont.*

youngest living Prince sons, now forty-three and thirty-five, have gone into business there. Exactly what they do together isn't clear, but we know they're there because in the typical skirmishes over minor debt that were happening all over Vermont they have been cited together a couple of times, and later they go after others for not paying them in turn. Mostly they pay their bills on time and seem pretty well settled in town.

At first I wondered why they moved so far away from the place where their land suits were being heard. The towns of Manchester and Bennington were much closer, close enough for their mother to ride there on horseback, and if they had wanted a more urban atmosphere, Albany, New York, was much closer than Vergennes. Then it hit me: New York was still very much a slave state, and therefore a less comfortable place for black men to live. Vergennes was in those days a congenial and bustling town, with waterfalls that made it a good place for mills and industry. Other black people lived there, and there was a flourishing Quaker community in the middle of what would soon become Underground Railroad territory. There were black heads of households there and numerous other African Americans living with white families.

But where were Lucy and her daughters and Festus? They were certainly close by, for both Festus and Lucy were receiving mail in local post offices. If Festus didn't build the cabin at this time, there's another intriguing and plausible possibility: four black people were living that year with Amos Chipman, a Revolutionary War hero who had fought in the Battle of Bennington and who lived near the disputed land in Sunderland.

Brownson's case against the Princes finally opened in December 1800, but was continued once again for six months. Perhaps this was because Brownson lost his wife, Abi, who had just died a miserable death that month. Six doctors performed an autopsy and discovered an enormous abscess weighing forty-four pounds. A man dealing with such a tragedy merited a continuation, and the case was rescheduled for June.

So it went on, with continuations and arguments, session after session. In June 1802, the case finally went to trial in Manchester's county court, and Brownson was awarded the victory. Fay's terse remark was simply, "I did not argue it." The Princes immediately appealed, and the following February it went to the Vermont Supreme Court, where the case was noted but continued to the next session. The folks at the National Archives were right: the case never went to the U.S. Supreme Court, as George Sheldon and others had written so many years ago and as many scholars unfortunately still assert today. All the pieces have been jumbled and miscommunicated down the long years. Lucy and the others did not win in the U.S. Supreme Court. After the Princes' appeal, the Vermont Supreme Court, in February 1804, proposed that both sides meet with referees and present a solution to the county court in four months. Lucy Terry never argued a case in front of the U.S. Supreme Court.

People often represented themselves in courts, just as Bijah had done several times in Guilford, and Lucy was no stranger to defending her family's rights in front of government bodies. The blind former slave Jeffrey Brace of Manchester may have had a chip on his shoulder when he wrote in his 1810 memoir that it would have been difficult for a black person in western Vermont at that time to hire a lawyer against a respected local citizen: "For what lawyer would undertake the cause of an old African Negro against a respectable widow in Manchester who had many respectable acquaintances?" But not only did Lucy take up the battle against a respected citizen, but she won.

It was time for us to get our own legal advice. We couldn't imagine that any modern lawyer had a working knowledge of eighteenth-century Vermont jurisprudence, nor did we know of an academic who did either. Anthony began asking around, and one name kept coming up: Paul Gillies, a practicing lawyer in Montpelier, was a legal scholar with a number of important published articles on early Vermont legal history. Gillies turned out to be very happy to meet with Anthony and set up a long appointment.

A bearded, graying man with a cheerful demeanor, Gillies struck Anthony as a cross between a rumpled lawyer and a well-dressed academic. He had served as deputy secretary of state, with oversight of the state archives, had been a speechwriter for the late Governor Snelling, and had written many articles for the

Vermont Bar Association Journal on historical aspects of the law. He was the perfect person to consult about the Princes, and he sat fascinated as he listened to the basics of the story. He nodded at each one and took notes. Then, wary of sharing our find, Anthony finally handed him a photocopy of Fay's notes from the turn of the nineteenth century.

"Where did you find that?" Gillies exclaimed.

Anthony just smiled and shook his head. They went over it line by line, Anthony telling the lawyer of our conclusions at each step of each case. Trial law, Gillies told him, "was a fishing expedition in those days," with both parties angling rather than presenting a highly structured case and behaving in ways that would shock modern people.

"There was a lot of drinking going on in courts in those days," he said. "It was customary for the winning lawyer to provide liquor and cigars to the jury."

Our conclusions looked right to him. He agreed to think it over and consult some books, then confer by e-mail. He got back to us in another week. The case fascinated Gillies, and he not only sent a digital photograph from an old law book as evidence for one of his points but indicated that he was "game for more, and more and more, as long as you'll tolerate my wandering. You are hardly wearing out your welcome."

He confirmed just about everything we thought about the first case when he said that we were right: "They took it to county court. There was a trial, judgment for defendants." Then that case, and the second case, went to the Vermont Supreme Court on appeal. Finally, the Princes would win.

Brownson, seeing things moving in favor of the Princes, didn't even show up when Lucy argued the appeal before the state supreme court in February 1803. She undoubtedly argued more than once, outlining her case to the judges and referees. Brownson's argument may have rested on something called the "quieting act," or the "betterment act," or "an act for settling disputes respecting landed property," which recognized the rights of those who had settled and cleared and claimed ownership during the tumultuous years of Vermont's birth. On the one hand, these "ancient settlers," as they were called, had worked hard to clear and cultivate the land, thereby making it more valuable. On the other hand, they might have purchased defective titles that could result in their eviction. The new laws were intended to assess the improved land and compensate them for their effort. To Lucy, however, it was straightforward: her husband had become a Sunderland proprietor way back in 1761. He never received a notice about taxes or tax sales, or he never saw an ad. Undivided lands often remained so for decades—Sunderland *still* hadn't divided all its land yet—and he had never legally forfeited the two lots drawn for him. Brownson may have bought the land forty years earlier, but it was not a legal sale, and he had no right to sue them.

She convinced them. The problem was determining what solution to offer. When the referees for the Vermont Supreme Court reported back in June, they declared that they had decided against Brownson and for the Princes. The settlement was as follows: Brownson got to keep the land, but the Princes got $200, a great deal of money at that time.

The gods must have smiled down at this, for that same month a widow in Bennington had their old nemesis, Oliver Waters, one of the Guilford attackers, arrested. His fortunes further declined the next month when a terrible thunderstorm struck late one night. The rain, the *Vermont Gazette* reported, "fell like a cataract, the thunder was almost one incessant peal and the lightning nearly a continued flash." Everyone was terrified, seeing the "scene of terror" as a sign of Jehovah's power. It looked to us literally like divine retribution when Waters, the man who had set fire to the Princes' hayricks, watched as his barn was struck by lightning and burned to the ground, just as Lucy was handed another court victory.

The Princes had won in court, but they still had no permanent place to live. With her residency established, Lucy resolved to make the town face up to its responsibilities to her. By now everyone in Sunderland must have known who they were: the black family that began showing up in 1794—eighteen years after the Revolutionary War and a full sixty-seven years before the start of the Civil War, claiming to be proprietors and taking on one of the most prominent families in the region, some of whom had administrative positions in the town. They must have watched the progression of the case with wonderment, bemused by the claims that surfaced after so many years. Even if the Princes kept to themselves, they would have been seen on shopping trips to nearby Bennington and Manchester when the courts met. Lucy surely attended church, and the post office listed her as residing in Sunderland. Over the years she would earn great respect from the locals.

Lucy, Caesar, and Festus took their $200—perhaps minus court costs—but though she might have viewed the payment as her sons' legitimate inheritance, the money did not appease her. It was clear to her that the town had wronged her family from the very beginning, so finally, with her options exhausted, she went to the town meeting as the widow of an original proprietor. With all of her considerable verbal force, she demanded that they make things right. Land in Sunderland was her right, both in the past and in the still-undivided lots, and they owed her a place to live. She had now been in the area for several years, waiting for a resolution. Since the courts had decided in her family's favor, the town needed to come up with a solution. If they didn't want to give her land, then they should fund a lawsuit to get back the original fifty acres.

The selectmen were dumbfounded. Then they did what all governments do when faced with a problem: they formed a committee to look into her claims. They wanted to do the right thing, but cautiously, and without giving up what they didn't have to. They were not bad people. We could read between the lines of the minutes and see them struggling with a problem that had sprung up from the distant past, before their time. They had taken no part in the land-jobbing machine of the 1760s and had no real knowledge of it. Now, using Lucy's evidence and digging back for the rest, they realized that Searles and the others had dealt out the original lots among friends like so many playing cards. Two weeks later the committee reported back that, sure enough, a tax had been levied in 1763, but that there was no record of proper notices of it, nor of its ever having been published or sent as personal notes to the proprietors, as directed. Even so, the town meeting voted down helping "the negroes."

The crux of the problem was not just the land itself but the fact that if Bijah and his heirs could be proven to have been legitimate proprietors, then the elderly and infirm—Lucy and Duruxa—were owed public support, the early equivalent of welfare. The selectmen went fishing for other ways out of the dilemma. Certain New England states had laws on the books preventing slave owners from freeing slaves in old age or illness in order not to have to support them. Might not Massachusetts have

SITE OF THE PRINCES' "NEGRO HOUSE" IN SUNDERLAND, VERMONT.
Courtesy of Vermont Historical Society.

a law that would force someone there to pay for their mainte-
nance? And might not Bijah's heirs have a right to it?

They came up empty, and at last, in the waning days of 1805,
they met to figure out "sum method for the Removal and Support of the widow Lucy Prince and Durackey Prince." A couple
of months later they appointed another committee to prepare a
petition to the legislature for a new trial against Brownson and to
take concrete measures to support Lucy and her disabled daughter. But no new court case or petition ever materialized, at least
not that we have been able to find.

Lucy was in her eighties when the town finally came through
for her. At the end of September 1806, the selectmen purchased
eighteen acres from Eli Brownson, part of the lot that was originally assigned to Bijah, "for the use and benefit of Lucy Prince &
her heirs." Trying to make things right for both sides, the town

paid him almost exactly the same amount that he'd had to pay the Princes when he lost the suit. Lucy and Duruxa did not settle there, however; the next year the selectmen commissioned a survey of another lot, which was where Lucy and some of her grown children would actually live. Since her sons had brought the original lawsuit, it was they who each received one of the lots that should have been Bijah's. One was held in trust for them; Festus later sold his fifty acres for $100. When the case was settled, forty-one-year-old Festus left again, going up to Addison County, where his brother Tatnai had remained, even though Caesar had settled in Sunderland, near his mother and sister.

Doors opened and closed. Down in Northampton, Lucy's old friend Scipio Smith died at sixty-eight, leaving behind a widow, a daughter, and a son. Up in Sunderland, Lucy was assured of support for the rest of her days. She was poor, but she was secure, and at last the achievements of her husband were recognized by law and by the public. Rumor has it that she regularly rode the fifteen or so miles between Bennington and Sunderland on horseback until her eyesight faded, and that every year she made a pilgrimage back to Guilford to sit by Bijah's grave and talk to the man she loved.

The timeline and the results of years of lawsuits had nearly crystallized. We sat back to compare what really occurred to the legend that grew up around Lucy, beginning even in her lifetime. As Lucy sat herself down to a much-deserved rest, her eyesight fading and her battles over, we closed her front door and turned our eyes to her children.

CHAPTER FOURTEEN

THE NEGRO HOUSE

It is March in Middlebury, Vermont, one of those New England days when you can almost, but not quite, believe that spring is coming. The sky is overcast and gray, but with the recent cold nights and days above freezing, it is good sugaring weather, and buckets hang from many of the maples along the road. Anthony and I are on our last research trip together, having spent all of the previous afternoon and evening reading documents and accounts in the Sheldon Museum. After nearly eight hours in the museum, the only thing we found was a single mention of Tatnai's working a few days for a stonemason who was putting up a new building in town. It seemed another signal that we were nearing the end of our road. We were certain that there was more out there, but we were running out of places to look.

Middlebury is a friendly college town surrounded by farming communities, and as we relaxed over dinner I commented that it was easy to see why Tatnai liked it well enough to settle there for the rest of his life. Unlike Caesar, Tatnai preferred town life and was no farmer, though all of them became proficient at it in their youth. The inn we were staying in overlooked a handsome little town green, and we could imagine him meeting friends at one of the taverns after a long day of work.

The next morning we set off again, driving two hours south to Bennington, where Anthony has another research appointment at the Bennington Museum. The views on the drive down charm us, with wide, flat valleys surrounded by the Green Mountains. We wind past all the towns that we now know Caesar, Festus, and Tatnai lived in over the years: Middlebury, Leicester, Shaftsbury, Sunderland, Danby, Manchester. It's our farewell tour, and we talk about the sort of life they had in these places, for it differed for each of them.

Anthony and I were fascinated by Festus and his sister Cill, and they are the ones we hope to find out more about on this trip. Where did they live and how did they support themselves during these years of the early nineteenth century? They shared a feistiness, a determination to live life in their own way. They also shared an artistic sensibility—Festus was a musician, and Cill was reputed to be a poet like her mother—but with rare exceptions they vanish from the public and private records during their forties. Cill drops out of the picture for many years. She may have taken a job in Sunderland, Manchester, or Bennington and remained with her mother and sister. She could have gone back to Deerfield, or up to Addison County, where Tatnai remained, or over to New York State. She apparently never married, but was she ever in love? I've always imagined that she kept her father's accounts in the Guilford days; somehow the handwriting and care suggest a woman who had worked in a shop. Then too perhaps she was bookish and imaginative. Both of us see her as outgoing, self-assured, and self-sufficient. Our inability to know more about her heads our list of regrets, but we are not destined to meet her again until she is an old woman.

We did learn, however, that Festus finally moved and was living in Jericho, near Vergennes and Middlebury. He had married a white girl from Leicester, Lucy Holman, in March 1805. He met her when both of them were living in Leicester. He was warned out of that town—it was a common practice to notify nonpermanent occupants that the town wasn't responsible for them—and went to Jericho; a few months later Lucy followed him to his new home, and they married. Perhaps it was at the insistence of his eighteen-year-old bride that they took the unusual step of announcing the marriage in the *Middlebury Mercury*. There were now two Lucy Princes, one black and one white, one elderly and the other young enough to be Festus's daughter and Lucy's granddaughter.

Festus had been married for a year and a half when the land in Sunderland was finally awarded to him. A year later he decided to sell; he hired a Middlebury lawyer to write up the deed, and then he and his wife moved farther south, closer to his family. Festus probably built a log cabin on the lot where his family was living. Over these years his wife gave birth to two sons and a daughter, whose names and fates we have never discovered. Five years later they moved from Sunderland across the state line into Cambridge, New York. Lucy must have come to the door when the census taker arrived, for it never occurred to him to ask the race of her husband. Consequently all of them, including the three children, are listed as white.

What sort of a life did they have? I imagine an unsettled one, for not being a landowner, Festus was warned out of several towns. Yet looking at the dates, we realize that that occurred less often than it seems. As Anthony points out, it happened whenever a town bestirred itself to make up a list, usually comprising dozens of names, and people may or may not actually have had to leave. He sees Festus as more comfortable than these moves suggest to me, while I see a more hand-to-mouth existence. Both of us agree that he probably made his living as a musician, traveling to wherever he was needed for the country parties and town balls that happened more often than we might expect. Even in this litigious age he never showed up for debt or legal scrapes. The fact that he only showed up in warnings out and censuses during these years means that he stayed out of trouble.

The Brownson conflict behind them, the community support for Lucy grew. Living in the center of town, she and her family were known by everyone, and at long last life went on peacefully for another decade or so, Lucy and at least one of her daughters living with Caesar in Sunderland on a beautiful piece of land on the fabled Battenkill trout stream, near the town center and church; Caesar farming and selling firewood and, as he moved toward his sixtieth year, working as a hired man; Festus and his family circling Sunderland and probably spending extended periods there; Tatnai working up in Middlebury, seventy miles away. Though peaceful, there were some difficult years. For instance, 1816 went down in history as "the cold year": a long cold season— a deep frost and a foot of snow in June killed off crops and froze the newly sheared sheep, whose fleece had to be tied around them to keep them warm—plunged the state into famine. In this year with no summer, Caesar was regularly forced to buy grain and meat to keep the family alive.

Tatnai moved to Middlebury when he was in his early forties, after Caesar left Vergennes to take up farming in Sunderland. Tatnai had a business partner, Joel Lawrence, but also did odd jobs, in positions requiring trust and competence, under prominent professional people. Middlebury seems to have been, at that time at least, a place where a black man could form a decent life for himself. Fifteen years later a man named Alexander Twilight would graduate from Middlebury College, the first African American to get a bachelor's degree from an American college.

Just as we saw the Princes easing into this new life, things began to go wrong again. The Brownson conflict resurfaced in November 1816 when he accused them of cutting timber on his remaining land, adjacent to theirs, and it reoccurred in March 1817. A few years later, in 1820, Lucy, who had been through so much and was now nearing the end of her long life, was about to face a double tragedy.

It began when illness struck Festus's family. We don't know what happened, but whatever it was, both Festus and his wife, Lucy, caught it. Lucy was terribly ill, and just as the new year dawned, Festus died at the age of fifty-seven. That very same month a case of smallpox turned up in Bristol, carried into that town by a stranger who was staying at a public house. It must have been the fear of contagion that sparked what is said to have happened next: Festus's widow and children were forced to leave Danby soon afterward. The town of Sunderland paid to transport the young family and their cow there and hired four women to nurse the young widow. They also voted to "repair the old house," which they now began to call the "Negro house," a term that was to stick until nearly the twentieth century, "or build some other house for the Negroes on the lot where the old house stands as soon as possible." This was probably the house that Festus had built earlier, and as his widow slowly recovered the townspeople threw themselves into the work, hauling in timber, stone, and other supplies to build a house for the "white negroes" next door to the rest of the Princes. Lots of people pitched in to supply the family with clothes, grain, firewood, and building labor, all paid for by the town. Among these people, ironically, was a Brownson woman.

While Sunderland remained untouched, by March Middlebury was infected when a schoolteacher caught the disease and exposed her entire class. They set up a hospital to quarantine and treat smallpox patients. Anyone presumed immune was needed to help in the crisis. Tatnai was hired as a nurse because he'd apparently had a mild case of smallpox in the past. Nursing was by no means a job relegated to those from the lower social classes; among those acting as nurse was a selectman from Burlington. By the beginning of May, the first smallpox death in Middlebury had occurred, and more followed steadily over the next week and a half. By then it had spread from Middlebury to Burlington, Colchester, and Georgia. Tatnai now was paid to dig a grave and clean the "pox house" as the city continued in the grip of illness and terror.

Then, just as the epidemic began to wind down, Tatnai caught it and died, only weeks before his fifty-fifth birthday. When Anthony brought home all this information, gleaned over several long days in front of microfilms of old newspapers in the New York Public Library, and spread it out across our coffee table, we sat in silence. This was *not* how it was supposed to turn out, with Lucy losing two of her sons within four months. We could only watch as the woman who had fought so long and hard to protect her family and give them a home experienced the deaths of her sons. For the first time in all the years of burying ourselves in their story, I cried.

Lucy Terry Prince, poet and orator, wife and mother, finally had had enough of this life. She lasted another year, and then she too died, on July 11, 1821, only a few years shy of one hundred. A Sunderland man named William Landon was paid for helping out during "the last sickness of the widow Lucy Prince," and Chauncey Bishop was paid to make her coffin. When Anthony read that, he too nearly cried. Her funeral was respectful, filled with people "who treated her with . . . deference." They remembered her for her ability to overcome adversities not of her making and to confront those in power. Laid to rest, she at last was freed from the earthly cares that began with her theft from her first family and that ended with the loss of too many of her second.

With her death, the long saga of Bijah and Lucy was nearly over. It had lasted for over one hundred years, in time for a new generation of American freedom fighters to take over. Down in Ulster County, New York, the Dutch-speaking Isabella Baumfree, who would later call herself Sojourner Truth, became free in 1828 along with the rest of that state's slaves. They never met, but Truth shared with Lucy Prince an ability to speak out publicly for rights and a love of God manifested by love for others. Probably almost blind in her last years, Lucy had nevertheless memorized and could freely recite much of the Bible, and she had named her children from its pages: Caesar, the proud king; Drusilla, the wife of Felix in Acts; Festus, who also appears in Acts; Tatnai, the governor in Ezra; Abijah, the ruler in Chronicles, after his father. Only Duruxa, the mysteriously ill daughter, had a name that is also a mystery.

It made sense that Rev. Lemuel Haynes, a man of color whose Manchester church she must have attended when he moved there from Rutland a few years before Lucy's death, delivered a eulogy that cited her Christianity, then moved quickly into an acknowledgment of her African birth with an angry antislavery message:

> *And shall proud tyrants boast with brazen face,*
> *Of birth—of genius, over Afric's race:*
> *Go to the tomb where lies their matron's dust,*
> *And read the marble, faithful to its trust. [. . .]*
> *How long must Ethaopia's murder'd race*
> *Be doom'd by men to bondage & disgrace?*
> *And hear such taunting insolence from those*

"We have a fairer skin and sharper nose"?
Their sable mother took her rapt'rous flight,
High orb'd amidst the realms of endless light:
The haughty boaster sinks beneath her feet,
Where vaunting tyrants & oppressors meet.

As we contemplate Lucy's final years on the day we leave Middlebury, Anthony and I idle our car on the road alongside the place where Lucy's final home stood in Sunderland. Across the road is a church, one founded during her time but with a spotty history of operation. Behind it lies a burial ground, with no stone for Lucy in sight.

Her troubles were over, but that wasn't true of those she left behind. About a year and a half after Lucy's death, her daughter-in-law, who was, with her children, still being supported by the town, remarried. With her mixed-race children, it made sense that her second husband, William McGowan, was black. Originally from Boston, McGowan moved the family to Washington County, New York. The relief that this second marriage must have brought didn't last long, for McGowan died in 1827, only five years after their marriage, leaving her with four additional small children. She tried to hold things together, but in May 1829, at the age of forty-two, she took the McGowan children— seven-year-old Jonathan, five-year-old Anne, and three-year-old twins Andrew and William—with her into the Washington County poorhouse for ten days. It wasn't the first time they'd been there. When they left, they moved back to Sunderland, back into the house next door to where Caesar, Drusilla, and Duruxa still lived. In a surprise that we can't explain away, Lucy now had an eighth child. Caesar was still working for others, but at the age

REV. LEMUEL HAYNES

of seventy-three he was less capable of the physical labor he used to perform and was now sometimes aided by the town.

These years saw the end of several of their old friends and adversaries as well. In Deerfield a very elderly Cato, the son of Jenny Cole, perhaps finally saw his mother's African home, in the afterlife, when he died in 1825.

The most surprising death was that of Lucy's first daughter, Duruxa. So little was known about her that I was astounded when one day Anthony brought home her obituary, which contained "some points of singularity in the Providential dealings respecting this woman." Duruxa, who had suddenly become "deranged and crazy" as a teenager, just as suddenly snapped out of it when she was sixty-three, just a few weeks before she died in September 1826; she spent the last three weeks of her life in "the clear exercise of all the faculties of her mind." What sort of a world came into focus for her after nearly fifty years? With her sister and brother at her bedside, they must have talked nonstop during this miracle, telling her everything that had happened in the family. On the last morning of her life she got up off her deathbed and went for a walk, unassisted. Then she climbed back into her bed and died peacefully half an hour later.

Even at this late stage of our research, the mysteries continued to mount. What sort of crime would put an old man in jail? For this is what happened to Caesar in 1823, for reasons we will never know. The town voted to support him and to petition the legislature to set him free. But we found no petition and could only assume that he got out of jail before the assembly met again.

Then too there was the mystery of the black man, a "transient person who sickened and died" in Caesar's house in 1830 or 1831. Who was he, why was he there, and why did the town vote to pay a doctor to treat him? Perhaps the Prince siblings were simply taking in black people who needed a place to stay as they passed through town. But might their house have been a station for the movement of fugitive slaves? There was a lot of Underground Railroad activity in their area, and western Vermont had stops running up from Bennington, through Vergennes, and to points north in Canada.

We will never know who this man was. However, it is striking how often in the past the Princes crossed paths with influential people later associated with the antislavery movement. Stephen Row Bradley, who was state's attorney when the men who attacked the Princes and set fire to their hayricks were prosecuted, had introduced a bill into the U.S. Senate in 1805 "to prohibit importation of slaves into . . . the United States." Gideon Olin, who in tandem with Bradley introduced the same bill into the

House of Representatives, was one of three judges in the Bennington county court during the legal battles with Brownson, and he sat on the bench virtually the whole time the Prince case was being argued. Royall Tyler, sitting on the state supreme court during their second trial, remarked, in response to a slave case before him, that "the only evidence of slavery that he was willing to accept would be 'a quit-claim deed of ownership from the Almighty.'" Loyal Case, the Middlebury attorney who wrote Festus's deed for the property sale, volunteered to defend a fugitive slave who was arrested after someone came up from the South to claim him. His brother-in-law represented the southerner, and when the case went to court in Middlebury, "half a dozen rows of ebony faces . . . lined the back part of the room during the trial." Tatnai may well have been among them.

Caesar lived another thirteen years, dying in 1836 when he was seventy-nine. Drucilla, whom we found so appealing although we knew little about her, lived on as the last of Bijah and Lucy's children. We pictured her chopping wood, drawing water, and caring for herself, with the help of her sister-in-law's children, into her old age. Like her mother, she was recalled as a poet whose eyesight finally began to fail, and two years after she lost her last sibling the town stepped in to help her too. Over the next several years a variety of people brought her meals and proffered health care. The woman who had loved clothes now got a new calico dress made up for her every year, along with stockings and caps. A month before she passed away at ninety-four, her mother's poem "Bars Fight" made it at last into print when it was published in the *Springfield* (Massachusetts) *Republican* in October 1854, and Lucy's name was indelibly associated, on the front page, with the history of Deerfield. Although designated a pauper, Drucilla was buried with all the respect shown to her mother:

a new cap, a shroud and "coffin trimmings," a coffin, a day spent in laying her out, and a full burial. Had she lived another seven years, she would have witnessed the outbreak of the Civil War.

The land Caesar farmed had long been rented out to other farmers, but even after the last of the Princes were gone, the place was known as "the Negro lot." As late as 1881, people still referred to it that way, just as the place where Bijah and Lucy first settled after their marriage in Deerfield remained for years on maps as "Abijah's Brook."

The story, as far as we can trace it, may end in Bath, New York, in the early twentieth century. There, living in the New York State Soldiers and Sailors Home in 1900, sat a black fifty-three-year-old Civil War veteran named Festus Prince. Although he was born in New York State, his parents were both born in Vermont. A Festus Prince who appeared in the 1830 census for Greenwich, New York, not far from Sunderland, may well have been his father and was probably the first of Festus's sons. The Civil War veteran was exactly the right age to have been the son of the Greenwich Festus, and the grandson of our Festus.

We don't know, but we like to think that he was one of ours, and that he was the same black Festus Prince who died twenty years later in Hornellsville, New York, and who has a plaque hanging in Washington's African American Civil War Memorial, commemorating his service in the Twentieth Infantry, Company D. In the final coincidence of this tale, this last Festus was discovered by the woman our older son married in Guilford during the final summer of our research, which also proved to be the final summer of our life there. Not just a great researcher, Carrie grew up in this same small town of Hornellsville. For a moment the generations of the Princes and of our own family may have crossed each other on the stage.

We will leave this last Festus there in Bath, rocking on the porch and telling his story to all the other veterans. We hope that his story includes Bijah's and Lucy's, and that he speaks of them freely. We hope that he proudly tells the other veterans of the remarkable family he's descended from, and of the parallels between his family's story and the nation's. We imagine him telling them that the story begins just over the century line of 1700, when his great-grandfather was born; that his great-grandfather joined forces with an African woman and that they rose from slavery to raise a proud and free family, teaching them to use American laws and traditions to protect their rights; that they had a hand and a voice in shaping a powerful nation, from the French and Indian Wars through the American Revolution, in which his great-grandfather, grandfather, and great-uncle fought; that his grandfather Festus was a natural musician who could play any instrument he picked up, and that his great-aunt Cill was a poet like her mother; that this family carried on to a fourth generation, his generation, through the Civil War, and looked forward into a world that would see World War I and the Jazz Age; that they all died respected by the white and black people around them. How many families, we hope he asks as he casts his eye around at his listeners, can say that?

A Tale

of Two Couples

Our years of searching for Bijah and Lucy came to an end nearly at the same time we left Guilford. We had learned about them shortly after we built our house, and we never expected to move away. Our search for them coincided with a life we had made for ourselves two centuries after their life there, but our life moved on.

At the beginning of our last summer in Guilford, our son Simon and his fiancée, Carrie, came up from New York to get married. One of our neighbors opened up the little 150-year-old village church, and Carrie's mother and sisters festooned it with flowers grown by a local college friend of mine. Our other son, Daniel, was there, as were several generations of family and friends. After the ceremony, everyone crossed the dirt road to the lawn of the B&B, where we all danced the night away next to the Green River, under the stars, on the other side of the mountain from where Bijah and Lucy had lived.

Only ten weeks later we were gone: I had accepted a wonderful job offer and expected to commute to it, while watching my future grandchildren play in the river next to the spot where their parents had married. I didn't want to leave behind a house we had built, and where we had made such important connections to the past and the future. But Anthony, in his wisdom, convinced me that it was time to go. He wanted us to have a full life in one place, rather than have me drive an hour and a half each way, in the snow and rain and ice. Once we made the decision, the house sold in a day. I wept through the listing and gave Anthony power of attorney so that I wouldn't have to be at the closing when our house was signed away.

He was right, though. We bought a beautiful old Vermont farmhouse just fifteen minutes from my new job, with acreage and barns. It was built in 1779, and I was comforted by knowing that it had been built in Bijah and Lucy's lifetime and that the minister who built it had known Lemuel Haynes, who visited our area more than once. There's a good chance that the man who preached Lucy's funeral sermon visited, and perhaps even slept in, our "new" house.

The last thing we did before we left Guilford for good was to say good-bye to Bijah and Lucy, the people we were now convinced had brought us there and were telling us to go. We stood on the tailgate of our yellow pickup truck and took each other's pictures by the street sign commemorating Abijah Prince. I finished writing this book a year later.

One evening shortly after the move we were driving home in separate cars, from separate places. I was thinking that if I hurried I might beat Anthony home, since he'd gone out to the state library in Montpelier for a last look at some records, while I was only coming back from my new office. It was a clear autumn night, and the stars were just beginning to show. Suddenly, right in front of me, something streaked brilliantly across the sky, expanding in its brightness, then went out as though someone had pulled a switch. I pulled off at our exit, right behind the only other car on the road, and when that car also turned onto our road, I realized it was Anthony driving. We jumped out of our cars at the same moment, still thrilled by the meteor we'd both just seen.

We stood quietly in the driveway for a few moments, looking up toward where it had been, knowing that we had just witnessed something brilliant and wonderful. It held us in its light, it blazed until we knew what we had seen, and then it let us go.

A Note
on the Legend

Lucy Terry Prince (1725?–1821) was admired by all who knew her. Years after her death, several men wrote down what they understood to be the facts about her long life, and this information forms what comes to us as the legend of Lucy Terry. Much of this information turns out to be largely correct, differing from the truth only in its details. However, it is in some of these details that her modern reputation rests and upon which scholars have based their work about her.

Pliny Arms wrote a history of Deerfield around the time of Lucy's death. It is an important document, revealing a town that was Puritan in its origins and stern in its punishments. He describes, for instance, the public whipping of Daniel Arms's slave Titus (not the same Titus hired by Bijah) for stealing rum from Elijah Williams's store and eggs, butter, bread, and chickens from others, in order to have a little feast among the slaves. Pliny Arms, descended from this slave owner, calls it a lynching, in which "every stroke drew blood." However, whipping was a common punishment for whites as well as blacks. His handwritten account gives the first rendering of the "Bars Fight" poem and says that "the boys of her children's age" went to the Princes' Deerfield home "to hear Lucy talk." He also gives information on the Sunderland land cases, saying that they went to federal court,

205

that "Gov Tichenor, then a lawyer, drew for Lucy the pleadings, and she argued the case against Stephen R. Bradley, who had been States Atty. and Royal [sic] Tyler afterwards Chief Justice of State of Vermont. Judge Chase of Maryland held the court, and observed Lucy made a better argument than he had heard from any lawyer of the bar of Vermont."

Everyone who has ever researched this information has come up empty. We were able to prove that Eli Brownson's case was argued by David Fay and that Judge Chase, who was on a traveling circuit, was in Vermont earlier than the Princes' case was heard and was not sitting on the bench during any of their court dates, since their case never went to a federal court. There are connections between the Princes and Royall Tyler and Stephen Row Bradley that may substantiate their being in the legend. An abolitionist, Tyler was for a time their neighbor in Guilford. Furthermore, he was sitting on the Vermont Supreme Court when the Sunderland case went before that body. There is no evidence that he stepped down from the bench to represent their opponent Brownson. Bradley, as state's attorney, had prosecuted the men who attacked the Princes and set fire to their hay in Guilford. Lucy did not, as many infer, argue in front of the U.S. Supreme Court, but the words of the judge—whoever he was— about the strength of her argument seem entirely plausible and probably refer to her pleadings before the Vermont Supreme Court.

It is also from Arms that the story about Williams College derives. This too seems a plausible story; Lucy knew at least one of the trustees and must have hoped that their respect for her would trump any racism toward her children. However, as Arms says, "he was refused on account of his color. The old lady was indignant, and addressed the Trustees in a most powerful appeal of three hours duration. . . . The Trustees were not a little perplexed and discomfited."

George Sheldon, who later picked up and greatly expanded the history of Deerfield into two exhaustive volumes, used Arms for much of the material. Both men were longtime residents and were descended from the town's earliest residents. For his research on Bijah and Lucy, Sheldon wrote letters to Giles Bacon, whose family had lived near Lucy and her children in Sunderland, Vermont, and Rodney Field, who had family information pertaining to the Princes. As so often happens with family stories, some of that information got tangled in the retelling. It is from them that we hear that Doolittle freed Bijah and gave him the Northfield land and that David Field honored his father's wishes and deeded the hundred acres in Guilford to Bijah. But in fact, Doolittle did not free Bijah, and Rodney Field, in assuming the land came through his father's and grandfather's side of the family, looks to the wrong side of the family and mixes up the story. He also thinks that the "Bars Fight" poem concerned the 1704 raid on Deerfield rather than the 1746 battle, and he calculates that Lucy was an astonishing 125 when she died. Other aspects, however, are right. Tatnai, for instance, did move to Northfield and probably worked for Capt. Hunt in his store.

None of what we discovered over these long years takes anything away from the legend of Lucy Terry Prince; if anything, our findings make it stronger and more poignant, if sadder. Our research also gives Bijah his due as a strong and assertive man, rather than one who received handouts and handled things badly. He was a clever and entrepreneurial man who got his lands through ingenuity, relationships, and hard work. The tale ends, then, as a dual story of a relationship built on love, in which each made the other stronger.

ACKNOWLEDGMENTS

This book would not have been possible without the help of many people and institutions. I would like to thank the National Endowment for the Humanities, whose grant allowed me to dedicate a year to the research. Research funds from Barnard College and Dartmouth College made much of the travel and research possible. My mother, Joyce Holbrook, not only proved herself to be a genealogist extraordinaire, but first brought Bijah to our attention. Neeti Madan, my literary agent, believed in this project even when it was just a possibility. And my editor, Dawn Davis, not only proved to be a dedicated, tireless, and true editor, but she gave Abijah Prince new life in a new generation by naming her first child after him. And finally, many thanks to Elinor Lipman for her novelist's ear for story and title.

We would like to thank the following librarians, libraries, archivists, historical societies, curators, and researchers—amateur and professional—for their invaluable assistance.

IN MASSACHUSETTS:

American Antiquarian Society

American Congregational Association, Boston: Dr. Margaret Bendroth, Librarian/Executive Director

Amherst College Library Archives and Special Collections, Amherst

Andover Newton Theological School, Newton

Baker Library, Harvard University, Cambridge

Berkshire Athenaeum, Local History Department, Pittsfield

Sue and Chuck Burt

Connecticut Valley Historical Museum, Springfield: Michele Plourde-Barker, Archivist, Genealogy and Local History Library

Deerfield Town Clerk

Dickinson Memorial Library, Northfield

W. E. B. Du Bois Library, University of Massachusetts, Amherst

Forbes Library, Northampton: Elise Bernier-Feeley, Librarian, Hampshire Room

Franklin County, Registry of Deeds, Greenfield

Greenfield Historical Society: Peter S. Miller

Hadley Historical Society: Eleanor Niedbala

Hampden County, Registry of Deeds, Springfield

Hampshire County Council of Governments, Northampton

Hampshire County Probate Court, Northampton

Hampshire County Superior Court Archives, Northampton

Harvard University Archives,
Cambridge
Historic Northampton
Jones Library, Amherst
Longmeadow Historical Society:
Linda C. Abrams, Curator, and
Erin Wilson, Intern
Massachusetts Archives, Boston:
John Hannigan, Reference
Archivist
Massachusetts Historical Society,
Boston
Massachusetts Supreme Judicial
Court, Boston: Elizabeth Bouvier,
Head of Archives
Massachusetts Trial Court,
Hampshire Law Library,
Northampton
National Archives and Records
Administration (NARA),
Pittsfield and Waltham
New England Historic Genealogical
Society, Boston: Timothy Salls,
Archivist
Northfield Historical Society: Joanne
Gardner and Betty Congdon
Northfield Town Clerk
Old Sturbridge Village: Jessica

Neuwirth, Jeannette
Robichaud, Library Assistant,
and Tom Kelleher, Curator
for Historic Trades and
Mechanical Arts
Prof. Robert Paynter, University of
Massachusetts, Amherst
Pocumtuck Valley Memorial
Association (PVMA), Deerfield:
Suzanne L. Flynt, Curator of
Memorial Hall Museum, Martha
Noblick, Library Assistant,
Sharman Prouty, Assistant
Librarian, and David C. Bosse,
Librarian
Robert Romer, Professor Emeritus,
Amherst College, Amherst
Stockbridge Library Association
Historical Collection: Barbara
Allen, Curator
Prof. Kevin Sweeney, Amherst
College, Amherst
Williams College, Williamstown:
Sylvia Kennick Brown, College
Archivist and Special Collections
Librarian
Williamstown House of Local
History, Williamstown

IN VERMONT:

Bailey-Howe Library, University of
Vermont: Christopher D. Burns,
Manuscripts Curator, Prudence J.
Doherty, Reference Specialist,
Jeffrey D. Marshall, Curator of the
Wilbur Collection, and Sylvia
Bugbee, Assistant Archivist,
Special Collections
Michael Bellesiles

Bennington Museum: Stephen
Perkins, Executive Director, Jamie
Franklin, Curator of Collections,
and Callie Raspuzzi, Collections
Manager
Martha Canfield Library, Arlington:
Bill Budde, Curator, Russell
Vermontiana Collection
Chittenden County Historical

Society, Burlington: Gail
Rosenberg
Virginia L. Close, Norwich
Danby Town Clerk
Paul Gillies, Esq., Montpelier
Guilford: Barbara Olds, Town Clerk,
and Kate Snow, Assistant Town
Clerk
Guilford Historical Society: Ann
Bonneville
Leicester Town Clerk
Manchester Historical Society: Judith
Ann Harwood
Norwich Historical Society
Rokeby Museum, Ferrisburgh: Jane
Williamson, Director
Rutland Historical Society: Patty
Pickett and James S. Davidson
Rutland Superior Court: Gay
Johnson, Court Clerk
Shaftsbury Town Clerk
Henry Sheldon Museum of Vermont
History, Middlebury: Jane

Ploughman, Research Center
Librarian
Sunderland: Rose Keough, Town Clerk
Vermont Department of Libraries,
Montpelier, newspaper and law
collections
Vermont Historical Society, Barre:
Paul A. Carnahan, Librarian, and
Marjorie Strong, Assistant
Librarian
Vermont Public Records Division,
Middlesex
Vermont State Archives, Montpelier:
Christie Carter, Assistant State
Archivist, Tanya Marshall,
Assistant State Archivist, and
D. Gregory Sanford, State
Archivist
Windham County: Sheila Prue,
former Sheriff
Windham County Superior Court:
Larry Robinson, Clerk

IN NEW HAMPSHIRE:

Dartmouth College, Hanover: Rauner
Library, Hazen Allen, Special
Collections Librarian; Baker-Berry
Library; Susan Bibeau, Manager,
Humanities Computing

Fort Number 4, Charlestown:
Barbara Bullock Jones
New Hampshire State Archives,
Concord: Brian Nelson Burford,
State Records Manager

IN CONNECTICUT:

Connecticut Historical Society,
Hartford
Connecticut State Library, Hartford
Enfield: Jean E. Blaser, Records
Manager
New Haven Colony Historical Society
Stonington Historical Society

Wallingford Historical Society
Yale University, New Haven:
Beinecke Library; Divinity School
Library; Kenneth Minkema, Yale
University Library; Lillian
Goldman Law Library

ACKNOWLEDGMENTS

IN NEW YORK:

Fort Ticonderoga
Simon Gerzina
Carrie McBride
New York Academy of Medicine,
    New York: Arlene Shaner,
    Reference Librarian
New-York Historical Society
    (NYHS), New York

New York Public Library, New York
New York State Library and Archives,
    Albany
Salem: William Al Cormier, Town
    Historian, and Dolores Phaneuf,
    Historian/Genealogist

IN WASHINGTON, D.C.:

Library of Congress

NOTES

INTRODUCTION: A QUEST

2 *"wildest flights of fiction"* George Sheldon, "Negro Slavery in Old Deerfield," *New England* (March 1983), 57. Reprinted in George Sheldon, *History of Deerfield. A facsimile of the 1895–96 edition published in recognition of the tercentenary of the town of Deerfield in 1973 with a new foreword by Amelia F. Miller and Donald R. Friary.* Deerfield, Mass.: New Hampshire Publishing Company, Somersworth in collaboration with the Pocumtuck Valley Memorial Association Deerfield, 1972.

5 *on legends and myths* See Hermione Lee, *Body Parts: Essays on Life-Writing* (London: Chatto & Windus, 2005), 6. Published in a shorter version by Princeton University Press as *Virginia Woolf's Nose: Essays on Biography* (2005).

CHAPTER ONE: THE ATTACK

11 *set fire to their hayrick* Stephen Row Bradley letter, October 4, 1785, University of Vermont, Manuscripts and Special Collections.

14 *on their "coasters"* See *Boston News-Letter*, July 24, 1704, and November 13, 1704, for examples of Samuel Prince's travels to and from the West Indies around the time when Abijah Prince was born.

17 *to keep out Indian attackers* The history of Indian and white relations in early Connecticut is a brutal one. What is now known is that the Pequot Wars began through a series of skirmishes, misunderstandings, and battles that left thousands dead when the English settlers went on the offense. The last battle ended horribly. There had been three thousand Pequot alive before the wars. In 1637, when they ended, half were dead. Thirty years after the Pequot Wars, Abraham Doolittle occupied a world that remained dangerous, but into which the English never hesitated to expand.

17 *at the heart of Bijah's story* This occurred in 1710. C. J. Hoadly, *Colonial Records of Connecticut*, vol. 5 (Hartford, Conn.: Press of the Case, Lockwood & Brainard, 1880), 177.

CHAPTER TWO: BIJAH'S LIFE WITH THE DOOLITTLES

21 *when he arrived in Northfield, Massachusetts* Try as I might, I cannot prove that Bijah arrived in Northfield at the same time as the Doolittles. There are no documents relating to the first forty years of his life, and it is possible that he came later, perhaps even as an adult.

21 *"Puritan outpost"* Herbert Collins Parsons, *A Puritan Outpost: A History of the Town and People of Northfield, Massachusetts* (New York: Macmillan, 1937), 99.

22 *since there was no meetinghouse* Ibid., 98.

22 *"as much wood as each man"* Ibid., 102.

23 *curtains on the windows* Letters from Mr. Lyman to Mr. Munsell, February 19, 1876, Northfield box, folder 14 (letters to Rev. Temple about Northfield and Northfield families), PVMA. Lyman was the son of Rev. Lyman, who succeeded Doolittle as minister to the Northfield church.

23 *at a profit* Probate of Benjamin Doolittle's belongings can be found on microfilm at the PVMA and also in the Northampton courthouse, Northampton, Mass. In 1726 he sold two pieces of Northfield property to Stephen Belding and Daniel Shattuck (Hampshire County Grantor Index, 1663–1786, book 1, 66 and 108), and in 1728 he sold more property to Belding (Hampshire County Grantor Index, book 1, 67).

23 *for six months each year* Parsons, *A Puritan Outpost*, 109.

24 *he had so recently left* J. H. Temple and George Sheldon, *A History of the Town of Northfield, Massachusetts, for 150 Years, with an Account of the Prior Occupation of the Territory by the Squakheags; and with Family Genealogies* (Albany, N.Y.: Joel Munsell, 1875), 442.

25 *who lived in his house* Parsons, *A Puritan Outpost*, 100, 108.

25 *"evil [that] grows worse daily"* Boston News-Letter, Judd Manuscripts, misc. 4, 118, May 27, 1724, Forbes Library, Northampton, Mass.

25 *he got the deliveries reinstated* Temple and Sheldon, *History of the Town of Northfield*, 230.

26 *annual salary as a minister* Judd Manuscripts, vol. 2, 106, Forbes Library.

26 *substantial slave population.* Listed as "Mr Doolittles Prince," Bijah bought a dozen pipes in Deerfield in August 1745. He surely made other purchases in other shops over the years. Elijah Williams daybook, vol. 1, 28, PVMA 5380.

26 *still rankled with them* Kenneth Minkema, "Jonathan Edwards's Defense of Slavery," *Massachusetts Historical Review* 4 (2002), 23–60.

27 *Edwards declared* Kenneth Minkema, "Jonathan Edwards on Slavery," *William and Mary Quarterly* (3d series) 54, no. 4 (October 1997), 832. The original letter is in the Edwards Collection, Andover Newton Theological School, Newton, Mass.

27 *forts closer to home* This journal is reprinted in Temple and Sheldon, *History of the Town of Northfield*, and was thought by Doolittle's descendants to have disappeared. One of my many discoveries in this project was that the military portion of the journal still exists: it is in the Massachusetts Historical and Genealogical Society, filed as "Anonymous."

27 *planks three inches thick* Letters from Mr. Lyman to Mr. Munsell, February 19, 1876, Northfield box, folder 14, PVMA.

28 *hanging out the town flag* Webster Collection, Town of Northfield, reel 5, "Accounts Against the Town," Dickinson Memorial Library. For the year 1751, Bijah was paid £1.5 ("to Abijah Prince to putting out ye flag").

29 *She was ninety-two* Mary Montague, letter to George Sheldon, 1874, Doolittle Family folder, PVMA.

30 *"it was then most terrible"* Epaphrus Hoyt, *Antiquarian Researches: Comprising a History of the Indian Wars in the Country Bordering Connecticut River and Parts Adjacents, and Other Interesting Events* (Greenfield, Mass.: Ansel Phelps, December 1824), 206–7.

31 *Abijah Prince joined the army* Elijah Williams account book, March 1, 1747, PVMA 5376.

CHAPTER THREE: BIJAH GOES TO WAR

32 *smoked a clay pipe* Elijah Williams daybook, vol. 1, 28, PVMA 5380. Bijah bought a dozen clay pipes from Williams two summers before he enlisted. This is the earliest mention of Bijah in Deerfield that I have been able to find, but certainly he often accompanied Doolittle there or went on his own.

33 *turning a buck on the side* Sibley's *Harvard Graduates*, vol. 9 (Boston: Massachusetts Historical Society, 1956), 236.

34 *on the Connecticut River* Kevin M. Sweeney, "River Gods in the Making: The Williamses of Western Massachusetts," *The Bay and the River: 1600–1900* (Boston: Boston University, Dublin Seminar for New England Folklife: Annual Proceedings, 1981), 101.

34 *not only sold locally* Kevin M. Sweeney, "Gentleman Farmers and Inland Merchants: The Williams Family and Commercial Agriculture in Pre-Revolutionary Western Massachusetts," *The Farm* (Boston: Boston University, Dublin Seminar for New England Folklife, Annual Proceedings, 1986), 71.

34 *goods for several units.* A short biography of Elijah Williams in the family papers collections binder at PVMA refers to him as "captain of the Snow Shoe men in the old French war."

37 *Elijah Williams's company in Deerfield* This company was made up of Nathaniel and Joel Ely, Timothy Day, John Whiteing, Phillip More, Charles Coats, Hezekiah Elmer, and Simon and Noah Georgau. Several others joined up as well while Bijah was serving, and it is possible that he had even been in the company for an earlier stint.

37 *"Colonel Bill"* "List of Certificates given by Govr. Shirley & Knowles to the Commission officers of the 2 Regiments raised in the p——of the Massachusets [*sic*], No. 31," November 17, 1747, Misc. Mss., Massachusetts, NYHS.

38 encouraged many men to enlist. Massachusetts Archives 12, no. 678 (July 12, 1743).

38 "Snow Shoes" John Stoddard to William Williams, March 1, 1747, William Williams Collection, 89, Berkshire Athenaeum, Pittsfield, Mass.

39 "blockhouses west of the Connecticut River" April 21, 1747, William Williams Collection, "Orders from Col. Dwight relating to the blockhouses," to Lieut. Col. William Williams, 82, Berkshire Athenaeum.

39 sometimes sold into slavery "Record of Indian Attacks," Phineas Stevens Papers, May 24, 1746–July 7, 1759, NYHS.

39 "stringing along" Samuel G. Drake. *Particular History of the Five Years French and Indian War in New England and Parts Adjacent, from Its Declaration by the King of France, March 15, 1744, to the Treaty with the Eastern Indians, Oct. 16, 1749, Sometimes Called Governor Shirley's War. With a memoir of Major-General Shirley, accompanied by his portrait and other engravings.* (Freeport, N.Y.: Books for Libraries Press, 1970).

39 they were in little danger John Stoddard to William Williams, July 20, 1744, William Williams Collection, 368, Berkshire Athenaeum.

40 "about as big as three fingers" Drake, *Particular History,* 146.

40 came from the garrison Boston Evening Post, June 8, 1747, issue 617, 4.

40 supply convoy Sibley's Harvard Graduates, vol. 7 (Boston: Massachusetts Historical Society, 1945), 642.

40 wrote to Deerfield to complain Kevin M. Sweeney, "River Gods and Related Minor Deities," diss., Yale University (1986), 377.

40 paying for their military service "Your Obedient Soldiers" to the Honorable Brigadier General Dwight, June 1747, William Williams Collection, 85, Berkshire Athenaeum.

42 Enfield in early May 1748 Stephen Williams diary, April 1748, 55 and 60, Storrs Library.

43 customers in other towns Elijah Williams daybook, December 12, 1749, PVMA 5382.

43 on horseback or by cart Ebenezer Hinsdale's book, October 13, 1748, PVMA 5333, 473.

43 He repaired fences Elijah Williams account book, May 20, 1748, PVMA 5376, 101.

43 delivered them to the store Elijah Williams, Enfield account book, March 19, 1751, PVMA 5376.

43 Bijah's shoes mended Elijah Williams, Enfield account book, July 1750, PVMA 5376.

43 He remained inconsolable for a time Stephen Williams diary, January 27, 1749, 108, and February 3, 1749, 109, Storrs Library.

43 *his share of their patrimony* Stephen Williams diary, March 15, 1749, 116–17, Storrs Library.

44 *"where ye Servant is free a^e his master"* Stephen Williams diary, January and February 1752, 176–78, Storrs Library.

44 *"comforts of his black people"* Sibley's Harvard Graduates, vol. 6 (Boston: Massachusetts Historical Society, 1942), 31. The *Sibley's* source for the information on Cato is from *Papers and Proceedings of the Connecticut Valley Historical Society*, vol. 1, 53n. Original source material on the second slave is "Early Files," Office of the Clerk of the Supreme Court of Suffolk County, 76, 356.

46 *"Persons Claiming Right to his Service"* Hampden County Registry of Deeds, vol. U, 221. The meeting took place on May 9, 1751. Because Sexton, one of the witnesses, was quite young and an employee of Elijah Williams's, and because Aaron Burt purchased something from Williams's shop on the same day, it is reasonable to assume that that was where the meeting took place.

CHAPTER FOUR: THE NEGRO NETWORK

48 *Burt and his wife, Miriam Elmer, in 1740* Corbin Collection, roll 35, New England Historic and Genealogical Society, Boston, p. 305 of notes.

49 *one less mouth to feed* Henry M. Burt and Silas W. Burt, *Early Days in New England: The Life and Times of Henry Burt of Springfield and Some of His Descendents* (Springfield, Mass.: Henry M. Burt, 1893), 417–19.

49 *served together in his company* Elijah Williams account book, PVMA 5376.

49 *town rolls for that year* Webster Collection, Town of Northfield, roll 2, Dickinson Memorial Library, Northfield, Mass.

49 *template for the document* Field Collection, Town of Northfield, reel 3, Dickinson Memorial Library.

49 *recorded by the registrar* Hampden County Registry of Deeds, vol. U, 221. It ended up in a highly unusual place for such a document: land records.

50 *reestablish his residency* "A List of the Polls and Estates Real and Personal Taken in Northfield, August 10, 1751," Dickinson Memorial Library. These lists were compiled by household and neighborhood. That Bijah's name appears immediately below Doolittle's is a strong indication that he lived in that household. His name is crossed out, since he left town a year later.

50 *send her family's genealogy* When it arrived, another mystery was solved: the reason for the alternative legend, repeated in some town histories, that David Field had once owned Bijah and had given him land in Guilford to fulfill his father's deathbed instructions. Field was another Deerfield businessman who speculated in land, and like so many in those years he overextended himself and went broke. But the closest he came to Bijah's story is that they were both residents in the same place for a time. There was no

other connection. The tale seems to have sprung from a simple mistake, the kind that is propagated through years of family hearsay. When a man named Rodney Field wrote in an 1877 letter that one of his ancestors once owned Bijah, he assumed the ancestor was a Field, but in fact his mother was a striking and stylish brunette named Pamelia Burt. He was looking at the wrong side of the family.

50 *his residency and his land* Bijah was paid for hanging out the flag for the town in 1751 (Webster Collection, Town of Northfield, reel 5, Dickinson Memorial Library) and for making a delivery for Pedajah Field's cousin, Dr. Ebenezer Field. A good bet is that he worked primarily for Lucious Doolittle's shop, since he had just spent the past couple of years working in Williams's Enfield shop.

50 *when the divisions were finally made.* Temple and Sheldon (*History of Northfield*, 282) gives a list of proprietors in the fourth division of land, but the list really depicts those who were taxpayers in 1751 and the acreage they did or should have received in 1753. The original documents, however, show that the fourth division didn't occur until April 1753, and the fifth division didn't occur until 1754. Stearns Collection, Town of Northfield, rolls 2 and 3, Dickinson Memorial Library.

51 *administered medicines with their own hands* For a detailed look at the Phelps family and slave ownership, see Elizabeth Pendergast Carlisle, *Earthbound and Heavenbent: The Life of Elizabeth Porter Phelps and Life at Forty Acres, 1747–1817* (New York: Scribner, 2004).

52 *while others decided his fate* Sezor Phelps to Charles Phelps, September 30, 1776, in Porter-Phelps-Huntington Family Papers (Box 4, Folder 12), Archives and Special Collections, Amherst College Library.

52 *the deal was null and void* Joseph Hubbard deed, January 20, 1767, filed by itself in folder, cataloged by Hubbard deed, Jones Library, Amherst, Mass.

52 *buy property and establish himself* Northampton, Mass., Registry of Probate book, reel 1.1, vol. 4, 110, Connecticut Valley Historical Museum, Springfield, Mass.

52 *an astonishingly long period of thirty years* James Avery Smith, *The History of the Black Population of Amherst, Massachusetts* (Boston: New England Historic Genealogical Society, 1999), 37.

53 *the case ended up in Superior Court.* Inferior Court of Common Pleas, 1732, book 2, 151, Hampshire County Court.

53 *back in 1695* Judd *History of Hadley*, 239.

53 *Ebenezer Hunt.* A listing of names that appeared in Ebenezer Hunt's account book shows "Abijah Freeman, Negro," with two notations: first appearance in 1752, and the second saying "here 1754." The word "here" was generally used

to describe people working for the account keeper. Judd Manuscripts, reel 15K, Forbes Library.

54 *Hull's wife, Bathsheba* The Northampton tax list appears to be arranged by household, and the men appear together. Northampton Town Papers, reel 146, 22, Forbes Library.

54 *Abijah Freeman* See, for example, the tax lists for Northampton in 1753–54, where they appear one after the other as "Abijah Negro" and "Amos Negro" (Northampton Town Papers, reel 146, Forbes Library), and Ebenezer Hunt's account book for 1754, in which Bijah appears as "Abijah Freeman, negro" (Judd Manuscripts, "Northampton Prices and Account Books," Slaves, misc., 305, Forbes Library).

56 *now look entirely possible* Northampton town Papers, reel 146, 1756 tax rolls, Forbes Library. With the birth of Amos and Bathsheba's first baby, Bijah moved on, but he now had a changed sense of his place in the world.

CHAPTER FIVE: LUCY ENTERS

60 *wrote to a number of people* Much of the misinformation about the Princes— that Bijah got his freedom and his Northfield land from Doolittle and his Guilford property from David Field—comes from letters that Sheldon received from Rodney Field and Giles Bacon (whose family owned land near the Princes' Sunderland home). These letters are in the PVMA, but it's now clear that both writers relied on family stories and hearsay for some of what made its way into Sheldon's account and remains ubiquitous in books and articles and on the Internet today.

60 *"comes down to us as a poet"* Broad Brook Grange, *Official History of Guilford, Vermont, 1678–1961* (Brattleboro: Vermont Printing Co., 1992), 146. See also George Sheldon, *History of Deerfield, Massachusetts*, vol. 2 (Deerfield: Pocumtuck Valley Memorial Association, 1896), 899.

61 *"expecting to find the answers to"* Undated letter from Bernard Katz to Mary Adams Ball, Katz microfilm, Schomburg Center for Research in Black Culture, New York.

62 *from this novel rather than from facts* One website, www.scholars.com, uses the Katz novel as the source for all erroneous information it gives on Lucy. Caveat emptor.

64 *Guinea slaves to be shipped to Barbados Sibley's Harvard Graduates*, vol. 6 (Boston: Massachusetts Historical Society, 1942), 11–18.

64 *"first steps of slave emancipation in Boston were taken"* Samuel Adams Drake, *Old Landmarks and Historic Personages of Boston* (Boston: James R. Osgood, 1817), 55, 127–35.

64 *their conversion to Christianity* In a letter from Barbados to Rev. Benjamin Coleman, Hall inveighed against those who treated "our poor slaves as if they had no more Souls than Brutes, & were really a Species below Us." Hugh Hall, letter to Rev. Benjamin Coleman, March 30, 1720, Benjamin Coleman Papers, Massachusetts Historical Society, Boston.

64 *kept up with each other* Williams and Hall had, in their salad days, gotten into trouble together for hazing new students and were forced by the administration to write out a formal apology. *Sibley's Collectanea Bioghica*, vol. 4, 47, Harvard University Archives, Cambridge, Mass.

65 *Stephen Williams . . . did the same* Hugh Hall account book, Massachusetts Historical Society. Another purchaser was Stephen Kellogg from Hadley, Massachusetts, who bought a "Negro girl" for £70.

65 *Terry had once lived in Bristol* It was Anthony who made the final link, making us as sure as we can ever be that this was how Lucy entered America. Two years before the purchase, Terry was living in Barrington, Bristol County, Massachusetts, a town that later became part of Rhode Island. Suffolk County land records show the purchase by "Samuel Terry, of Barrington, Bristol County," of property in Uxbridge, Massachusetts, near Worcester. Suffolk County land records, March 2, 1726, vol. 39, 197, Massachusetts Archives, Boston.

66 *public drunkenness* Terry's financial and professional troubles began shortly before Lucy's arrival. First he and his father were taken to court for a jointly held debt (Hampshire County court records, book 1, 235, Superior Court, Hampshire County). Only months later, on April 18, 1729, he sold most of his properties to Hall, for the enormous sum of £700, to pay off debts to him (Suffolk County judicial records, Supreme Court record 22685, Suffolk Files Collection, Massachusetts Archives). Two years before Lucy arrived, he lost his job as the minister in Barrington, then held successive jobs as cleric and schoolmaster in Middlesex, Massachusetts (*Sibley's Harvard Graduates*, vol. 5 [Boston: Massachusetts Historical Society, 1937], 542–43). When Terry's father died in 1730, his will forgave the younger Samuel's debts to him but left his son no other assets. Samuel had received the benefits of an expensive education and apparently other assistance over the years, so his father attended to the future of his younger sons, who had not had these privileges, leaving Samuel with expensive tastes but straitened circumstances (Hampshire County probate records, box 146, no. 26, Hampshire County Probate Court). A few years after Lucy's arrival, Terry's fortunes worsened. A sawmill he'd owned burned under mysterious conditions. A year later he was convicted of drunkenness (*Sibley's Harvard Graduates*, vol. 5, 543). The next year he and his brothers co-signed on one of his debts, hoping to help him

with a debt he owed to two Connecticut men, but Terry failed to repay it (Hampshire County court records, 1735, vols. 3, 26 and 40).

66 *going into the slave-trading business* Stephen Williams diary, vol. 2, 189, June 18, 1730, Longmeadow Historical Society.

CHAPTER SIX: LUCY GROWS UP

67 *including a number of slaves* George Sheldon, "Negro Slavery in Old Deerfield," *New England Magazine* (March 1893), 51; also in George Sheldon, *History of Deerfield*, vol. 2, 893.

67 *at least one of them was an adult* Deerfield church records, PVMA.

69 *"a prodigy in conversation"* Lemuel Haynes, obituary of Lucy Terry Prince, *Vermont Gazette* 12, no. 41 (July 14, 1821).

72 *"anything she could string"* Sheldon, "Negro Slavery in Old Deerfield," 55; also in George Sheldon, *History of Deerfield*, vol. 2, 897.

73 *strings of beads* Elijah Williams daybook, vol. 1, April 26, 1742–January 16, 1746, PVMA 5380.

73 *credit at the shops* Elijah Williams daybook, vol. 1, December 1743, April 26, 1742–January 16, 1746, PVMA 5380.

74 *theft, drunkenness, and lewdness* Deerfield church records, October 2, 1738.

75 *she was capable of deep irony* George Sheldon, *History of Deerfield*, vol. 1, 905.

77 *"woefully unprepared to war"* All of the information about the wars and periods of peace comes directly from an August 4, 2005, e-mail from Kevin M. Sweeney, history professor at Amherst College and co-author with Evan Hacfeli of *Captors and Captives: The 1704 French and Indian Raid on Deerfield* (Amherst: University of Massachusetts Press, 2003).

77 *on the quiet Monday morning* Epaphrus Hoyt, *Antiquarian Researches: Comprising a History of the Indian Wars in the Country Bordering Connecticut River and Parts Adjacents, and Other Interesting Events* (Greenfield, Mass.: Ansel Phelps, December 1824), 241–42.

78 *the other two decapitated* Judd Manuscripts Collection, misc. 13, 146, Forbes Library. Judd copied this from the *Boston Weekly Post-Boy*.

80 *thirty-three years after Lucy's death* *Springfield Daily Republican*, November 20, 1854. The only other known early version appears as a handwritten copy in Pliny Arms's papers at PVMA (Arms Family Papers, box 13, folder 17). This is therefore undoubtedly the first time it was published. The entire article appeared as part of a series on towns in western Massachusetts. This article so closely resembles the version later published in George Sheldon's *History of Deerfield* that he probably either wrote it himself or gave a reporter his notes.

80 *a long familiarity with the form* Sharon Harris, "Lucy Terry: A Life of Radical Resistance," in *Executing Race: Early American Women's Narratives of Race,*

NOTES

Society, and the Law (Columbus: Ohio State University Press, 2005), 150–81. Whether Harris is right or not, the poem offers clues about Lucy's speech and the speech of those around her. That Lucy rhymes "lack-a-day" with "Canada" shows that the territory to the north was probably pronounced "Canaday" by these frontier people, for instance.

81 *admitted to the fellowship of the church* Deerfield church records, PVMA.

81 *Lucy had to be treated by the doctor* Thomas Williams daybook, PVMA 5406. Dr. Williams treated Lucy with a "blistering plaster" on November 1, 1748.

81 *"he that is called being free is the servant"* Ashley's sermon can be read in full in the Jonathan Ashley folder, PVMA. George Sheldon also includes long extracts from it in *History of Deerfield* and in "Negro Slavery in Old Deerfield."

82 *got him back Boston Weekly Post-Boy,* New England no. 775, October 2, 1749.

82 *Barnard paid £2 for Prince's coffin* Joseph Barnard, June 1752, paid to James Couch, PVMA 5302, 93.

82 *£225 in old currency, or $100* Deerfield manuscripts, box 5-VIII, folder 1, PVMA, and John Williams [Conway] account book, AA.18.27, Historic Northampton.

83 *known as Heber Honesty or Honestman* William L. Chaffin, *History of Easton* (Cambridge, Mass.: John Wilson and Son University Press, 1886), 433–34.

83 *Heber and Susannah knew Lucy and Bijah* Ibid.

83 *Heber and Susannah in their old age* Albert M. Phillips, *Phillips Genealogies* (Worcester, Mass.: Charles Hamilton, 1885), 136.

CHAPTER SEVEN: COURTSHIP AND MARRIAGE

87 *not very successful treatments* Dr. Thomas Williams account book, October 14, 1755, PVMA 5408.

87 *a more dangerous and exciting time* George Sheldon, *History of Deerfield*, vol. 2, 896.

87 *He worked there during the summer* Joseph Barnard account book, July 1738–69, microfilm, PVMA microfilm.

87 *he wasn't a legal resident* Court of Sessions, Hampshire County, book 5, 251.

87 *She bought a fan* Elijah Williams daybook, May 29, 1751, PVMA 5282.

87 *She bought pins and chocolate* Ebenezer Hinsdale account book, January–May 1750, PVMA.

88 *five yards of checked cloth* Ebenezer Hinsdale account book, January–May 1750, July 1, 1751, PVMA.

88 *enough to make a handkerchief* Elijah Williams daybook 1751–53, December 3, 1751, PVMA 5383.

88 *A sheet of drawing paper* Records of Lucy's purchases in Elijah Williams's store can be found in his account books and daybooks, PVMA 5384 and

222

PVMA 5385, for the following dates: June 27, 1754, October 17, 1754, February 28, 1755, May 3, 1755, May 9, 1755, May 26, 1755, May 29, 1755, June 7, 1755, October 17, 1755, November 18, 1755, and November 25, 1755. She also got cash from David Hoyt on August 28, 1754 (David Hoyt account book, PVMA 5341).

88 *three sheets of paper.* Elijah Williams daybook 1751–53, December 3, 1751, PVMA 5383.

89 *a pair of shoe buckles* Elijah Williams daybook, vol. 6, November 13, 1755–May 10, 1756, March 31, 1756, PVMA 5386.

89 *Ishmael bought a pair of gloves* Elijah Williams daybook, vol. 6, April 2, 1756, PVMA 5386.

90 *married on Monday, May 17, 1756* Deerfield town records, PVMA.

91 *Elijah—now Major Williams* Capt. Elijah Williams was promoted to commissary and major on September 27, 1754. *Sibley's Harvard Graduates*, vol. 9 (Boston: Massachusetts Historical Society, 1956), 238.

92 *starvation of people and livestock* Israel Williams Papers, microfilm 923.273 in Deerfield. The originals are in the Massachusetts Historical Society.

92 *severe and often deadly whippings* Fred Anderson, *Crucible of War* (New York: Vintage, 2000), 140.

93 *to buy his wife's freedom* Elijah Williams daybook, vol. 7, May 11,1755–September 27, 1756, PVMA 5387, and Elijah Williams account book, PVMA 5381.

94 *within one of the four forts* For more information on fifers and drummers in early America, see Regimental Drum Major Association at www.drumma jor.net; Metropolitan Museum of Art, "Timelines of Art History: Military Music in the European and American Tradition," at www.metmuseum .org/toah/hd/ammu/hd_ammu.htm; David K. Hildebrand, "About Early American Music," at Colonial Music Institute, www.colonialmusic.org /Resource/DHessay.htm; Folkstreams: The Best of American Folklore Films, www.folkstreams.net.

94 *behind his property on the street* All signs point to this as the way in which Lucy became free. There is no manumission to be found, but the fact that Bijah returned with a soldier's salary and afterward Lucy is no longer listed as Wells's servant strongly suggests that Bijah paid Wells, or that the injured and childless master no longer saw a reason to keep her in bondage, especially since she remained on his land.

94 *Abigail kept up after his death* See Barnard Family Papers, box 9, folder 15, August 15, 1767, PVMA.

94 *across the road that now leads to Greenfield* Pliny Arms, Arms Family Papers, box 13, folder 17, 31, PVMA.

94 *the first freeborn black in Deerfield* Deerfield church records, PVMA.

98 *"Titus & Cato to How & a horse to harrow"* All of these entries, and others, are from Jonathan Ashley's account book, PVMA 5301.

98 *in the style to which they were accustomed* Bruce McClellan, "Grapes and Thorns: A Study Centered upon Parson Jonathan Ashley of Deerfield, Massachusetts, 1712–1780," unpublished book manuscript, PVMA, 136–37.

99 *Ashley would in fact never grant them* See, for example, Elijah Williams daybook, vol. 6, November 13, 1755–May 10, 1756, PVMA 5386.

99 *dismantled a beaver dam for him* Elijah Williams account book/ledger book, May 20, 1757, PVMA 5377, and Elijah Williams daybook, vol. 9, May 28, 1757, PVMA 5389.

99 *it was time to plant crops* Jonathan Ashley account book, July 1, 1757, PVMA 5301, 37 passim.

99 *the doctor, Thomas Williams* Thomas Williams daybook, June 24, 1757, PVMA 5410.

100 *a pair of spectacles* Daybook fragment, February 23–March 27, 1758, attributed to Elijah Williams, March 20, 1758, PVMA 5426.

100 *sealing wax* Joseph Barnard account book, July 1738–69, April 1757, PVMA, and Elijah Williams daybook, vol. 9, August 4, 1757, PVMA 5389.

100 *parrot in a cage* Elijah Williams daybook, August 11, 1757, PVMA 5389.

100 *an inkpot* Elijah Williams daybook, vol. 9, August 26, 1757, PVMA 5389.

101 *Fort Massachusetts* Much of the information on Dr. Thomas Williams's life comes from Mark C. Kestigian, "Early Medical Care in Deerfield," *Historical Journal of Western Massachusetts* 7, no. 2 (June 1979).

101 *when she still served the Wells couple* See, for example, October 23, 1754, Thomas Williams daybook, PVMA 5407, although he also treated her on previous occasions.

102 *To pay the good doctor* Thomas Williams daybook, June 24, 1754, PVMA 5410.

103 *spring-loaded knife* See Oscar Reiss, *Medicine in Colonial America* (Washington, D.C.: University Press of America, 2000), 173–75 and 193–95, and Lester King, *The Medical World of the Eighteenth Century* (Chicago: University of Chicago Press, 1958), 124–29.

103 *lead oxide astringent* All of the Princes' medical records are in Thomas Williams ledger, BV Williams, NYHS.

103 *to buy a mare on Christmas Day* Daniel Arms account book, December 25, 1757, PVMA 5299.

104 *a man named Aaron Scott* Elijah Williams daybook (tavern book), December 4, 1757–January 22, 1761, June 1, 1758, PVMA 5390.

104 *a boat of his own* Caleb Sharp account book, accounts of 1754–95, August

11, 1758, Lucious H. Boltwood Historical and Genealogical Collection, Jones Library.

105 *"Abijah Prince"* Thomas Williams ledger, October 1, 1758, BV Williams, NYHS.

105 *morning sickness and headaches* Thomas Williams ledger, February 8, 1760, BV Williams, NYHS. Most women delivered their babies with the help of midwives, but in the eighteenth century well-trained doctors had a surprising cache of obstetrical procedures at their disposal, and the instructions for postpartum women's care were strict. The mother was to stay in bed for at least ten days, for movement, even sitting up, could cause the uterus to drop and lead to disaster. She was to eat very lightly, mainly sips of broth or wine or ale concoctions, to avoid internal pressures. The room had to be kept either moist or dry, depending upon the weather and the woman's condition. Doctors were on the lookout for the danger signs of hemorrhaging, tearing, or fever, all of which could lead to death.

More startling are the ways in which doctors and even trained midwives dealt with difficult deliveries. The accepted maxim was that if the lives of the mother and baby were both threatened, it was the mother who was to be saved. If the delivery could not proceed naturally because of pelvic obstruction or a similar cause, the only remedy was to perform what we today call partial-birth abortion in order to save the mother's life. Cesarean sections were almost never performed on living women, since none of those attempted (with the exception of one performed by a midwife in England who was rumored to have managed a successful one with the use of a razor, a tailor's needle, and silk thread) had succeeded. If the mother died, a cesarean would be performed immediately to save the child. Above all, doctors watched for puerperal fever, the cause of so many childbirth deaths, especially later in the nineteenth century, before physicians learned to wash their hands when moving from the autopsy table to the childbirth bed. See J. Kirkpatrick, M.D., *Advice to the People in General, with Regard to Their Health* (London, n.p., 1767).

105 *by delicate spoonfuls* Elijah Williams daybook, vol. 2, September 18–December 1, 1760, PVMA 5392.

105 *women who had just delivered babies* Kirkpatrick, *Advice to the People in General, with Regard to Their Health*, 13.

106 *dressed her injuries* Dr. Thomas Williams ledger, BV Williams, NYHS.

106 *she was finally baptized* Deerfield church records, PVMA.

106 *Stockbridge, Massachusetts* Dwight Collection, Hampshire/Franklin County Papers, 22, Norman Rockwell Museum, Stockbridge, Mass.

106 *William Williams in Pittsfield* William Williams Collection, December 16, 1766, Berkshire Athenaeum, 219.

CHAPTER NINE: GETTING TO GUILFORD

112 *building a house* Broad Brook Grange, *Official History of Guilford,* 12.

112 *building a small house* David Field contract with Moses Brooks, January 1, 1743, Field Family Papers, folder 7, PVMA.

113 *into his personal holdings* Broad Brook Grange, *Official History of Guilford,* 9–10.

114 *"fines and broken windows"* Sibley's Harvard Graduates, vol. 6 (Boston: Massachusetts Historical Society, 1942), 113.

114 *"a great deal of insolence & ill manners"* Ibid., 114.

114 *"Spanish bankrupt"* Ibid., 116, 117.

115 *some of the most prominent New Englanders of his time* For more on the land speculators, see Roy Hidemichi Akagi, *The Town Proprietors of the New England Colonies* (Philadelphia: University of Pennsylvania Press, 1924), 209–10.

116 *Elijah's purchases from Searles* See Elijah Williams, ledger B, PVMA. On January 7, 1755, Williams made purchases from several Northampton people, including Isaac Searles, from whom he bought 100 pounds of tobacco.

116 *twenty other complainants* Israel Williams to A. Oliver, Israel Williams Papers, microfilm 923.273, PVMA; original housed in the Massachusetts Historical Society as 71-D-235.

116 *"spared no pains to obtain their designs"* The others whom Williams cites include "Hudson—Warren—three Staffords Searls and Vanowen." Israel Williams to A. Oliver, July 20, 1756, Israel Williams Papers, microfilm 923.273, PVMA; original housed in the Massachusetts Historical Society as 71-D-235.

116 *He begged Williams to withdraw punishment* Israel Williams Papers, microfilm 923.273, PVMA; original housed in the Massachusetts Historical Society.

117 *Searles did indeed manage to take it over* Matthew Thornton letter, November 17, 1760, Peter Force Collection, series 9, container 9, Library of Congress.

117 *the story of Sunderland's origins in 1761.* The Sunderland grant is not housed in the town clerk's office but can be found in *New Hampshire Provincial and State Papers,* vol. 26, 481–84.

118 *a New Hampshire grant for Guilford back in 1754* Charles Coates of Northampton, who had served in Bijah's 1747 regiment, needed the Guilford property for his own family and was glad to move there, but most of the others had no plans to live there themselves. Several other Deerfield men became proprietors of Guilford in a tangle of holdings, sales, and trades that later gave nightmares to their executors. Broad Brook Grange, *Official History of Guilford,* 115.

118 *the entire grant was likely to be forfeited* Broad Brook Grange, *Official History of Guilford,* 15.

119 *"nothing done by the grantees thereon"* New Hampshire Records and Archives, 47, (n.d.).

119 *Wentworth . . . gave it to them* Wilmington Regrant, 1763, Albert Stillman Batchellor, *The New Hampshire Grants Being Transcripts of the Charters of Townships*, vol. 26, Town Charters, vol. 3 (Concord: Edward N. Pearson, 1895), 560–64.

119 *whites who had known him when he was a slave* Leaving our own Guilford house each morning, Anthony began the tedious tracking of intricate and multiple land transactions. Kate Snow, who worked in the town office, made space for him as he went through the bound volumes of Guilford land records. Even here the history of Vermont warfare stymied him: when the violent divisions between Yorkers and Vermonters, two factions vying for the territory that would eventually become the state of Vermont, heated up, Guilford had two competing governments, each keeping separate records. The earliest documents, buried for safekeeping underneath the old Guilford town pound, eventually rotted or disappeared.

The confusion stemmed from the claim, published by Sheldon in his exhaustive history of Deerfield, that a man named David Field had honored his father's wishes and given Bijah one hundred acres in Guilford; Field's descendants declared this as well. We finally understood that the claim was wrong: it turned out that Elijah Williams originally had owned their land and that Field had nothing at all to do with it.

120 *"hetcheling"* Hetcheling required pulling the stalks through nails protruding from a board, progressing to finer nails, and then using what's called a comb, until they were fine fibers that could be spun and woven into fabric.

122 *Lucy survived her fertile years* It is possible, however, that they lost a child: Lucy's obituary states that she had seven children, but I have been unable to corroborate this.

122 *register the births of the five children* I am grateful to David Proper, who, in his booklet *Lucy Terry: Singer of History*, notes the coincidence of these dates. David Proper's booklet is published by Deerfield, Mass.: Pocumtuck Valley Memorial Association and Historic Deerfield, 1997.

123 *a third primer* Elijah Williams daybook, vol. 14, June 22, 1764–July 31, 1765, 5, PVMA 5394.

123 *they disappear from the records again* Elijah Williams daybook, vol. 5, August 10, 1765–November 14, 1772, March 21, 1766, PVMA 5395.

124 *Ralph Way* Salah Barnard daybook, January 23, 1767, PVMA 5306. "Indenture" was a word that meant simply contract and covered all sorts of commitments, but it also could refer to an apprenticeship. Later circumstances strongly suggest that Caesar was indentured to Ralph Way.

125 *several weeks afterward* Thomas Williams ledger, April 27, 28, 29, and 30, 1767, May 1, 2, 5, and 10, 1767, NYHS.

125 *a man and horse to transport him* Salah Barnard daybook, May 18, 1767, PVMA 5306.

125 *Lucy spun flax for the doctor* Salah Barnard daybook, PVMA 5306, and Dr. Thomas Williams ledger, NYHS, both June 22, 1767. The flax was sold to Dr. Williams. Thomas Williams ledger, May 1, 1767.

126 *Darby* Salah Barnard account book, PVMA 5306.

126 *"his Estate torn in pieces"* Stephen Williams diary, book 7, April 16, 1768, 65, Storrs Library. For more on Elijah Williams's financial troubles, see Sweeney, "Gentleman Farmers and Inland Merchants," and "River Gods in the Making."

127 *to rescue the overextended businessman in 1769* Stephen Williams diary, April 11, 1769, vol. 7, 154, Storrs Library.

127 *in the process of settling* Hampden County land records, book 9, 664–66.

127 *leaving his lands in the hands of his creditors.* Town of Guilford land records, book 4, 94.

128 *castrated* Deerfield town papers, 4, meeting house and church, box 1, 4-I, C, Pastors and Ministers 1729–2000, PVMA.

128 *Ashley had had his slave "cut"* Ashley Papers, box 3, titled "To the church of Christ in Deerfield, May 25, 1780," PVMA.

128 *an enormously unpopular man* George Sheldon, *History of Deerfield*, vol. 1, 537.

129 *"Cato's money"* George Sheldon, "Negro Slavery in Old Deerfield," 55; see also Sheldon, *History of Deerfield*, vol. 2, 898. Cato spent his entire life in the Ashley household until his death in 1825 when he was nearly ninety. George Sheldon, a small child when Cato was an old man, recalled "seeing him often sitting on a bench in an outhouse, where he would spend hours singing in a gruff voice the famous ballad of Captain Kidd, drumming an accompaniment on the board at each side, with both hands; his finger nails were long and thick and each one gave a blow which sounded like the stroke of a tack hammer." As a younger man, Cato had loved dancing and riding horses, fast, protesting if admonished that he had been unable to stop the animal. But in old age he could never get warm, particularly after the family replaced the fireplace with a cookstove; in freezing frustration, he would race to the fire in Dorothy Ashley's room.

129 *"dead as a hammer"* George Sheldon, "Negro Slavery in Old Deerfield," 55.

130 *the happiest years of the two women's lives* 2003 conversation with Bob Romer.

130 *arrested and sentenced for attempted rape.* Hampshire County court records, Court of Sessions, November 1772, book 13, 59.

CHAPTER TEN: BATTLES ON THE HOME FRONT

132 *"gone to school with the white children"* A schoolteacher's account of his students in Sunderland, Vermont, in 1826 refers to one as "Miss Negress." Is it possible that this was Festus's daughter? Samuel McKee, diary, February 7, 1826, 119, Dorothy Canfield Library, Arlington, Vt.

133 *service on the loyalist side* For more information on what happened to these soldiers, see Gretchen Holbrook Gerzina, *Black London: Life Before Emancipation* (New Brunswick, N.J.: Rutgers University Press, 1995).

133 *exempt . . . Harvard faculty and students, from conscription* O'Reilly Papers, vol. 5, case 40, 11, NYHS.

133 *on the Lexington Green* Henry Weincek, *An Imperfect God: George Washington, His Slaves, and the Creation of America* (New York: Farrar, Straus & Giroux, 2003), 200–203.

133 *under the famous Thaddeus Kosciusko Massachusetts Soldiers and Sailors in the War of the Revolution*, vol. 8 (Boston: Wright & Potter, 1904), 64, 477; see also Bernard A. Drew, *If the Door Closes on You, Go in the Window* (Great Barrington, Mass.: Attic Revivals Press, 2004), 16.

133 *a striking figure in old age* Agrippa Hull's portrait, the only image of any major black figure in this book, hangs in the Stockbridge Library Association Historical Collection, Stockbridge, Massachusetts. His descendants still reside in Stockbridge.

133 *July 11, 1777 Muster Rolls of the Revolutionary War*, vol. 21, 95, Massachusetts Archives. Caesar enlisted on July 11, 1777, in Capt. Caleb Montague's company, Col. Samuel Williams Regiment of Militia, as a private, and served until August 12. He reenlisted in 1779. Wherever he went in 1777, it was as much as 60 miles from the location where he enlisted.

134 *Battle of Saratoga.* Most of this information, including the quotation, comes from "Burgoyne Campaign of 1777," at www.u-s-history.com/pages/h1298.html.

134 *"if no large force could be permanently maintained"* William Hubbard pension file S29914, NARA.

136 *mustered into the Continental Army* At his first enlistment, Festus is described as among those "detached from the Militia of the County of Berkshire to Serve in the Continental Army" (Walter Rockwell Papers, box 1, NYHS). We can safely conclude that he was already living in Stockbridge and serving as part of its militia, rather than joining from afar. He enlisted after the Continental Congress directed Massachusetts to raise two thousand men for nine-month terms. The Massachusetts Resolve reflecting this dictum said that towns were barred from enlisting any who were not its residents. For this initial service, he was paid £60.

136 *Stockbridge, Massachusetts, company* Massachusetts Soldiers and Sailors of the *Revolutionary War* (Boston: Wright & Potter, 1904), 790.

136 *collected a bounty* Walker Rockwell Papers, box 1, NYHS, source for Isaac Marsh account book, 71–170.2, Stockbridge Library.

136 *Caesar reenlisted that autumn* Muster Rolls of the Revolutionary War, vol. 21, 39, Massachusetts Archives.

136 *Agrippa's brother Amos* Peter Force Papers, series 7E, reel 27, Library of Congress.

136 *a catering bill . . . for "musick"* S. C. Sedgwick and C. S. Maynard, *Stockbridge 1739–1939: A Chronicle* (Great Barrington, Mass.: Berkshire Courier, 1939), 170. It was a bill submitted for a ball.

137 *threw a party* Sedgwick and Maynard, *Stockbridge 1739–1939*, 145.

137 *Agrippa never lived it down* "An Uncommon Man's Bicentennial," in "Bygone Berkshire" column, *Berkshire Eagle*, August 15, 1959.

137 *old horse, with a saddle and bridle* George Sheldon, "Negro Slavery in Old Deerfield," 35. Also published in George Sheldon, *History of Deerfield*, vol. 2, 900.

137 *listed his occupation as fiddler* Justice of the Peace case files, box 105, Windham County courthouse.

137 *inspiring them in battle* Muster Rolls of the Revolutionary War, vol. 27, 62 (microfilm), Massachusetts Archives.

138 *the same rate as corporals* A bill in Congress in 1778 set the pay rates. A fifer or drummer made about $7.30 a month, the same as a corporal, as opposed to a private, who got $6.65 or so. Peter Force Papers, series 7E, reel 27, Library of Congress.

138 *full musical bands* Robert K. Wright Jr., *The Continental Army* (Washington, D.C.: U.S. Army, Center of Military History, 1983), 38.

138 *they marched back to West Point* This information courtesy of John Hannigan, the archivist at the Massachusetts Archives. An officer at Camp Totoway in New Jersey, where Festus may have spent part of his time, wrote to his superior to look into a complaint that a man (probably a slave owner who resented not having the use of his so-called property) raised about "two Nogres [*sic*] In the Massachusetts Line Held as soldiers for the War; contrary to his Inclination." Orderly books, reel 13, 129, October 7–November 19, 1780, NYHS.

138 *center of the action at West Point* Muster Rolls of the Revolutionary War, vol. 4, 229, Massachusetts Archives.

139 *keeping deserters in as enemies out* See the National Park Service website for Fort Stanwix, New York, "Soldier's Day Program," at www.nps.gov/fost/edpackets/fourthsoldier.htm. The educational packet gives much of this valuable information for the use of teachers and students preparing to visit the fort.

139 *their liquor was confiscated* Information about duties for Festus's company and the others while he was stationed at West Point comes from the orderly books, reel 8, 89.2; reel 12, 118.1, 122, and 123; reel 13, 125, 128, 129, 130, and 131; reel 14, 144; reel 15, 151, 153, 154, 155, and 156; and reel 17, 176; all at NYHS.

139 *mending his uniform* National Park Service, "Soldier's Day Program."

140 *eventually tried and hanged* John André Collection, New York State Library, Albany.

140 *"passion and temper."* Maj. Gen. Alexander McDougall letter, December 15, 1781, McDougall Papers, reel 3, NYHS.

140 *in the frigid winter.* Ibid.

141 *Lafayette, under whom Festus probably served* On the horse guard, see *Massachusetts Soldiers and Sailors in the Revolution*, 790; on Festus serving indirectly under Lafayette, orderly book 130, reel 13, NYHS.

141 *he served as a drummer Massachusetts Soldiers and Sailors in the Revolution*, 790.

141 *to work in the shop of a cooper* See the court case Bijah brought against Abner Turner for nonpayment of wages, *Prince vs. Turner*, 1780 November term, Hampshire County Court of Common Pleas.

141 *reputed . . . to be a poet* Broad Brook Grange, *Official History of Guilford*, 146.

141 *everyday life in an established town* Entries in David Hoyt account book, 1768–1803, September 1782–November 1783, PVMA 5342.

142 *Zadock Hawks, the shoemaker* Zadock Hawks account book, July 1783, PVMA 5329.

142 *she bought him a mug of flip* All of the entries for these transactions appear in David Hoyt account book, PVMA. Cill Prince began purchasing things at his shop in September 1782 and worked until November 1783.

142 *plea for civility and unity* Broad Brook Grange, *Official History of Guilford*, 28.

146 *"greatly Despaired of"* Tateny *Prince vs. Joseph Stanton*, Justice of the Peace case files, box 105, Windham County courthouse, and *Abijah Prince Jr. vs. Joseph Stanton*, Justice of the Peace case files, box 105, Windham County courthouse.

146 *if he didn't pay Prince v. Turner*, 1780 November term, Hampshire County Court of Common Pleas.

146 *destroy the Princes' crops Abijah Prince vs. John Nois*, Justice of the Peace case files, box 105, Windham County courthouse.

147 *never paid them John Noyes vs. Abijah Prince*, Justice of the Peace case files, box 110, Windham County courthouse.

147 *no land was assigned to him* Town of Northfield records, reel 3, Dickinson Memorial Library.

148 *a cash settlement of £5* "A List of the Polls and Estates Real and Personal take in Northfield, August ye 10:1751," Town of Northfield valuation list, reel 1, Dickinson Memorial Library. Abijah's name is crossed out on this list. He

doesn't appear before this year, nor in 1752, suggesting that they may have removed him immediately after he gained his proprietorship and left town. Perhaps the reason he settled for such a small amount is that taxes would have accrued over the thirty years.

148 *sealing wax* Northfield town papers, Stratton family misc., PVMA, and Hampshire County Grantor Index, 1787–1889.

148 *recording the sale the next year* Northfield town papers, Stratton family misc., PVMA, and Hampshire County Grantor Index, 1787–1889, book 16, 117.

149 *her family attended services* The fact that Bijah's death was recorded by the church's minister indicates that they participated in the church. Lucy certainly would have attended church services. There is a "Caesar," no last name, listed among the early church members, but Caesar Prince probably never lived in Guilford, and his last name was always used in documents—the Prince family always insisted that their last name be used in all documents. There was, however, another Caesar in the town, probably a hired hand or servant to a white family. Anthony found a case in which this Caesar, no last name, sued a Guilford resident named Thomas Cutler for twelve shillings. Windham County court records, Justice of the Peace case files, box 110.

149 *known to see angels and have visions* Gertrude S. Richmond Thayer, "The Noyes Family of Guilford, Vermont," in *The Vermonter* 41, no. 11 (November 1936), 230–31. At the time of Nathan's conversion, he saw a white throne "and one seated upon it clothed in white," surrounded by twenty-four elders singing his praises and casting golden crowns at his feet (Nathan Noyes, *A Short Account of the Life and Experience of Nathan Noyes* [Detroit: Bagg & Harmon, 1847], 14). There was a less religious aspect to some of this as well, for close by, near to both families, lived "Old Mother Honeywell," a Noyes relative rumored to be a witch and blamed for a series of otherwise inexplicable occurrences. Some were delighted when a white owl was shot and Mother Honeywell fell and hurt herself badly at the same time, and even more so when they discovered a stuffed white owl standing on the Noyes mantelpiece.

150 *debt, trespass, destruction of property David Burros vs. Abijah Prince*, Justice of the Peace case files, box 110, Windham County courthouse. Noyes encouraged Burrows to sue for nineteen shillings that Bijah had borrowed, but because Burrows lived outside of Vermont, the law required that a bond be given by the plaintiff in order for him to be able to prosecute the case. Noyes paid that bond so that Burrows could take Bijah to court. Furthermore, Burrows now was demanding more than thirty-nine shillings, adding the extra twenty for damages.

150 *a list of witnesses to call Abijah Prince vs. James Burrows*, witnesses summons, November 22, 1784, Justice of the Peace case files, box 105, Windham County courthouse.

151 *entered it as evidence. Abijah Prince vs. James Burrows,* Justice of the Peace case files, box 105, Windham County courthouse. The page from Abijah's book is found in a separate file.

152 *seize his property* Justice of the Peace case files, box 105, Windham County courthouse.

152 *decided for Bijah once again* Judgment of *C—Burrows vs. Abijah Prince,* Justice of the Peace case files, box 105, Windham County courthouse. It turned out that their lawyer, Samuel Knight, was the justice of the peace who had decided in their favor in the previous Burrows suit.

152 *living on their own* Tatnai, who was living in Northfield the following year, probably had already moved down there to Bijah's old town, perhaps working in either the tavern of Benjamin Doolittle's son Lucious or that of Elisha Hunt.

152 *Scipio Smith* Windham County court records, 1772–1789, box 1.

152 *setting his livestock upon the crops Abijah Prince vs. Amos Noyes,* summons, Justice of the Peace case files, box 105, Windham County courthouse.

CHAPTER ELEVEN: LUCY GOES TO COURT

154 *with whom she could stay* A black man named Peter Thomas was warned out of Thetford, Vermont, on May 5, 1786 (Thetford town papers, Thetford Historical Society) and often shopped in Norwich; some of his purchases suggest that he may have been living in Norwich at that time. Peter Olcott account book, in "Account Books Norwich 91," Rauner Library, Dartmouth College.

156 *"fall upon the Charity of the Town"* E. P. Walton, ed., *Records of the Governor and Council of the State of Vermont,* vol. 3 (Montpelier: Steam Press, 1875), 66.

156 *breaking into the Princes' property Abijah Prince vs. Amos Noyes,* witnesses summons, July 22 and 25, 1785, Justice of the Peace case files, box 105, Windham County courthouse. The sheriff was told on July 25 to summon witnesses for the case. Josiah Bennet, Aaron Bennet, David Culver, all neighbors, had been summoned three days earlier, and on the twenty-fifth Gershon Noyes, John Noyes, William Burrows, John Burrows, and Rufus Fisk—all of whom had been involved in previous legal battles with the Princes—were called, as were John Stafford and Stukely Stafford.

156 *that the fence was covered with frost and snow* Amos Noyes statement, no title, Windham County, *Abijah Prince vs. Amos Noyes,* Justice of the Peace case files, box 105, Windham County courthouse.

156 *pay Bijah for damages and the court for costs Abijah Prince vs. Amos Noyes,* Justice of the Peace case files, box 105, Windham County courthouse.

157 *"a countenance that bespoke authority"* William Tyler Arms, *History of Leyden, Massachusetts* (Orange, Mass.: Enterprise and Journal, 1959), 92.

157 *a genteel and well-liked sawmill owner [Zerah] Brooks vs. [Oliver] Waters,* Windham County court records, box 1.

157 *at Joseph Martin's house [Elizabeth] Goulding v. Oliver Waters,* Windham County court records, box 1.

157 *a black man named Robert* This took place in Leyden, Massachusetts. Hampshire County court records, Court of Sessions, August 1784, book 14, 161. Joseph Martin pled no contest.

157 *His brother went free* Hampshire County Court of Inferior Common Pleas, docket 68, May 18–22, 1784, 210, and August 31–September 8, 1784, 8.

157 *two jailers were hired to guard him* Hampshire County court records, Court of Sessions, August 1784, book 14, 161.

158 *broke down the Princes' door and attacked Scipio Smith* Windham County court records, 1772–89, box 1. Scipio was forty-seven at the time of the riot, according to the age given at his death in the Northampton church records, Forbes Library.

158 *fled for Leyden* Windham County court records, Justice of the Peace case files, 1781–1806, box 107.

159 *Bigelow asked that the dispute be allowed to die quietly* William Bigelow to Stephen Row Bradley, Bradley Family General Correspondence to S. Bradley, 1780–81, box I, Special Collections, University of Vermont.

159 *until his fine was paid* Windham County Court, vol. 257, 156.

159 *Noyes bailed him out* Windham County court records, Justice of the Peace case files, box 124.

160 *the nephew of Aaron Burt* Windham County court records, Justice of the Peace case files, 1781–1806, box 107, and Windham County court records, 1772–89, box 1. The judges in Rufus Fisk's trial were Luke Knowlton, John Bridgman, Samuel Fletcher, and Benjamin Burt.

160 *"slave plantation country"* Telephone conversation with Warren Perry, August 2005.

160 *wealthy farmers, professionals, and clergy* Guocon Yang, "From Slavery to Emancipation: The African Americans of Connecticut, 1650s to 1820s," PhD diss., 1999, 237, quoted in Kari J. Winter, ed., *The Blind African Slave, or Memoirs of Boyrereau Brinch, Nicknamed Jeffrey Brace* (Madison: University of Wisconsin Press, 2004), 35.

160 *at least one Indian* The probate for John Noyes, who died in 1751, shows that he left an Indian girl named Mary Woppleton to his wife. New London probate packets, reel 997, Connecticut State Library.

161 *to get ahead politically* This letter, dated November 15, 1804, and written from Washington, D.C., by Congressman James Elliot, was leaked to the

newspaper and was later reprinted in *The Green Mountain Patriot* (Peacham, Vermont), August 27, 1805.

CHAPTER TWELVE: BIJAH'S LAST YEARS

162 *were expecting a baby* They married on January 24, 1786. Hadley town records, 10, Forbes Library microfilm.

162 *its tiny coffin* Samuel Gaylor Jr. of Hadley account book, 179, PVMA.

162 *a quart of rum* "'Historical Sketch' read by Phineas Field of Charlemont at the Meeting of the PVM Association, February 25, 1879," in bound volume of PVMA meeting records.

163 *during these difficult times* Winter, *The Blind African Slave*, 172–76, 168–69.

163 *wood for fires and fencing* Guilford town records, book 4, 94, Guilford Town Office.

163 *was not leaving his family homeless* We were puzzled by not being able to find the Princes in the U.S. census for 1790. However, it turned out that for the census that year, instead of the census taker going from house to house, residents were expected to report to the marshal for their district to give their information. Obviously, there was a lot of room for slippage in such a system. See Ruby Coleman, "Outsmarting the Census Enumerator, Transcriber and Indexer, Part 2," at New England Historic Genealogical Society, www.newenglandancestors. org/education/articles/research/special_guests/rc_outsmart_census2.asp.

164 *Cill was once again living there* Drucilla Prince and a number of others, including the sons of some prominent Deerfield residents, were on the list of warnings out for 1790. "Warning out of town 1752–1792," Deerfield Manuscripts, PVMA, box 4, folder 2, town offices.

164 *Anna Harris from Coventry* First Coventry Congregational church records, reel 463, Connecticut State Library. We know that Anna was African American because in 1830 she asked to be released from her church in order to join the Temple Street Church in New Haven, "the church of colored persons." Woodbury First Congregational Church records, reel 419, vol. 2, 47.

164 *Abijah Jr. and Anna's baby died* Columbia Congregational (Lebanon Crank), 1722–1917, vol. 5, 359, Connecticut church records, State Library Index, reel 159.

164 *Abijah Jr. himself died* Connecticut church records, State Library Index, Columbia Congregational (Lebanon Crank), 1722–1917, vol. 5, 360.

165 *during the January thaw* Jeremiah Lyons diary, Colrain, Mass., diaries, box 1, New York Public Library Special Collections.

165 *Bijah died* Guilford church records, Vermont Historical Society.

165 *one of Guilford's most important early residents* Broad Brook Grange, *Official History of Guilford*, 146.

165 *"committing other enormities"*Windham County court proceedings, June 1793–June 1795, vol. WMC 258, 245. John Noyes Jr. was arrested in June 1795.

166 *come to avenge his family* Broad Brook Grange, *Official History of Guilford*, 146–47.

167 *"old colored pioneer"* Ibid., 333, 146.

167 *Noyes and his wife died* Connecticut Herald, obituary, November 20, 1827.

168 *"my wife Sally has eloped"* Vermont Gazette, December 5, 1794, vol. 12, issue 28, 4. This wording differs from the version given by Marcia Hoffman Rising, in *Vermont Newspaper Abstracts 1783–1816* (Boston: New England Historic Genealogical Society, 2001), 132.

168 *administrators of his estate* Marlboro District Court, Brattleboro, Vt.

CHAPTER THIRTEEN: BETRAYED

174 *months passed between sessions* All the information about when the various court sessions met, and where, comes from *Laws of the State of Vermont Revised and Passed by the Legislature in the Year of Our Lord 1797* (Rutland: Josiah Fay, 1798).

175 *"villas are destined to rise"* John A. Graham, *A Descriptive Sketch of the Present State of Vermont* (Bennington: Vermont Heritage Press, 1987; first published 1797), 44–45.

176 *or thought it unimportant* Boston Post-Boy, September 7, 1761.

176 *land sold at "vendue"* Boston Post-Boy, August 8, 1763.

176 *a slave for sale* Boston Post-Boy, August 22, 1763.

176 *was present to make a bid* Paul S. Gillies, "The Vendue: The Exercise of Geo-Catharsis." "Ruminations" column, *Vermont Bar Journal* (Summer 2005), 9–12.

177 *Caesar, Festus, Duruxa, and Drucilla decades later* Sunderland town records, book 4, 226, Sunderland Town Clerk Office.

177 *two sets of minutes* All of this appears in the various books at the Sunderland town clerk's office. See Sunderland proprietors records, 50 (the original version of the minutes is on p. 11) and an unpaginated page; Sunderland town records, book 4, 225, 226. The Boston Post-Boy advertisement appeared on August 8, 1763.

177 *not on the Sunderland land* Vermont Gazette, September 4, 1783, vol. 1, issue 14, 4.

178 *where they all lived when they arrived* The ad that Caesar put in the newspaper about Sally leaving him in 1794 indicates that he lived in Manchester. It is not clear how long he stayed there. Festus showed up in Guilford in 1798 to collect some money the town owed him, so perhaps he and Lucy and her daughters stayed on longer than we imagined. Tatnai probably stayed behind for a while: he was assessed at one poll in Northfield for the

year 1796 (Northfield Papers, box 1, PVMA). By 1800 Caesar and Tatnai were living in Vergennes.

178 *faced Brownson in county court* All the information concerning these lawsuits comes from the two-page notebook entries in David Fay's daybook. David Fay daybook, Park McCullough Collection, Sec. 101, box 101–A, item 101–3, University of Vermont Special Collections. Why, though, do we find Festus back in Guilford at this time, being paid a large amount of money by the town? Guilford town treasurer's book, 1800–1839, September 13, 1798, Guilford Town Office.

179 *a sizable amount in back wages* Jedediah West, Manchester District Probate Court, microfilm 2740, vol. 2, 153, Vermont Public Records Office, Middlesex, Vt.

180 *for not paying them in turn* According to an advertisement (giving notice to debtors and creditors) in the *Middlebury Mercury*, Bissel Case, merchant, went into bankruptcy sometime before February 22, 1804. *Middlebury Mercury*, vol. 3, issue 13, 4. See also Vergennes town records, vol. A, 140 and 201, for Case keeping an inn; January 1801, Addison County judgments, box AS-00102, Vermont State Archives; Thomas Byrd daybook 4, 386, Rokeby Museum, Ferrisburgh, Vt.; Smith & Woodbridge account book, vol. 1, 9.

181 *living with white families* Some of the African Americans living in Addison County were William Ferris, Peter Hunter, Trovo Newport, and Brewster Nichols. Second Census of the United States, Addison County, Vt.

181 *receiving mail in local post offices* Festus's letter was notified in the *Vermont Gazette*, November 17, 1800, vol. 1, issue 36, 1. The letter was waiting for him a month earlier than this date, so perhaps this was a second notice. Lucy's letter was notified in *The Ploughman, or Republican Federalist* (Bennington newspaper), vol. 1, 7, August 24, 1801.

181 *an enormous abscess* Vermont Gazette, December 21, 1800. See also Rising, *Vermont Newspaper Abstracts 1783–1816*, 207.

181 *rescheduled for June* I cannot be sure that this was the reason for the continuation, but it makes sense that having just suffered his wife's terrible final illness and death, Brownson would not have been in court.

182 *never argued a case in front of the U.S. Supreme Court* We still couldn't quite make other pieces of the legend fit either. Royall Tyler, the famous writer who had lived in Guilford when the Princes did, and was said to have been Brownson's legal counsel, was serving on the state supreme court in those years. He took on private cases in the Bennington region, but there is nothing to link him to this particular case as a lawyer, though he did serve as a judge when the second case went to the supreme court. A letter from Tyler dated February 14, 1800, refers to his needing to travel for court business in Rutland and needing

to go to Bennington the next week to argue cases. The Princes were not in court during these months (letter from Royall Tyler to an unknown correspondent, quoted in an unpublished biography written by his son, Thomas Pickman Tyler, "Memoirs of Hon. Royall Tyler—Late-Chief Justice of Vermont" [Royall Tyler Collection, Vermont Historical Society]). Tyler served on the Vermont Supreme Court from October 1801 to October 1806 (and perhaps beyond).

Also sitting during the second case were Jonathan Robinson and Theopholus Herrington, the man who went down in Vermont history for supposedly declaring about this time in a fugitive slave case that if the master had a deed for a slave, it had better be "from God Almighty" (Vermont Anti-Slavery Society, annual report, Vermont Historical Society).

Tyler too was an ardent abolitionist. His son described his views on slavery as "decided, pronounced, and far in advance of those then prevalent" and ascribed the "God Almighty" statement to Tyler rather than to Herrington; he asserts that all the judges shared this strong antislavery sentiment (Tyler, "Memoirs of Hon. Royall Tyler—Late-Chief Justice of Vermont," 96). It seems extremely unlikely that a man who held such beliefs and who, as a Guilford resident, must have been aware of the attacks there against the Princes would travel all the way to Bennington to represent their opponent. Might he have represented the Princes? It wouldn't be the first time during those years that he took on a case being argued before the court on which he served, as other judges also did, stepping down from the bench to act as lawyers. In Tyler's paper is an account for a case he represented over a four-year span, while also serving as a judge on the supreme court (Royall Tyler Papers, doc. 45, folder 14, Vermont Historical Society).

182 *"many respectable acquaintances"* Winter, *The Blind African Slave,* 171.

183 *"wearing out your welcome"* E-mail message from Paul Gillies to Anthony, March 28, 2006.

183 *before the state supreme court, in February 1803* There were so many things that seem to be incorrect about the legend. The case was argued before the Vermont Supreme Court, not the U.S. Supreme Court. David Fay was Brownson's lawyer, not Royall Tyler or Stephen Row Bradley. Indeed, the Princes had probably known these two men in Guilford, and both men were now serving on the state supreme court. Festus's trip to Guilford back in 1798 may have been a chance for him, and not Brownson, to consult with one or both of them. Later, when Bradley became a U.S. senator, he introduced anti–slave trade legislation to that body, matched in the House of Representatives by a similar bill introduced by another Vermonter, Gideon Olin (*Middlebury Mercury,* January 8, 1806, 3; see also Raymond B. Zirblis, *Friends of Freedom: The Vermont Underground Railroad Survey Report* [State

of Vermont, Vermont Department of State Buildings and Vermont Division for Historic Preservation, December 12, 1996], 21). This is at the same time that Britain was introducing anti–slave trade bills into Parliament.

According to the legend, Bennington lawyer Isaac Tichenor (or Ticknor), who was on the state supreme court until the year before the Princes first brought suit and then governor for the duration of the cases, helped Lucy to prepare her case. A perfectly dressed and much admired man known as "Jersey Slick" because of the place of his birth and his impeccable manners, he had gone to Guilford to explain to the town the act passed to quell the Yorker and Vermonter difficulties during the last war (Walter Hill Crockett, *Vermont: The Green Mountain State*, vol. 5 [New York: Century History Co., 1923], 66–67).

He was also strongly antislavery, remarking in his gubernatorial inauguration address of 1805 that "it cannot, I flatter myself, be necessary that I should impress on your minds that the genius of universal emancipation ought to be cherished by Americans; that there is not complexion incompatible with freedom." Walter Hill Crockett, *History of Vermont*, vol. 2 (New York: Century History Co., 1921), 596.

184 *compensate them for their effort* The Settlement Act is given in *State Papers of Vermont*, vol. 3, *Journals and Proceedings* (Bellows Falls: Wyndam Press, 1928), 153; the Betterment Act is from *Records of the Governor and Council of the State of Vermont*, vol. 3 (Montpelier: Steam Press of J & J.M. Poland, 1875), 349; the Quietening Act is discussed in Daniel Chipman, *The Life of Hon. Nathaniel Chipman, LL.D.* (Boston: Charles C. Little & James Brown, 1846), 62–65.

185 *just as Lucy was handed another court victory* Vermont Gazette, August 7, 1804.

186 *voted down helping "the negroes"* Sunderland town records, book 5, 474–75.

187 *have a right to it* Sunderland town records, book 5, 474–75.

187 *"Lucy Prince and Durackey Prince"* Sunderland town records, book 5, 475.

187 *Lucy and her disabled daughter* Sunderland town records, book 5, 476, 477, 478.

187 *"Lucy Prince & her heirs"* Sunderland town records, vol. 5, 225.

188 *when he lost the suit* The town paid Brownson $220 on September 3, 1806. Sunderland town records, book 5, 225.

188 *sold his fifty acres for $100* Festus sold his fifty-acre lot, number 20, to Remembrance Sheldon of Williamstown, Mass., for $100 on September 26, 1807. Sunderland town records, book 5, 240.

CHAPTER FOURTEEN: THE NEGRO HOUSE

189 *a new building in town* Paul Champlin ledger, vol. 1, Henry Sheldon Museum of Vermont History, Middlebury.

190 *a white girl from Leicester, Lucy Holman* Leicester is near Middlebury.

191 *announcing the marriage in the* Middlebury Mercury *Middlebury Mercury,* vol. 4, no. 16, Wednesday, March 27, 1805, 3. Festus's name is misspelled, a fairly common problem with typesetters in those days.

191 *a Middlebury lawyer to write up the deed* Sunderland town records, vol. 5, 240.

191 *the three children, are listed as white* Federal census for 1810. Tatnai (misspelled as "Falnae") is listed as living alone in Middlebury (federal census, Middlebury, Addison County, 73). Amos Chipman, previously listed with four black people in his household, no longer has them there, another indication that it may have been Lucy, Caesar, Duruxa, and either Festus or Drucilla who were living with him. Lucy appears on the census as head of household in a family or group of four (Vermont 1810 Census Index [Bountiful, Utah: Accelerated Indexing Systems], 24). These were handwritten censuses, so because a *y* in the line above hangs down over their name, the printer erroneously transcribed "Prince" as "Pricher." The spelling is correct on the actual page. The account of Festus's moves to New York State in 1815 and 1817, in *The Official History of Guilford, Vermont,* based on the account given by Giles Bacon, is probably erroneous, as are many of the "facts" Bacon recalled.

192 *working as a hired man* In 1815 Caesar was working as a hired man for Ben Lathrop. Much like his father before him in Deerfield, he planted, dug post holes, drew flax, and harvested (Ben Lathrop, accounts of general merchandise, Sunderland, Vt., 1809–31, Russell Collection, Canfield Library). He bought supplies like potatoes, butter, pork, and whiskey from the same man.

192 *plunged the state into famine* Walter Hill Crockett, *History of Vermont,* vol. 3 (New York: Century History Co., 1921), 134.

192 *to keep the family alive* Ben Lathrop, accounts of general merchandise, Sunderland, Vt., 1809–31, 369–73, Russell Collection, Canfield Library.

192 *also did odd jobs* That April he went to work for a doctor named Darius Matthews, who had also been a justice in one of the earlier cases in Vergennes. Darius Matthews daybooks, Matthews Family Papers, Sheldon Museum.

192 *a decent life for himself* According to Paul Gillies, things didn't remain so hospitable. When the great African American abolitionist Frederick Douglass visited Middlebury in 1843, the college students "placarded the town with violent aspersions of our characters and the grossest misrepresentations of our principles, measures, and objects. I was described as an escaped convict from the State prison, and the other speakers were assailed not less slanderously." Frederick Douglass, *Autobiographies* (New York: Library of America, 1994), 771–72.

193 *Festus died at the age of fifty-seven* Giles Bacon to Rodney Field, February 27, 1877, Prince family folder, PVMA. Bacon is frequently wrong, but the removal of "the widow Lucy Prince" and her children to Sunderland coincides

with this information, except that Bacon gives the death date as February 1819, off by two years.

193 *staying at a public house National Standard* (Middlebury), January 11, 1820.

193 *forced to leave Danby soon afterward* This is another claim by the notoriously incorrect letter from Giles Bacon to Rodney Field (February 27, 1877, Prince family folder, PVMA), but for once it makes some sense when lined up with the information gleaned from the Sunderland town records.

193 *to transport the young family* Sunderland town records, vol. 7, 85.

193 *"as soon as possible"* Sunderland town records, vol. 7, 63.

193 *"white negroes"* Sunderland town records, vol. 7, 87.

193 *a Brownson woman* Sunderland town records, vol. 7, 69.

193 *exposed her entire class* Letter from Dr. Fanshaw to Judge Aldis, March 24, 1820, Vermont Papers, box 1, folder A-Goelet, New York State Library.

194 *a mild case of smallpox in the past* Samuel Swift, *History of Middlebury* (Middlebury: A. H. Copeland, 1859), 322.

194 *a selectman from Burlington National Standard*, vol. 7, issue 39, 3.

194 *in the grip of illness and terror* Middlebury town records, vol. 87, Sheldon Museum.

194 *his fifty-fifth birthday National Standard*, May 9, 1820.

194 *make her coffin* Sunderland town records, vol. 7, 87.

194 *"who treated her with . . . deference" Vermont Gazette*, vol. 12, no. 41, July 14, 1821.

196 *"Where vaunting tyrants . . . meet"* Lucy Prince obituary, *Vermont Gazette*, vol. 12, no. 41, July 14, 1821.

196 *Washington County, New York* Sunderland proprietors records, Town Clerk's Office. Giles Bacon asserted that Tatnai married a woman named Quack in Northfield and that Festus's daughter married a grocer in New York State. He seems to have mixed up Festus's widow, who married William McGowan and moved to Washington County, New York, with Festus's daughter. Perhaps he looked up black men living there and discovered a black grocer named Quack Boston (probably derived from the ubiquitous "Quackenbush" or "Quackenboss" name) who lived in Salem, New York.

196 *first time they'd been there* They went in on May 4, 1829. Jonathan had been placed there the previous June, and the others the previous August. Laura Penny Hulslander, ed., *Washington County, New York, Poor House Accounts* (El Paso: Sleeper Co., 1997), 35.

196 *where Caesar, Drusilla, and Duruxa still lived* Vermont 1830 census.

196 *Lucy now has an eighth child* Vermont 1830 census.

197 *when he died in 1825* Sheldon, *History of Deerfield*, vol. 2, 897–98.

197 *"dealings respecting this woman" Vermont Gazette*, September 12, 1826.

198 *before the assembly met again* Sunderland town records, vol. 7, 91–92.

198 *Caesar's house in 1830 or 1831* Sunderland town records, vol. 7, 128.

198 *"importation of slaves into . . . the United States" Middlebury Mercury*, January 8, 1806, vol. 5, no. 5, 3.

199 *House of Representatives* Raymond P. Zirblis, *Friends of Freedom*, written for the State of Vermont (Vermont Division of Historic Preservation, December 12, 1996).

199 *Prince case was being argued Journal of the General Assembly of the State of Vermont* (Bennington: Anthony Haswell, 1800), 60, and (1801), 16.

199 *"from the Almighty"* Frederick Tupper, "Royall Tyler, Man of Law and Man of Letters," in *Biographical Sketches of Vermonters*, vol. 1 (Montpelier: Vermont Historical Society, 1947), 66–67.

199 *"during the trial" St. Albans Messenger*, November 7, 1850, 2. See also Swift, *History of the Town of Middlebury*, 274.

199 *stockings and caps* In the 1840s she was living in Zenas Warner's house in Sunderland; in 1850 she was living in Pardon Davenport's Arlington house. Census for 1840 and 1850.

200 *the grandson of our Festus.* The 1830 census shows a Festus Prince as a Greenwich head of household that included a multiracial group of people: one white female under five; one white female age ten to fifteen; one white female between thirty and forty; one black male between ten and twenty-four (the right age to be Festus's son); two black females between ten and twenty-four. The possibilities are fascinating. He could have had a white wife who brought two daughters into the marriage; perhaps his sister was living with them too.

200 *Twentieth Infantry, Company D* www.itd.nps.gov/cwss/soldiers.htm. Buried in Hornellsville, Robertson Cemetery, Festus Prince died on February 25, 1920 (source: www.rootsweb.com/~nysteube/hv/hv4b.html). The Twentieth served in Florida, Alabama, Louisiana, and Texas (microfilm M589, roll 70, NARA).

SOURCES

Most of the sources on Lucy Terry and Abijah Prince are unpublished and are located in the archives noted in the acknowledgments section of this book. Endnotes also give the precise location of particular materials. While most published sources include repeated factual errors, there are a number of useful sources on New England, slavery, and town histories. These include:

Akagi, Roy Hidemichi. *The Town Proprietors of the New England Colonies*. Philadelphia: Press of the University of Pennsylvania, 1924.

Arms, William Tyler. *History of Leyden Massachusetts*. Orange, Mass.: Enterprise and Journal, 1959.

Broad Brook Grange. *Official History of Guilford, Vermont, 1678–1961*. Brattleboro, 1992 (reprint).

Carlisle, Elizabeth Pendergast. *Earthbound and Heavenbent: The Life of Elizabeth Porter Phelps and Life at Forty Acres, 1747–1817*. New York: Scribner, 2004.

Cottrell, Robert J., ed. *From African to Yankee: Slavery and Freedom in Antebellum New England*. Armonk, N.Y.: M. E. Sharpe, 1998.

Crockett, Walter Hill. *History of Vermont*, vol. 3. New York: Century History, 1921.

Farrow, Anne, Joel Lang, and Jennifer Frank. *Complicity: How the North Promoted, Prolonged, and Profited from Slavery*. New York: Ballantine, 2005.

Gillies, Paul S. "The Vendue: The Exercise of Geo-Catharsis." In "Ruminations," *Vermont Bar Journal* (Summer 2005), 9–12.

Graham, John A. *A Descriptive Sketch of the Present State of Vermont*. Bennington: Vermont Heritage, 1987 (first published 1797).

Guyette, E. A. "The Working Lives of African Vermonters in Census and Literature, 1790–1870." *Vermont History* (Spring 1993), 69–84.

Haefeli, Evan, and Kevin M. Sweeney. *Captors and Captives: The 1704 French and Indian Raid on Deerfield*. Amherst: University of Massachusetts Press, 1973.

Hahn, M. T. *Alexander Twilight: Vermont's African American Pioneer*. Shelburne, Vt.: New England Press, 1998.

Harris, Sharon. "Lucy Terry: A Life of Radical Resistance." In *Executing Race: Early American Women's Narratives of Race, Society, and the Law*. Columbus: Ohio State University Press, 2005.

Hemenway, Abby Maria. *Vermont Historical Gazetteer*, 5 vols. Burlington, Vt.: 1867–91.

Hoyt, Epaphrus. *Antiquarian Researches: Comprising a History of the Indian Wars in the Country Bordering the Connecticut River and Parts Adjacents, and Other Interesting Events.* Greenfield, Mass.: Ansel Phelps, December 1824.

Judd, Sylvester. *History of Hadley, Including the Early History of Flatfield, South Hadley, Amherst, and Granby, Massachusetts . . . Also Family Genealogies by Lucius M. Boltwood.* Springfield, Mass.: H. R. Huntting & Co., 1905.

Katz, Bernard, and Jonathan Katz. *Black Woman: A Fictionalized Biography of Lucy Terry Prince.* New York: Pantheon, 1973.

Kestigian, Mark C. "Early Medical Care in Deerfield." *Historical Journal of Western Massachusetts* 7, no. 2 (June 1979).

Massachusetts Soldiers and Sailors in the War of the Revolution. Boston: Wright & Potter, 1904.

Minkema, Kenneth. "Jonathan Edwards's Defense of Slavery." *Massachusetts Historical Review* 4 (2002), 23–60.

———. "Jonathan Edwards on Slavery." *William and Mary Quarterly* (3d series) 54, no. 4 (October 1997).

Noyes, Nathan. *A Short Account of the Life and Experience of Nathan Noyes.* Detroit: Bagg & Harmon, 1847.

Parsons, Herbert Collins. *A Puritan Outpost: A History of the Town and People of Northfield, Massachusetts.* New York: Macmillan, 1937.

Piersen, W. D. *Black Yankees: The Development of an Afro-American Subculture in Eighteenth-Century New England.* Amherst: University of Massachusetts Press, 1988.

Proper, David. *Lucy Terry Prince: Singer of History.* Deerfield, Mass.: Historic Deerfield, 1997.

Rising, Marcia Hoffman. *Vermont Newspaper Abstracts, 1783–1816.* Boston: New England Historic Genealogical Society, 2001.

Saillant, John. *Black Puritan, Black Republican: The Life and Thought of Lemuel Haynes, 1753–1833.* New York: Oxford University Press, 2003.

Sheldon, George. "Negro Slavery in Old Deerfield." *New England* (March 1983), 57.

———. *A History of Deerfield. A facsimile of the 1895–96 edition published in recognition of the tercentenary of the town of Deerfield in 1973 with a new foreword by Amelia F. Miller and Donald R. Friary.* Deerfield, Mass.: New Hampshire Publishing Company, Somersworth, in collaboration with the Pocumtuck Valley Memorial Association Deerfield, 1972.

Smith, James Avery. *The History of the Black Population of Amherst, Massachusetts.* Boston: New England Historic Genealogical Society, 1999.

Sweeney, Kevin M. "River Gods in the Making: The Williamses of Western

Massachusetts." In *The Bay and the River, 1600–1900.* Boston: Boston University, Dublin Seminar for New England Folklife, Annual Proceedings, 1981.

Swift, Samuel. *History of the Town of Middlebury.* Middlebury, Vt.: A. H. Copeland, 1859.

Temple, J. H., and George Sheldon. *A History of the Town of Northfield, Massachusetts, for 150 Years, with an Account of the Prior Occupation of the Territory by the Squakheags; and with Family Genealogies.* Albany, N.Y.: Joel Munsell, 1875.

Thayer, Gertrude S. Richmond. "The Noyes Family of Guilford, Vermont." *The Vermonter* 41, no. 11 (November 1936).

Winter, Kari J., ed. *The Blind African Slave, or, Memoirs of Boyrereau Brinch, Nicknamed Jeffery Brace.* Madison: University of Wisconsin Press, 2004.

Zirblis, Raymond B. *Friends of Freedom: The Vermont Underground Railroad Survey Report.* Montpelier: State of Vermont, Vermont Department of State Buildings and Vermont Division for Historic Preservation, 1996.

OUTLINE OF LOTS IN SUNDERLAND, VERMONT.
NOTE HOW THE MAPMAKER WROTE "NEGRO" TO IDENTIFY THE LOT
WHERE THE PRINCES' HOUSE STOOD. *Courtesy of the Vermont Historical Society.*

INDEX

Page numbers in *italics* refer to illustrations.